STUCK WITH VIRTUE

RELIGION AND CONTEMPORARY CULTURE

Series Editor
PETER AUGUSTINE LAWLER

STUCK WITH VIRTUE

The American Individual and Our Biotechnological Future

PETER AUGUSTINE LAWLER

ISI BOOKS
WILMINGTON, DELAWARE
2005

© 2005 ISI Books

Lawler, Peter Augustine.

    Stuck with virtue : the American individual and our biotechnological future / Peter Augustine Lawler. — 1st ed. — Wilminton, Del. : ISI Books, 2005.

        p. ; cm.
        (Religion and contemporary culture)

        ISBN-13: 978-1-932236-84-2
        ISBN-10: 1-932236-84-8
        Each chapter was originally prepared as a lecture or presentation.
        Includes index.

1. National characteristics, American. 2. Individuality. 3. Liberty. 4. Political science. 5. Biotechnology. 6. Technology and civilization. 7. Social evolution. I. Title.

JC311 .L39 2005   2005932319
320.54/0973—dc22   0511

Book design by Kelly Cole

Published in the United States by:

    ISI Books
    Intercollegiate Studies Institute
    Post Office Box 4431
    Wilmington, DE 19807-0431
    www.isibooks.org

CONTENTS

PREFACE

The two subjects of this book are the American individual and biotechnology. The other principle of unity is that each of these chapters was prepared as a lecture or presentation for a diverse group of intelligent, educated, and active citizens and students of American moral and political life. Each chapter has a wide scope, comes to controversial conclusions, and is meant to influence opinion—and not just scholarly opinion. I hope that these chapters reach a much, much larger and wider audience through their publication together. The introduction and the first two chapters offer overviews of our present situation as modern individuals and function here as something like orientation sessions. I have made them as informal as possible, even dispensing with distracting notes and all that. Some of the later chapters are a bit more technical, but that only means you might want to read them a bit more slowly.

Each chapter is meant to stand on its own, so there is some unavoidable redundancy. It also means that if you don't like one, you can move on to the next, or even just skip around without missing anything essential to your reading pleasure. I've not tried to impose a uniform style upon the chapters just for consistency's sake.

Most of them appeared in print somewhere else first, and I appreciate the generosity of *Society, Modern Age,* the *New Atlantis,* the *Intercollegiate Review, Perspectives on Political Science,* and Lexington Books in allowing me to use them, with some revision, again here.

I want to thank Jeremy Beer for being a skillful and encouraging editor, and for allowing my own book to introduce this series on religion and contemporary culture. Eric Cohen, editor of the *New Atlantis,* did a fine job of tightening and clarifying two of the chapters, especially the one on caregiving. Several Berry College students, especially Elizabeth Amato, Kelly Walsh, and Keri Libby, did some expert proofreading. Diane Land, as usual, lavished her incomparable attention to detail on every word. If this book isn't perfect, it's because something changed when Diane wasn't looking. If I really thought this was the last book I would do with Diane, I would dedicate it to her with a sappy and sincere testimonial.

This book talks up friendship here and there, so let me mention some of my best writer/professor friends. Dan Mahoney, Paul Seaton, Marc Guerra, Mark Henrie, and Ralph Hancock each read and talked me through much of what's written here, not to mention all sorts of other controversial issues and perennial questions. If I added just a few more names—such as my friends Bob Kraynak and Joe Alulis—I could cover the whole "crowd" of American faith-based, non-libertarian, Strauss-influenced thinkers. We're not yet famous enough to merit Ann Norton's or Shadia Drury's critical attention, but watch out! I have to add—and not just because this paragraph might leave you with the impression that I don't have any women friends—that I wouldn't know anything at all without the orientation Delba Winthrop gave me more than a few years ago.

I've also learned a lot from and enjoyed my time with an unusually fine group of students who have been enrolled in my seminars over the last few years. Here I should start a list, but it would simply be too long. And my apparently legendary inability to remember names when I need them might accidentally cause me to slight some of my friends.

This book also talks up love, which may be for suckers, but is certainly not only for them. Let me give the place of honor to Rita, Catherine, and my parents.

A final word of thanks belongs to the Earhart Foundation. Without Earhart's generous support I never would have found time to finish this book.

The American Individual Today

The guiding premise of this book is that we tend to think of ourselves today as *individuals*—as opposed to parents, children, friends, citizens, or creatures. I have a very particular definition of the individual in mind: To think of oneself as an individual is to think in the first person, or to think that everything exists for me. To be an individual is to be a free agent, unencumbered by church, country, family, friendship, love, or any other form of social or communal duty. The individual—as individual—is the center of the universe. Nothing existed before me, and when I am gone, all is gone. Every moment of my life should be determined by calculation concerning what is best for me, and so all my human connections should be the product of conscious and selfish consent. I surrender my freedom as soon as I think of myself as part of a whole greater than myself or lose my mind in love with someone else.

We individuals believe, in fact, that we live freely and truthfully only when we live in the first person. That's why as our famous French observer, Alexis de Tocqueville, says in *Democracy in America*, "Americans are pleased to explain almost all the actions of their life with the aid of self-interest rightly understood" (volume 2, part 2, chapters 8–9). A free and enlightened individual, we take pleasure in bragging, "resists instinct in all encounters and reasons coldly about all the acts of his life." Rather than "blindly yielding" to love or any other passionate enthusiasm, the individual as individual has the habitual capacity for "sacrificing without effort the pleasure of the moment to the permanent interests of his whole life." Individual sacrifices of momentary passion or enjoyment are not really blind, because they are not really sacrifices at all: They only defer gratification with the intention of maximizing and prolonging it. Genuine sacrifice is for suckers, for bees, ants, ignorant and superstitious monks, and the other mindlessly communal animals.

The individual, the product of theorizing by liberal philosophers such as John Locke, is an abstract being without many of the natural social qualities characteristic of real human beings. When he or she boasts, Tocqueville notes, the individual exaggerates the freedom or ability to govern himself or herself (that is, not to be governed by other human beings, nature, or God) with his or her individualistic "philosophy." And our Constitution is largely based on this individualistic, Lockean philosophy of self-government. We Americans consent to be governed as *individuals.* Sovereign individuals, from this view, are like sovereign states, and therefore government is nothing more than a treaty or compact among sovereigns. Just as sovereign states, in fact, can withdraw from treaties without being invaded, sovereign individuals can withdraw from any or all of the social ties to which they have consented to be bound when those ties no longer serve their self-interest.

As the unionist Orestes Brownson complained in *The American Republic* (1865), Lockean theory could provide no argument against the Southern states' assertion of "the right of secession" that was the cause of the Civil War—and the Lockean argument used by the Confederate states was destructive not only of government but of all social life. The theory of the individual, in fact, has no argument against the individual's assertion of a "right of secession" from whatever binds him to other human beings or to God. Brownson, almost a century and a half ago, saw clearly what Lockean theory could do to marriage, the family, friendship, and churches, not to mention nations and citizens. He saw that the theory of the individual gives no adequate account of the citizen's loyalty to his country, no adequate account of human loyalty or responsibility at all. That is why Brownson attempted to explain why the Lockean theory of our framers could not really account adequately for the enduring Constitution they had created. They must have built better than they knew, or thought they knew. In truth, of course, our founders were more than Lockean theorists, and more than sovereign individuals.

Nobody, or almost nobody, really believes that Locke teaches the whole truth any more. Few really believe that Locke was right when he said that human beings exist freely and rationally in some state of nature, and that government, the family, in fact, all social life are merely products of our rational, self-interested consent. The partial truth taught by contemporary Darwinism lies in its recovery of the Aristotelian insight that we are by nature gregarious, social animals. That is why our efforts to replace the natural world with one consciously constructed with individuals in mind tends to make us happier in some ways and more miserable in others. An account of the whole truth about human beings would incorporate both the partial truth about our freedom that we see reflected in the theory of the individual and the partial truth about our sociality we see reflected in the extremely clever chimp described by the sociobiologists. It would also include our common experiences of loving openness to the truth about all things, including ourselves, and our incurable longing for God.

But as Brownson and John Courtney Murray in *We Hold These Truths* (1960)—the best American Catholic or Thomistic political thinkers we have had—both noted, the paradox is that the history of America is, in large part, the gradual but real infusion of seemingly untrue Lockean principles and self-understandings into all areas of our lives. All of our experiences, it sometimes seems, are being reconfigured in terms of calculation and consent. Lockean theory, allegedly refuted time and again by Marxism, Freudianism, sociobiology, evolutionary psychology, deconstructionism, post-structuralism, neuroscience, and so forth, seemingly explains more human behavior than ever. Perhaps our progress toward individualism is simply in accord with Locke's comprehensive intention. His description of the human individual was less an account of what we are really like by nature than a project to free us from our natural and social limitations. Locke aimed to *make* his view of the human individual true, to reconstruct all of human life with the individual in mind. Locke understood, Pierre Manent reminds us in *The City of Man* (1998, in English), that *the* distinctively human faculty is the power of abstraction, and that the greatest evidence of our freedom is our capacity to make our abstractions real. He knew that his description of the free individual expressed only part of the truth about being human, but he also knew that it was possible that it would express more of that truth all the time.

The sense that we live in a theoretical time is strange; it is more unclear than ever whether the sovereign individual with individual rights is a natural fact or a historical construction. It surely is more clear than ever that we might have indefinite power to free ourselves from all that we have been given by nature. It seems that the more sovereign we become, the less natural we are. And we attempt to free ourselves from nature partly because we see ever more clearly how hostile nature is to individual aberrations from her reasonable, impersonal laws. In other words, the more we war against nature, the more obvious we think it becomes that nature is at war with us.

We are the only species that acts to privilege the good of particular individuals over the species as a whole. Sociobiologists can lament the way in which increasingly child-free Europeans are choosing for themselves and against the species, choosing not to produce the replacements nature intends them to produce. But sociobiologists can praise and blame only because we are not really governed—not completely, anyway—by the evolutionary process the sociobiologists describe. Human beings have never been species survivalists. When Carl Sagan told us to populate other planets to maximize the probability of species survival (because an asteroid might pulverize any particular planet), most of us just shrugged. Why should we care how long the species lasts after we're gone? Christians, for example, have never thought that the human species is or should be immortal; when it comes to long-term survival, each of us should trust in God. In fact, it might be said that any animal smart enough to think in terms of species serves its species less well than those too stupid to have such thoughts. When the history of our planet is written by some brilliant extraterrestrial, the beginning of the end of our species may well be identified with the emergence of the individual—the self-conscious mortal.

OUR LIBERTARIAN SOCIOBIOLOGY

The power of individuals today to choose not to be citizens or parents or creatures is remarkable and certainly unprecedented. But thinking of ourselves as free individuals and nothing more surely is bad even for the preservation of individuals, not to mention nations or species, over time. Yet that sociobiological criticism of our perverse individualism carries little weight with us. The truth about nature allegedly discovered by the sociobiologists can only increase our obsessive individualism.

The Americans who have the most stable families and the most children—who live as nature intends—are those least likely to believe that sociobiology teaches the truth, or the whole truth, about human existence. They are our most observant religious believers. A study could easily show that the Americans who say they believe in Darwin and not the Bible are no more fecund than the French, who share the chance-and-necessity premises—the hopelessly dogmatic atheism—of our evolutionary theorists. Sovereign individuals have always known that what Darwin teaches is right about everything but individuals, and that it is the job of individuals to prove him wrong about them. But the most sociobiologically sound Americans—orthodox religious believers—think that neither Locke nor Darwin understood the deepest truth about human existence. They reject the notions that they are either deeply autonomous individuals or clever chimps.

At first glance, then, we have every reason to affirm Tocqueville's praise of our religion as a reasonably effective antidote to our individualistic excesses. Religion helps to ease our self-obsession, gets us to take our souls seriously, acts to protect women and children from exploitation, and inspires acts of relatively disinterested virtue. Tocqueville certainly would not have been surprised to see that the progress of individualism in our time had generated an impressive countercultural response. "Man," he explains, "did not give himself the taste for the infinite and love of what is immortal. These sublime instincts are not born of a caprice of his will; they have their immutable foundation in his nature; they exist despite his efforts. He can hinder and deform them, but not destroy them" (volume 2, part 2, chapter 12). Even the allegedly autonomous individual cannot really legislate the soul into or out of being, and he or she has no choice but to address its needs somehow.

A solid minority of Americans are more thoroughly dedicated in their religious devotion today than the conflicted American Christians Tocqueville described. But another difference between Tocqueville's time and our own may be more telling: In the America he described, Christian religious belief and moral doctrine commanded almost universal respect; dissenters kept quiet for fear of suffering all the consequences of moral isolation. But our countercultural Christians are today openly viewed with some combination of contempt and condescension by most of our sophisticates—including our mainstream media and many of our rather conservative intellectuals, such as Mark Lilla (the darling of the *New York Times*).

According to Lilla, "The leading thinkers of the British and American Enlightenments hoped that life in a modern democratic world would shift the focus of Christianity from a faith-based reality to a reality-based faith." But, Lilla complains, "American religion is moving in the opposite direction today, back toward the ecstatic, literalist, and credulous spirit of the Great Awakenings." He adds ominously, "Nobody can know how long this dumbing down of American religion will persist" or what its antiliberal or anti-individualistic consequences might be. Certainly, "citizens should probably be more vigilant about policing the public square, not less so" ("Church Meets State," *New York Times Book Review*, May 15, 2005).

The opinion in Tocqueville's day was that our religion served our political liberalism by showing us that the individual's pursuit of happiness might culminate in happiness itself, that liberal politics and economics plus a belief in a personal God and the immortality of the soul might combine to produce a realistic or comprehensive view of human goods. Now we're told that religion has become too dumb and fantastic to do us any good, and so we must privatize and isolate belief as much as possible. The solution to dumb, anti-individualistic religion is an aggressive extension of the spirit of individualism to religion.

This dumbing down of religious believers is partly reflected, of course, in their "ignorance of basic science," or in their refusal to recognize the fact that Mr. Darwin teaches the whole truth about our origin and destiny. Lilla, along with most of our intellectuals, disagrees with Tocqueville about whether our religion should keep us from obsessing over the consequences of what scientists tell us is a reality-based view of our place in nature. He also disagrees with Tocqueville about whether our preachers know something about the soul, about the reality of being human, that our scientists do not. For Lilla, the fact that our evangelicals present a view of reality counter to the dominant secular or "Enlightenment" individualism— which has morphed into a sort of libertarian sociobiology—is decisive evidence against them. But at first glance, "libertarian sociobiology" would seem not to be reality based at all, but rather a ridiculous oxymoron, presenting us with something like an autonomous chimp. It would seem to be evidence, as our evangelical and orthodox thinkers say, that neither libertarianism nor sociobiology expresses the deepest truth about being human. Especially untrue and obnoxious is Lilla's implication that today's "secular humanists" live more "reality-based" lives than our religious believers.

To give Lilla his due, evangelical Christians do not tend to give reality-based arguments to defend their relatively reality-based lives. They tend to think in terms of opposing "worldviews," biblical and secular. And they often claim that if it were not for the absolute truth of biblical revelation, relativistic individualism would be the truth we would all share in common. Our evangelicals lack the confidence to say that what we can see with our own eyes about nature and human nature supports their dissent from the individualistic excesses of our time. They concede too much to the individualism they criticize, and the result is that they do not really engage in dialogue with their fellow citizens, such as Lilla, about the human goods we all—believers and nonbelievers alike—share in common. Lilla is right to criticize them for their faith-based secession from the intellectual life of our country. But that does not mean that our evangelicals have nothing real and valuable to offer that life.

According to the astute British observers Adrian Wooldridge and John Micklethwait, America, largely because of the influence of religion, is the only reality-based nation in the enlightened world. They write in *The Right Nation* (2003) that Europeans tend to live in a postreligious, postfamilial, and postpolitical fantasy, and that they do not think clearly with their futures in mind. By contrast, we relatively conservative Americans think of ourselves as parents, creatures, and citizens, as well as free and productive individuals. So we refuse to reduce all moral questions to merely technical ones, and we take responsibility for our futures as real human beings. The evangelicals' dissent from the dominant libertarian sociobiology of the intellectuals is actually connected to the truth about the way people really are.

Neither libertarianism nor sociobiology is completely reality based, and the one incomplete and superficial understanding of reality generates the other. Nature, the sociobiologists teach us, is blind and pitiless, and the self-conscious individual is a cosmic accident who ought not exist. Finding ourselves homeless in the cosmos described by the biologists or the physicists, we individuals also find ourselves free to transform nature to make ourselves more at home. Our job, it appears, is to replace natural evolution—which uses individuals (denying, in effect, their dignity or real existence) to benefit the species—with conscious and volitional evolution— the result of our free efforts to impose our will on nature for the benefit of individuals. The dignity of the individual, from one view, resides in his unconstrained assertion of himself against natural indifference.

We generally call the effort to transform nonhuman nature for the good of individuals *technology*, and the newly emerging effort to transform our own human nature *biotechnology*. Increasingly, we define ourselves by our technological and biotechnological efforts to replace inhospitable natural reality with a world made by and for free individuals. We might say that we middle-class Americans work to create a middle-class world, one not appropriate for the other animals or gods but for the free beings with bodily needs stuck between those two extremes.

One consequence of this way of approaching the world is that the individual—as individual—is ungrateful, because he too readily believes there is nothing for which to *be* grateful. God and nature have given us nothing good, except for the mysterious capacity to work effectively to free ourselves from their domination. And the more successful we are in securing our freedom, the more ungrateful we become. As Gregg Easterbrook explains in *The Progress Paradox* (2003), a time traveler from a past century would surely find it strange that we whine so much about remarkably little. Our anxiety, paranoia, and other forms of neurotic unhappiness have less material foundation all the time. It's not the case that people used to be happy because they enjoyed the various forms of pain, poverty, and tyranny that technological progress and good government have alleviated or eradicated. Not only is there no going back to more low-tech times, very few of us would really want to go back. We shouldn't forget all the good that thinking of ourselves as individuals has done for us.

People now are freer than ever to do whatever they want; they are less chained to economic necessity and social repression than ever before. Things are also generally more just. We are constantly inching closer to the meritocracy for which Jefferson hoped, that natural aristocracy in which the best would rise to the top and everyone else would still do well enough. Nor has the expansion of freedom produced a corresponding increase in criminality or vice: divorce, drinking, and crime rates have recently been in decline. We are getting healthier. IQs are on the rise. And thanks to smarter technologies, the environment is getting cleaner without our having to curb our consumption. If you ignore the fecundity problem—which may be alleviated by regenerative medicine's promise of indefinite longevity for each individual—the individual, the species, and the environment, Easterbrook shows us, are all in surprisingly good shape. The more we become dependent on technology, of course, the more we worry about some crisis that would reveal our inability to control what we do not really understand. But there probably is not any such crisis on the horizon; even some acts of bio- or even nuclear terrorism probably would not alter much the progress we have come to take for granted.

OUR HAPPINESS PROBLEM

We're not as grateful as we should be for all this genuine progress because we're not as happy as we believe we should be. For one thing, we're more anxious than in the past because we high-tech individuals are more concerned than ever about controlling the future. "Anticipation-induced anxiety," as Easterbrook observes, is now commonplace. So the cliché that we "are shallow and live for the moment" is pretty much the exact opposite of the truth among middle-class Americans today. We may, in fact, mouth shallow phrases and platitudes, but our freedom shines forth in our obsession with our futures as individuals. The inability of the anxious individual to live anywhere but in the future (not in the past or present or eternity) is the foundation of David Brooks's poetic celebration, in *On Paradise Drive* (2004), of our driven and productive lives; it is our national greatness; it is what motivates us to dominate the whole world.

Our increasing individualistic obsession actually makes sense. The shape of one's future is, more than ever, the product of one's own choices. Our unprecedented medical knowledge—characterized by one breakthrough after another when it comes to diet, exercise, supplements, and so forth—means that we have an increasingly long list of things to do in order to fend off death as long as possible. Because we know so much, we must work harder than ever against death. In fact, sickness and death seem today to be shameful evidence of personal irresponsibility. After all, death might be avoided simply by attending with proper prudence to all the known risk factors.

The example of our health obsession—which, of course, is mostly good—shows how confused libertarian sociobiologists are. Are we trying to free ourselves from natural necessity—which the sociobiologists say is impossible? Or are we trying to free ourselves from chance—from being utterly contingent, mysterious, and hopelessly vulnerable exceptions to the laws that govern the rest of nature, from being individuals? We individuals certainly have no interest in making sociobiology completely right! We want to free ourselves from the nature that might (or might not) strike us down with disease or death at any moment. In so doing, we make the mistake of identifying nature with chance, and bringing nature under our control with the overcoming of chance. But the non-technological animals do not, in truth, experience themselves as governed by chance. The theory of evolution might explain their development that way, but that is our theory, not theirs. The more we free ourselves from necessity, the more we subject ourselves to chance, and so the more anxious and contingent we control freaks become. Our obsessions tend to make us more obsessive; the harder we work in response to them, the more completely we become individuals.

We cannot transcend completely the realms of necessity and chance and become personal gods; in winning some victories against one, we in some ways enter more deeply into the other. And who can believe we'll really get more happy and more virtuous if disease and death are no longer experienced as necessary—but still as always possible—outcomes for us individuals? So becoming more healthy doesn't necessarily make us more happy, which is not a problem that can be solved by obsessively deciding to eat, drink, smoke, take recreational drugs, and be merry, not to mention deciding, as some do, barely to eat at all.

Eric Cohen defends the more subtle view that we see nature "as both *orderly* and *absurd.*" Nature, we know, is governed by impersonal necessity. And we're happier when we admit that, sooner or later, we individuals will have to surrender our particular existences to that necessity. From one non-individualistic view, the best way to live happily is by acknowledging that all our victories over death and disease are temporary, whereas all our losses, as Cohen adds, are inevitably "final" ("The Tragedy of Equality," *The New Atlantis*, Winter 2005). Still, it strikes us as absurd and worthy of our correction that death and disease seem to strike capriciously; good children often die miserable, lingering deaths, and everyone knows bad, healthy, old people. Nature doesn't *care* about any of us; it strikes blindly or at random against some but not others (for a long while). But it remains the case that all our victories over nature are contingent and provisional.

We work, most of all, to bring less order and necessity into the world through our technological interventions. Our view of nature as amoral or immoral or cruelly disordered depends upon our individual perspective; nature does not intend and can only to a very limited extent be made to serve individuals. Anything, of course, that spares little children horrible deaths and gives them long lives is good, but those wonderful victories over nature both give us and rob us of happiness. We let them undermine the natural capacity given to our species alone to love contingent and mortal beings in this world. It would be best, of course, to encourage and embrace the victories of modern medical science in full awareness of their limitations, but that requires being grateful both for what we can do for ourselves and for the invincible necessity that seems to make each of our lives so contingent and temporary. We would have to care for individuals, but not too much, which, I think, requires seeing human beings as more than individuals.

As the debate over the Terri Schiavo case reminded us, defending the individual's autonomy at the expense of other human considerations can actually end up justifying the killing of particular human beings. We cannot bring death under our control by annihilating it; no matter what we do, we must die. But through annihilating ourselves, we can, in a way, bring annihilation under our control. We can choose not to be dependent or irrational or to suffer; we can brag that we would rather be dead than endure those miserable indignities. And we can say that no individual should be made or even allowed to live without a certain degree of autonomy. Thinking of human beings as individuals and nothing more, as Paul McHugh observes, is the source of "our own, homegrown culture of death, whose face is legal and moral and benignly individualistic rather than authoritarian or pseudo-scientific." In our increasingly individualistic time the authority of the prudential judgment of the physician is being displaced by the bioethicist—the expert at maximizing individual autonomy. "To most doctors and nurses," McHugh adds, "the idea that one can control the manner and pace of one's own death is largely a fantasy"; their "training and experience" keeps them from privileging autonomy over other ways of understanding what a human being is ("Annihilating Terri Schiavo," *Commentary*, June 2005).

Consider what thinking of ourselves as individuals has done to marriage. Today a woman who chooses the wrong spouse can only blame herself, whereas someone stuck in an arranged marriage can direct her anger in a cathartic way toward others. Knowing that I'm not stuck in my unhappy marriage—that I have the freedom or the chance to correct my bad choices—only makes matters even worse. I, the individual, must show my courage by accepting the burden of choosing against my most intimate social bonds and for my personal happiness. People might be happier when they accept that marriage has a lot to do with both necessity and chance, neither of which can be completely replaced by choice.

We might even be grateful for having to live well with what we have been given, but for our choices we are rather unreasonably stuck with blaming ourselves completely. The truth is that the attempt to free marriage from necessity has subjected it more to *both* choice and chance. What is more whimsical and uncertain than basing a merely human institution on love and convenience alone, especially in a time when our individualistic experts tell us that love is an illusion? More people than ever deny today that marriage is a necessary institution with a secure human future.

One result of the deterioration or individualistic reconstruction of key social institutions in today's meritocratic world of choice is that rejection is more personal than ever. Those who are slighted or ignored can't blame social prejudices or "the system." It is devastating to know that I am just not that interesting or attractive or useful to others. The downside of a meritocracy—a classless society—is that nobody has to like me. Fewer thoughts produce more anxiety than knowing I live in a world where people have to work harder than ever just not to be alone. Libertarian Virginia Postrel, in *The Substance of Style* (2002), celebrates the contemporary world, in which we have more ways than ever to choose to be "smart and pretty." But we had better choose well, because it's more hellish than ever not to be smart and not to be pretty.

The individual, of course, is free to choose to pursue happiness, and he is free to define happiness for himself. Individual opinions on happiness, as Locke explained, are quite variable and subjective. So any public attempt to define happiness is repressive. But Locke actually privileged freedom over happiness; the free being is always in an ever elusive pursuit. Happiness itself, Locke suggests, is not characteristically the experience of a free individual. He knew that we are not completely in the dark about what happiness is, and it generally requires being more than a free individual. The sociobi-ologists teach us that for most people most of the time happiness is something like the opposite of loneliness. A few people—the most rugged of individuals—really do want to be left alone. But in general married people are happier than single people, people from larger families happier than people from smaller ones, and so forth. There is something inescapably unrealistic and elitist about Locke's privileging of personal freedom over social and familial happiness.

Thomas Jefferson, our intellectual founder, seemed to part from Locke on the happiness issue. He said in his letters that the Epicurean philosopher who lives beyond hope and fear does not only pursue happiness. He is actually happy. And Jefferson also thought that we find happiness, as the sociobiologists explain, by acting in accord with our unconscious social instincts. But that didn't mean that Jefferson had the solution to the problem of happiness in America. Epicurean happiness, he readily admitted, is both very rare and very selfish, and our social instincts weaken as we become more sophisticated and self-conscious, which is why Jefferson peri-odically engaged in the impossible mission of keeping most Ameri-cans down on the farm. We are tempted to conclude that the Jeffersonian history of America is the weakening of social instinct in most people without any compensatory growth in Epicurean or philosophic happiness. The obvious problem with Jefferson's twin peaks of human happiness theory is that one—the Epicurean's—is above and the other—natural instinct—is below most of the expe-riences of the self-conscious mortal. Jefferson did not really explain how middle-class Americans—those beings who cannot help but hope, fear, and love—might find happiness. He finally seems to agree with Locke that happiness is not for the being who exists some-where between the serene philosopher and the unconscious animal.

But Jefferson might add that our unhappiness is partly caused by the hypocritical laxity of middle-class aspiration. What we want, of course, is to be able to choose all the benefits but none of the burdens of being individuals. We individuals want to live long, healthy, and free lives without being anxious and lonely. We all want all the warmth and emotional security of "community" without any of its suffocating demands or constraints. We want all the love and sense of belonging that comes with family, faith, patriotism, and so forth without really thinking of ourselves fundamentally as parents or creatures or citizens. We do not want to be alone, but we do not want love to turn us into suckers. Our ambivalence reflects the complexity of our free human natures.

Guided by our insipid communitarian and therapeutic writers, we indulgently allow ourselves to imagine the coming of an anxiety-free world that would justify and reward all our work. But at the same time we find that we cannot not know that such a world exists only in the realm of fantasy. We're far too aware that it would be bad for us to feel *too* warm and secure. Our anxiety does us the favor of reminding us of the truths that other people are unreliable and that nature does not care about us as individuals at all. (According to Easterbrook, studies have even shown that people who are somewhat depressed predict the future better than those who are not because they are more realistic in their expectations.) People who are happy and well adjusted, we fear, are not concerned enough about controlling themselves and their environment. Those who nostalgically long for low-tech nobility and contentment—for the agrarian simple life, Native American wisdom, and so forth—are basically losers. We can never really fool ourselves into ignoring the fact that without real work and its attendant anxieties, life would be hell for us individuals.

Our world remains full of therapeutic happy talk about how to reconcile autonomy with community. To listen to us talk it is even easy to believe that the therapeutic view of the world has triumphed. Christina Hoff Sommers and Sally Satel, authors of *One Nation Under Therapy* (2005), conclude that our experts' "therapism" is at odds with "the American Creed," which is marked by the "values" of "self-reliance, stoicism, courage in the face of adversity, and valorization of excellence." They worry that our nation "will . . . continue to slide into therapeutic self-absorption and moral debility." But Hoff Sommers and Satel do not see that our therapeutic language doesn't correspond to our actions; despite what we say, we're not really sliding down the slippery slope to serfdom or soft despotism. Our individualistic lives are in some way harder than ever, in part, because our "self-absorption" is less in some therapeutic reverie than both survivalist and competitive or meritocratic self-obsession. Nobody with eyes to see can say that our American virtues such as courage and stoic self-reliance have to become obsolete to live well, although the therapists may actually have a point that, by themselves, they are not nearly enough for happiness in most cases. Perhaps the therapists should be blamed most for attempting to deprive us of the pride we should take in the virtues that make life worth living.

PARANOID PARENTING

Nobody really believes, for example, that the therapism of the experts has made parenting any easier. Sophisticated Americans are having fewer children than ever, but our individualistic reluctance to think of ourselves as parents is only part of the reason. In fact, being more consistently individuals has given us a new incentive to want children. Adult experiences of passion and love, as Frank

Furedi observes in *Paranoid Parenting* (2002), have become "particularly short-term and insecure," and all the "emotions that adults invest in one another are tempered by expectations of impermanence." As the ideas of *man* and *woman* have been displaced and distorted by the ideal of the genderless individual, we have found it more difficult to speak or act with confidence as either a man or woman. Because we have so little respect for what comes naturally, even "love between man and woman is often treated in a calculating and pragmatic fashion." At the same time, we still desire to be recognized and loved as more than individuals, as men and women. The result is that "the validation of self through one's child assumes a new importance." The child, "one of a few permanent facts in one's life," increasingly becomes "a unique emotional partner." An individual—or a pair of individuals—can escape some of the disorienting pain of modern isolation by focusing on his child (or perhaps children), who is stuck with his parents and cannot help but love them. In a sense, the child acts as an involuntary therapist, but not one who makes life easy.

Maybe the main reason that sophisticated parents have so few children today is that they perceive parenthood as harder than ever before. The reasons, according to David Anderegg in *Worried All the Time: Overparenting in an Age of Anxiety and How to Stop It* (2003), that parents give for that perception "are that the world is so much more *competitive* today, so much more *unsafe* today, and so much more *confusing* today." All the social policies and safety regulations designed to make children more safe have had virtually no effect on parental worry. Much more effort than ever before must be devoted to preparing children for the hard and disorienting world of American individuals. Most sophisticated parents choose to have small families not to spoil their children but to be able to prepare each of them to flourish in a particularly tough world. Parents think they have to be more responsible than ever.

The decision to have just one or two children both originates out of worry and produces more worry still. We know that parents have always been most anxious about their firstborn children, and then eased up and chilled out when it came to subsequent arrivals. So in a world full of families with nothing but firstborns, parental worrying would rise to its highest possible level. That conclusion even makes sense according to the evolutionary theory of sociobiology: The natural job of parents is to produce offspring that survive, and so their goal would seem always to be to get as many genes as possible into the next generation. That goal, as the sociobiologists (and even St. Thomas Aquinas) say, is the same for all animals. The one-kid strategy of perpetuating one's genes is too high risk a strategy to have much natural support.

"Evolutionary psychologists," Anderegg concludes, "are murky, at best, when trying to explain the current trend toward smaller families." There are some plausible hypotheses: Smaller families make more resources available for each child, making survival and success more likely in each case. Modern medicine makes it more likely that even sickly "runts" will turn out well. Certainly each child is more likely to become a healthy and fertile adult than ever before. But each child is still subject to death by accident, and so from another view parents have left their gene spreading—not to mention the emotional satisfactions of being parents—more to chance than ever before. In the final analysis, "evolutionary psychology . . . has only one prescription for parents worrying, and that is to have more children." Much parental anxiety is an unnatural product of individual choices; that doesn't mean we can or should actually relax enough to follow the psychologists' advice. But most of us still long to love or fear loneliness enough to resist the obvious individualistic solution to the problem of parental anxiety: Be an individual, not a parent, all the time. We parents remain more than individuals.

THE END OF THE ENDURING SELF?

One result of us incomplete individuals rejecting that sociobiological advice is the overprotection or overregulation of each particular child. That is bad, of course, for the development in children of some of the virtues, at least, they will need to flourish as happy and responsible adults. As Anderegg explains, "goals like developing courage, which are thought to flow from letting children take risks, are meaningless when the literal survival of the sole offspring is at stake." So our sophisticated parenthood, we can expect, will increasingly privilege individual survival over virtue or reduce virtue to those emotionally tough qualities required for individual success. It will tend to produce what David Brooks complains he found at Princeton—constantly calculating careerists who tend to reduce friendship to networking and amusement and sex to stress release.

We also cannot be surprised that our parenthood plays a part in turning college life itself into the emotionally sterile state of nature described by Tom Wolfe in *I Am Charlotte Simmons* (2004), where each individual is left alone with nothing but his or her wits to fend for him- or herself. The pleasures of conquest connected with hooking up go to the strong; the weak are condemned to "sexile," and nobody, especially not the professors, talks about the character required to live an admirable and authentic life, to be what Wolfe calls "a man in full," a real stoic, an outstanding example of courageous human individuality under difficult circumstances. One of Wolfe's big points seems to be that the contemporary elite campus is tougher on the soul than prison. Even a brilliant girl raised well in "Sparta" by her admirable—or simple and virtuous—parents does not have enough virtue to maintain her identity in the world shaped by what passes for Athenian enlightenment in America today, an enlightenment that began for her with the vulgar Nietzscheanism of her well read high school teacher and continued with the combination of radically politically correct nonjudgmentalism and soulless neuroscience of her college administrators and professors.

The deepest question Wolfe raises about the modern individual concerns where he or she is supposed to get the point of view, the character or virtue, the inward life or conscience to resist degrading social conformity. It turns out that the words "I am Charlotte Simmons" had no enduring meaning at all. The characteristic American, our critics have always said, is both an anti-social rebel and a social conformist, both James Dean and the man in the gray flannel suit (to use the relatively tame images from the fifties). Both extreme positions seem to come from excessive concern with the opinion of others, from a lack of a point of view by which to stand apart from and judge public opinion or fashion or "peer pressure."

The American individual, as Tocqueville explains, thinks he or she is free only if he or she relies solely on his or her own judgment, rejecting the authoritarian repression of authority, parents, tradition, nature, God, and so forth. It is much more clear what a radically free judgment is *not* than what one *is*. Be yourself and be unique, we are told. But as Tocqueville explains, the individual human mind is anxious, disoriented, and paralyzed if it has to work all by itself. To be conscious, to think clearly and well, is to think with others. The solitude of radical freedom makes human thought and action impossible. And because the individual looks up to no authority, he's stuck with looking around for some orientation from fashion, from public opinion, from whatever the reigning experts are saying.

The Individual and
Biotechnological Enhancement

One theme of this book is the modern individual who worries incessantly about achieving personal authenticity and self-fulfillment yet is more anxious than ever about being alone. Another concerns the individual's relationship to the various technologies now becoming available to improve, if not perfect, our natures. On the one hand, we worry that by using technology to change our bodies and even our souls—our moods—we might change our very identities and so fail to achieve authenticity. On the other hand, we also believe that we have a duty to pursue happiness and enhance our security according to the latest studies and technological advances. As *Beyond Therapy* (a report of the President's Council on Bioethics, 2003) puts it, "Only a person utterly at peace with himself would be beyond temptation at the prospect of having his troubles effortlessly eased," and we must add that the individual as individual always chooses freedom and comfort over virtue.

Most of all, however, our main experience of technology and biotechnology has not and will not be the effortless easing of our troubles. Enhancement is and increasingly will be part of the "designer" work we'll have to do just not to be alone. It will be harder than ever for sovereign or self-sufficient individuals to choose against what's generally regarded as useful or effective. It is really hard to be yourself if you really believe or hope that the "self" is just a chemical reaction to be altered at will. You know of no way of keeping public opinion or social forces or politically correct experts from making a pharmacological determination of what you should be.

Consider the way in which the American individual increasingly identifies self-fulfillment with bodily obsession. Carl Elliott, in *Better Than Well: American Medicine Meets the American Dream* (2003), calls attention to a study chronicling the way the diaries of adolescent girls have changed over the last century. Before World War I, girls "rarely used the language of self-identity and improvement when they wrote about their bodies. In comparison to today, they were far less likely to mention their bodies at all." They tended to regard obsessing about one's physical appearance as vain and undignified, and they would resolve to think more of others. Today a girl bent on becoming a better person is likely to focus her private thoughts on diet, exercise, and various beauty enhancements. She really believes she can *change* herself by losing thirty pounds. That also means, of course, that a girl thinks that how she looks to others is who she is; gone is much of her authentically inward life.

Our perky libertarians—such as Virginia Postrel—say that enhancement technologies allow us to re-create our outward selves to correspond to our inward identities. Such enhancement does not reflect anxious social conformism but a way of being authentic or, as Postrel says, "special." If a generously endowed girl nevertheless thinks of herself as a being with small breasts, for example, she can now become one. Soon enough, those who think of themselves as tall will no longer have to be short. Even men who think of themselves as women already can become women, and vice versa. More Americans than ever, Elliott reports, believe that being "born in the wrong body" is, in effect, tantamount to being "deprived of an identity." We increasingly identify ourselves with our bodies—not so much the bodies we have now, but the bodies we would *like* to have.

The man who becomes a woman cannot be accused of social conformism. But even s/he wants to be recognized as a woman by others. Being "inwardly" a woman is not enough because s/he is not a genuinely self-sufficient individual. In most cases, people are dissatisfied with their bodies because their physical appearance has socially isolated them. The individual, in truth, too readily identifies authenticity with emptiness and isolation and will use every means available to avoid it. For the most part, biotechnological enhancement will be used to allow and often compel us to surrender our stigmatizing physical or psychological differences. The choice for a new body—or even a new soul—will not be so "special" at all. Biotechnology may well most powerfully act to decrease genuine human diversity.

The paradox is that the disappearance of genuine inwardness is largely the result of the individualistic focus on the self, on getting in touch with one's own feelings or needs. "Finding yourself," Elliott observes, "has replaced finding God." Or perhaps they are the same thing: We are told that we will find God by looking within; when we have discovered our true selves we will also have found God. But of course such a self-obsessive search really yields nothing, and the individual finds to his dismay that authenticity turns out to be emptiness. Self-discovery therefore must become self-invention. We must make ourselves as God made the whole world—out of nothing. But how does one do *that*? It is impossible. That is why even our self-inventing postmodern artist cannot escape fashion or public opinion or dominant ideologies.

The self-inventor is left with a guilty conscience. He wants to distinguish his self-constructed identity from the inauthentic shows most people put on for others. After all, nobody wants to believe that self-construction is nothing but a flight from the truth into social conformism. The so-called postmodern theorists from Erving Goffman to Richard Rorty claim to have solved this problem by eliminating the distinction that was the basis of this conscientious objection. They say that there is no true self that stands apart from the social roles one plays. We are all performers and nothing more, and successful people consciously develop multiple, flexible identities without giving a moment's thought to which is true and which is false. In this way, the theory of the individual culminates in the denial of the possibility of the sovereign individual, even while it continues to assume that success and failure is by individuals. So it seems there can be no real objection to the biotechnological reconstruction or transformation of one's identity, as long as individual success and the pursuit of happiness are our only goals.

The most promising form of biotechnological enhancement aims to free us from our anxiety by transforming our identities or souls, to make our moods—and so our beings—something other than those of individuals. The promoters of relatively effective antidepressants such as Prozac claim that I will discover my true self once my anxiety is gone. The premise is that I was never really an anxious individual after all, that all my greatness and misery is the result of a correctible chemical imbalance. We cannot help, Elliott concludes, but be both enthusiastic *and* anxious consumers of such psychopharmacological remedies. Paxil's slogan is "Relieve the anxiety, and reveal the person," but nobody really believes that chemical manipulation is a reliable source of revelation.

My argument in this book is that all of our efforts at mood control will, paradoxically, reveal our pursuit of happiness to be more futile than ever. It just might show us that happiness is more than a chemical problem that has a technological or biotechnological solution. Remember the contemporary American part of the problem that the novelist-philosopher Walker Percy emphasizes in *The Message in the Bottle* (1975): "One tires of the good life and the best of all possible worlds one has designed for oneself. One feels anxious without knowing why. One is at home and yet feels homeless. One loves bad news and secretly longs for . . . catastrophes." Catastrophes bring necessity to the forefront, and it becomes clear what we're supposed to do, what virtue is. The anxiety connected with the illusion of infinite possibility—the illusion expressed extremely or ideologically by communism and the other forms of designer utopianism (including the ones described by our utopian poet David Brooks) of our time—makes virtue more necessary than ever to live well and far more difficult to acquire. The illusion is that it is possible or good to live wholly as an autonomous individual, or not as a creature, friend, citizen, parent, or child. But the truth is we will never live in a world without the reality of catastrophes, without sin, suffering, loneliness, profound disorientation, dementia, and death.

Stuck with Virtue

All in all, I don't think that we need fear the advent of a posthuman future. We will not become so content, so happy, that virtue, love, friendship, and God are no longer necessary. I disagree with *Beyond Therapy* that "[w]hat's to be particularly feared about the common and casual use of mind-altering drugs" is "that they will seduce us into resting content with a shallow and factitious happiness." We are clearly not going to be either too shallow or too happy. We are going to remain stuck with the tough demands of living in a very high-tech, very meritocratic, very competitive society, and we will remain all too aware of what other people think about and expect from us. So here's the good news—and the bad news: The Brave New World is not lurking around the corner. The human soul— that nonmaterial principle of motivation and aspiration—shines forth in and transforms all our thought and action, including our wonderful but finally futile efforts to free ourselves from nature and God. Neither God nor the soul will die just because we who misunderstand ourselves as individuals and nothing more have forgotten for the moment how to talk about them.

Besides, I have exaggerated somewhat the predicament of today's American individual by neglecting the social or at least non-individualistic virtue of pride. It should go without saying that today's successful meritocrat takes pride in how he or she has distinguished him- or herself by living a tough and productive life. Pride in one's ingenuity and industry is more pronounced today than ever. And today's child of sophisticated parents is sometimes a remarkable work of art; such parents love to be recognized for what they have accomplished through their child. Because it is never easy, pride is always taken in the virtue of governing oneself and others. Lurking beneath the surface argument of this chapter has been Pascal's account of the misery of our mortality, but Pascal also says that pride counterbalances human misery. One of the toughest indictments of our excessive individualism is that it has even turned against proper pride.

There is also plenty of evidence that what Joseph Ratzinger has called, in *God and the World* (English translation, 2002), our "attempts to manufacture man's inner fulfillment, his happiness, as a kind of product" will fail. Perhaps, Ratzinger (now Pope Benedict XVI) goes on, "we are beginning to see again that freedom from work, that freedom which is a gift of God's service, stepping outside the mentality of mere achievement, is what we need."

That freedom from work—experienced by the first Benedictine monks—does not, of course, entail the abolition of the ennobling necessities of labor and achievement in this world. For Ratzinger also reminds us, Christians, even before the Lockeans, overcame "the ancient prejudice against manual labor, hitherto regarded as fit only for slaves," and so abolished the distinction between "slave and free man." Because we are all free beings who work, we are all called to cultivate or improve what we have been given with both the needs of our bodies and the needs of our souls in mind. None of us, in one sense, is free from work, but in another sense, we all are. Freedom from work means freedom from the illusion that we can or must make everything worthwhile for ourselves.

"The true God," Gilbert Meilaender observes in *Bioethics: A Primer for Christians* (2004), "will . . . always disappoint our desire for independence and self-sufficiency." Our trust in the "perfection and power of God is displayed in the acceptance of neediness, dependence, and suffering." Certainly we have plenty of reason to be grateful for, and to acknowledge our dependence upon, what we have been given. Certainly the mysterious gift of Being and especially human being demands the reasonable response of wonder.

In this book I use the word *individual* in a very specific way. As Walker Percy says, the dilemma of the modern individual lies in constituting himself against the modern science that denies the reality and goodness of any particular human being's particular experiences. The unlimited attempt to achieve autonomous, sovereign control over an indifferent nature is both impossible and self-destructive. But at the same time I write on behalf of the true dignity of the individual rightly understood: each of us is constituted by nature—through the capacity of language or speech—as a "wayfarer," a homeless, displaced being in search of the truth about his or her situation. We search with each other, but finally each of us must use his or her capabilities to be the judge of the truth of his experiences. Those judgments are not possible if we experience ourselves as either too alone or as too much at home. Individuals, in the sense of dignified and particular human beings, cannot be at home with their homelessness by listening to our libertarians, who make us too homeless, or our sociobiologists, who make us too much at home.

I also agree with Walker Percy that there is a true and proper way to speak of the sovereign individual, the being who can tell the truth to himself about his strange or alienated experiences and act accordingly. But the sovereign—in the sense of autonomous—individual, as I have explained, characteristically defers to public opinion or impersonal authority rather than attempting the lonely and impossible task of self-invention. The genuinely sovereign individual—the being genuinely aware of his predicament as a particular human being—knows that words like autonomy, creativity, and self-fulfillment have no meaning without some foundation in the capabilities we have been given by nature or God.

CHAPTER 1

COMMUNISM TODAY

We are on the verge of a realignment in American political life today, one that will produce libertarian and anti-libertarian factions. The anti-libertarian faction can also be called communitarian, as long as that term is defined with some precision. These communitarians will not be opposed, in general, to the free market. The Evil Empire has fallen, after all, and almost nobody really believes any more that we are slouching toward socialism. Alexis de Tocqueville's fear that democracy tends to evolve toward a benevolent despotism of meddlesome schoolmasters to whom we surrender thought and concern about our futures no longer seems so prescient. And neither does Tocqueville's hope that the Americans would continue to resist individualism through vibrant, participatory local political institutions. The truth is that American individuals are more obsessed with their futures than ever, while the communal attachments that help take people's minds off themselves and provide the safety nets that keep them from falling too hard are weaker than ever.

The new anti-libertarian faction will have the modest aim of moderating the self-destructive excesses of our self-obsession. It is true that more Americans than ever are now forming, and will continue to form, countercultural, "whole-life" small communities, and most of these communities will have a religious foundation. But that sort of thoroughgoing communitarianism will remain an "alternative lifestyle" that will not be embraced by most of us. The socialist hope that America as a whole could eventually become a "Great Community" founded on the activist, egalitarian pursuit of justice remains nowhere except in the world of professors. Most of our new communitarians will be happy if they can moderate the excesses of the libertarian view of liberty, if they can direct the future of human freedom well enough to encourage or at least not discourage those human experiences connected with love, family, friendship, faith, citizenship, responsibility, and even death—experiences that make life worth living. In other words, the new communitarians will be united more by their opposition to libertarian extremism than any shared, comprehensive view of human community.

The new anti-libertarian faction will oppose the comprehensive and indiscriminate claims for personal liberty made by libertarian ideologues. That view of the world—which until recently was shared only by a few intellectuals—is now emerging as the modern American consensus, cutting across the mainstream of our two political parties. A libertarian, for my purposes here, is pro-choice on everything, or almost everything—a free-marketer economically and an anti-prohibitionist, even an antimoralist, when it comes to social and cultural issues. The libertarian wants the principles of calculation and consent to inform every facet of each of our "designer" personal lives. And today, the ideology of libertarianism is being reinforced and reinvigorated by the promise of unfettered biotechnological development: we will soon be able to design our lives ever more completely in opposition to the various tyrannies and indignities nature imposes upon us.

To be clear, this ideological libertarianism is not characteristic of all or perhaps even most Americans who call themselves libertarians. Nor do I wish to imply that our self-proclaimed libertarians were in any way soft on Marxist totalitarian tyranny. But the kind of libertarianism I am describing here is a creeping cultural phenomenon that is affecting us all.

As I will explain, what libertarian ideology promises today is strangely close to what Marx promised would come with communism—freedom from alienation and oppression, a life constrained by nothing but personal choice, the withering away of religion, and the withering away of the state. The "old" communism of the Soviet empire was, in a certain sense, a strangely conservative ideology rooted in tyranny and historical quackery. It eventually collapsed because it futilely opposed itself to what libertarians call the "dynamism" of human initiative or free human action. Insofar as the hopes of communism present themselves now in a more clearly libertarian and technology-friendly form, they are in some ways more seductive.

Thus, while the title of this chapter will no doubt alarm some readers and irritate others, taking that risk seems necessary in order to help us think more clearly about the peculiar ideological threat that confronts us today. The new anti-libertarian coalition will obviously contain diverse elements. It should include all lovers of human liberty who see that libertarian ideology—like all ideological extremism—may generate rampant statism. I write, largely in the tradition of Hayek, Acton, and Tocqueville, against big government and for the enduring responsibility of fallible mortals.

IDEOLOGIES

We are all still living in the modern world, a world that has not changed in fundamental orientation for hundreds of years. The world, in fact, continues to become progressively more modern. One of the great founders of the modern world—Niccolo Machiavelli—thought that the great obstacle to human beings seeing the truth was their propensity to be suckered by tyrants, especially those employing the seductive charms of Christianity. For Machiavelli, people get so caught up in the illusions of an otherworldly imagination that they do not notice how much they are being taken advantage of in this world.

But despite the great success of Machiavelli and others in freeing human beings from that otherworldly imagination and directing them toward the pursuit of wealth and freedom in this world, it is not true that the main effect of his thought has been to liberate us from lies and direct us toward the truth. Even Machiavelli would have to admit that the unprecedented lies of our so-called enlightened era are the most tyrannical ever told. The twentieth century was—and the twenty-first century probably will be—a mixture of unprecedented freedom and unprecedented tyranny.

The name rightly given to a specifically modern lie is an *ideology*. An ideology is a form of popular science, and so not a form of real science. It is a comprehensive and easy-to-understand account of all that exists. Ideologies are the dogmas that fill the vacuum created by the discrediting of religious dogma. They are, in fact, usually meant to be replacements for Christianity's central tenets. But they never really free themselves from Christianity altogether: The future paradise promised by the personal God of the Bible, we are told, can be achieved in a more human—but still more impersonal—way.

Ideologies are offered as replacements for all personal claims of authority—the claims of particular poets, priests, philosophers, princes, and God. The Machiavellian view—which is the democratic view—is that to defer to someone else's wisdom is to be suckered into being ruled by that person. The claims of ideology, on the other hand, are never personal; ideologies teach that we are not controlled by persons but by forces, such as history or matter or the economy or technology. That is why ideologies are always promulgated by experts who never say "I think" or "I believe" but "history shows" or (nowadays) "studies show." Ideologists always call upon the impersonal authority of science. But is it really more degrading to accept the personal authority of God or a philosopher like Aristotle than to defer to, or be controlled by, no one in particular?

It is true that to be controlled by forces is more democratic than to be controlled by people, since in the former case everyone is at least equally unfree. But that does not change the fact that ideologies such as Marxism and evolutionism make us all seem less truly free than we really are. The libertarian ideologues are at least right to say that we are not determined completely by the division of labor or nature, although they too ideologically imagine a future in which we will be deprived of much that genuinely characterizes our liberty. They, with the Marxists, imagine an unalienated, "designer" or choice-filled future, a kind of techno-paradise on earth. The libertarians, in their own way, imagine that we are less free than we really are.

All ideologies, in fact, oppose the foundational Christian claim, although one that does not necessarily depend on religious faith, that human beings are alienated by their natures. We experience ourselves as to some extent "displaced persons," as somewhat homeless, as aliens or pilgrims in this world. The very existence of human beings—the very existence of myself as a self-conscious being—is a mystery that eludes systematic explanation. My self-consciousness—and so my openness to the truth about all things—cannot be explained by any ideology: Even Marx could not account for his own love of the truth or his own love of freedom—both of which were quite real—through his materialistic, systematic account of history.

COMMUNISM

Modern ideologies all deny that human alienation is natural, that it is part of the human condition and therefore something we cannot completely overcome on our own. So, all ideologies also oppose the Christian and classical view that false hopes about the effectiveness of human effort always end up intensifying the human alienation that they mean to remedy. Ideological programs to eliminate alienation end up undermining those ways we really do have to ameliorate and live well with our homelessness without providing any real replacement for them.

The claim of communism, for example, is that human alienation is not natural but historical. Human beings alienated themselves through their historical or economic activity—through their development of the division of labor. From the communist standpoint, the bad news is that we unwittingly messed ourselves up. The good news is that we can free ourselves through revolution by bringing the division of labor, and so history, to an end.

Surely, we might object, communism is dead: no one but North Koreans, Cubans, and a few out-of-touch professors buys that ideology anymore. Yet, in my view, while the hard side of communism is dead, the soft side is very much alive. True, nobody really still thinks that the communist revolution is coming, and almost everyone now knows that the totalitarian terror designed to provoke or complete such a revolution was, at the very least, a monstrous mistake. But the seductive lie of communism lives on, in that many people still think that it is too bad that communism could not work, that Marx's beautiful dream could not become real, that we cannot free ourselves through economic or political action from our miserable human alienation.

We can begin deconstructing this lie by looking at Marx's description, provided in *The German Ideology*, of the unalienated life promised by communism: "in communist society, where nobody has one exclusive sphere of activity but each can become accomplished in any branch he wishes, society regulates the general production and thus makes it possible for me to do one thing today and another tomorrow, to hunt in the morning, fish in the afternoon, rear cattle in the evening, criticize after dinner, just as I have a mind, without ever becoming hunter, fisherman, shepherd, or critic." Here Marx predicts that under communism you will be able to do whatever you want whenever you want, with no reason at all to take one activity more seriously than another, no reason at all to take any of them seriously at all. The sign that alienation has been overcome is that no one is consumed or obsessed with any activity at the expense of others. Life has become a series of easygoing hobbies—what we now call playing golf badly, philosophizing or shooting the bull badly, and so forth. If you start to take golf and philosophizing seriously, then alienation has returned. Under communism, Tiger Woods's obsession with perfecting his short game would be unthinkable, as would Socrates's relentless obsession with questions that have no answers. Under communism, surely Tiger would relax, and Socrates would chill out and realize that he is just shooting the bull.

Now, we busy and very alienated Americans sometimes do yearn for weekends much like the communist life described by

Marx—weekends of casually terrible fishing and golf followed by shooting the bull after dinner. But if Marx's communism really described all of human life, it would not be heaven on earth but an inescapable hell. It would be worse than the hell experienced by Bill Murray's character in *Groundhog Day*. We would be stuck with lives even more hellish than living the same day over and over again; there would be *nothing* impelling us to choose in one direction rather than another.

Here is one way of explaining why life under communism would actually be hellish. Marx says that human alienation in some ways becomes magnified under capitalism. In capitalist societies, human beings have become more self-obsessed and individualistic than ever. Our devotions to God, family, friends, country, and so forth define less of our lives than ever before, and it seems that the only human distinctions left that bear any weight concern money. And obsession with money—a most selfish obsession—isolates us and pits us against one another. But the pursuit of money—which is required not just to live well but to live at all under capitalism—at least gives us something difficult and interesting to do, something that can moderate the neurotic self-obsession that can otherwise overwhelm us when we have nothing at all worthwhile to do. The money-based productivity of us capitalists, after all, really has made all our lives more comfortable, secure, and free. Our productivity is surely worthy of pride, but pride—a social virtue that connects one with others—would disappear if hard work, like everything else, became a pointless option.

Marx says that under communism our self-obsession will disappear. But why should that be? It is not that Marx believes that our old devotions to God, country, friends, and family would reappear: these alienating illusions, he thought, would never return. Our need for and devotion to money would of course also be gone. So there would be nothing to orient or direct our lives; all of life would become a personal whim. It is not even clear why Marx calls communism communism, because under it we would not be guided or limited in our choices by any community at all. There would be no sense of duty or love to limit our "designer" lives; the attachments presupposed, and created, by duty and love limit our options and make us obsessive. Under communism, the good and bad news is that each human being would be both more free and more alone than ever.

There would be nothing to limit our self-obsession, to get our minds off of ourselves, under communism. And in that case, human beings would very likely be more death-obsessed than ever. Marx, a good materialist, never says that the coming of communism will bring human mortality to an end, and he never says that human beings will stop being self-consciously mortal. But no being aware of his or her own death can help but be moved by that fact. Under communism, if Marx is right, we would simply be deprived of the means—religion, love, virtue, political life, and so forth—with which human beings have always availed themselves in order to live well enough in the face of death. More than ever, we will be stuck with dying pointless deaths alone. The communist lie also would make it impossible to find the words to explain to ourselves our experiences of alienation in the midst of the paradise we had created for ourselves, and being deprived of such explanations would make us yet more alienated. Communism is not the remedy for, but merely an intensification of, characteristically capitalistic or individualistic alienation. What is psychologically tough about capitalism—and who can deny that Marx explained pretty well at times why we capitalists are anxious and restless in the midst of prosperity—would be worse under communism.

We might explain Marx's unrealistic imagining of life under communism as a possible *human* reality by referring to the intensity of his own distinctively human longings. He deeply desired to become wise, and so he imagined a world in which all mystery would disappear. He imagined away the mystery of death (not to mention birth), and he imagined away the mystery of love—or being dependent on another human being whom we find good despite (or because of) the fact that he or she eludes our complete comprehension and control.

Marx also longed to be completely free. He longed for a world without any trace of servility. That world too would have to be without love, death, or any form of human neediness or contingency, because it would have to be without anything that makes one human being dependent on another. Marx's characteristically modern longings for perfect wisdom and freedom were so strong that he did not see that a world without mystery and dependence would be hellishly inhuman. That world is both impossible and undesirable, at least as a human creation. More deeply still, Marx mistakenly imagined that he himself could be satisfied or even happy in a world of his own construction in which his longings for wisdom and freedom would be completely satisfied. It is part of the mystery of Marx's own being that we cannot really imagine him—that amazingly intense thinker and activist—as anything but miserable in the society full of slackers he worked so hard to bring into being.

Is Communism Already Here?

Communism as Marx describes it could never, as far as we can tell, become real, because neither he nor we could ever imagine a world full of unalienated human beings. But we *can* imagine a society where something like communist ideology—the hope for a society in which everyone would live unalienated in the present without the oppression of religion and morality—exerted a great deal of intellectual appeal. Such a society would be not so different from our own—at least its more sophisticated sectors. And it would tend to have the following qualities:

The morality taught by its experts and repeated by its well-educated members would be marked by an easygoing tolerance or nonjudgmentalism. Those in the know would say that they are very indifferent when it comes to issues that used to be connected with the soul. Even choices that used to be regarded as fundamental or life-forming—like who to have sex with and why—would be regarded as mere preferences. Anything "consenting adults" do would be beyond reproach; nonconsensual sex would be less criminal than insane. That sort and all sorts of obsessive sex are evidence of wounded souls or at least chemical imbalances, and they would need to be eradicated through therapy in the interest of safety. More generally, anyone who deviates very far from moral indifference would be labeled as dangerously outside the "mainstream," and perhaps also in need of therapy to get in touch with the truth of the times. If such deviants could not be talked into seeing the truth, drugs might be prescribed. If the medication did not work very well, they would just be ignored. There would, in fact, be no need to be so obsessive as the Soviets and put those moral fanatics—such as Aleksandr Solzhenitsyn—into psychiatric prisons, which would only call attention to their crazy whining. (American novelist Walker Percy once wrote that he had Solzhenitsyn envy: the Russian dissident was at least taken seriously enough to be thrown into the Gulag.)

Education increasingly would become merely technical and

careerist, and Percy's and Solzhenitsyn's books would be ignored. But our indifference to the soul would often make it not even particularly good technical education. Teachers would become increasingly nonjudgmental about their students' academic performance, and grades would continue to inflate. People would occasionally grouse but not really worry about what unearned self-esteem would do to students' souls. But there would also be a growing consensus that the report card should also include genuinely stern news about the student's body mass. Grade inflation does the student no physical harm. The real problem would be students inflating physically, too, and the obesity epidemic would become the number one educational concern. In the BMI category, there would be no masking the student's true performance. And the school would have every right to demand that parents discipline their kids toward a more physically risk-free life. The tough goal would be no child left with a big behind.

Education would become technical in order that students acquire the means to live however they please. Their mastery of technology would be in the service of diversity, of expanding the menu of individual choice. But how can they design lives according to mere preferences or whims? How can I choose to be a Christian or a Spartan or a philosopher when I know so clearly that there is no foundation to Christianity, being a warrior, or the way of life of the philosopher? Education would be largely technological because people's true view would be that the only real or weighty choices would be for health and safety, for maximizing one's own security and minimizing risk, for maximizing one's own independence and minimizing one's dependence on others and on nature. That choice for individual independence, of course, would also be to maximize dependence on technology. So for all the talk of education for diversity, the tendency would be to empty the moral contents out of all non-technological ways of life. And so technology—the mastery of nature with individual control and security in mind—would move from being a means to an end. The real conclusion would be that all the diverse ways of life that resist the domination of technology are equally weightless. Nothing would arouse people enough to direct technological means effectively toward non-technological ends.

The seeming inability to be aroused over issues as fundamental as love, death, and God that would pervade a society such as the one we are imagining would lead some writers to believe that we really had become as passion-free as Marx hoped we would. Whiny or out-of-touch moralists would write books about people having become flat-souled or virtue having come to an end. These moralists would be dismayed that people seemed to be able to live well without reference to what used to be regarded as distinctively human obsessions. The world, to hear people talk, would seem to be composed of nothing more than soulless hobbyists or chatty tourists. More generally, theorists would be divided into those who like the communism Marx described and those who hate it, but they would all agree that such an apathetic world had come about.

There really would be some evidence, even if it were not entirely compelling, that people, by becoming unobsessive, had also become pretty unerotic: In the times of the Victorians or the Puritans, the sight of an ankle filled a man with desire; now we would see beautiful, virtually unclothed young women on MTV and yawn. It is not surprising that Viagra would have to be invented. People would actually believe that, as liberated individuals, they are no longer defined by "gender," by being men and women. So they would also believe that marriage need not be between a man and a woman.

Redefined as a contract for caregiving between any two individuals, marriage would be detached from any necessary connection to sex and babies at all.

Sex would continue to exist, of course, but more as a form of mildly diverting recreation disconnected from the "necessity" of procreation or the alienating constraints of marriage. Instead of "same-sex" marriage elevating gay relationships by leading them to conform to the traditional standards of heterosexual monogamy, promiscuous and relatively casual gay sexual behavior would increasingly become the model for all human sexual activity. Married couples would be increasingly reluctant to admit to obsessing over one another's fidelity. Love would continue to exist, but it would be perceived as more and more unreliable as a guide to human behavior. Disconnected from common human responsibilities and intimations of eternity or at least relative permanence, people would count on love less and less. The withering away of love, Marx sort of predicted, would accompany the withering away of the state and religion. The less erotic people become, the less dangerous, unpredictable, and discontented they become.

OBSESSIVE COMMUNIST PROHIBITIONISM?
Despite the logic of the argument against the future of love, those theorists who would believe that they see human beings becoming unobsessive and apathetic would be almost as wrong as Marx. They would confuse what people have been taught to say by ideological experts with what they really experience. People would not really be unerotic, just confused, and that confusion would make them more angry and litigious when it comes to matters of the heart than ever. No matter what the law and the experts might say, nobody really would believe there is such a thing as a "no fault" divorce.

And gay men would have as great a capacity for jealousy as heterosexual women. Even though thinking about death would disappear from polite conversation, all sorts of human activity would still reveal our personal obsession with our mortality. People would be more death haunted than ever before, and so traumatized by the fact of their inevitable extinction that they would often be unable to bear being with people who are obviously near death.

Sophisticated people would have very few children, not only because babies are clearly an alienating constraint on one's freedom, but because they refuse to endorse the idea that they would eventually need to be replaced. Rather than producing replacements, they would sometimes focus their attention completely and most scientifically on their own indefinite perpetuation. But out of love or fear of loneliness they would often still have one or two children, and they would become obsessive about their children's safe, healthy, and productive futures too. They would be so worried about their children that they would barely know that they loved them and would find it especially tough to be in love with them in the present. They would be deprived of the words to know that children—like all of us—are lovable, in part, because they will die, because they are aliens or pilgrims in this world. Childhood would be hell under communism, which may be why Marx never described it. Either parents would utterly ignore their children in the interest of remaining unalienated, or they would define their whole lives around the only beings left in the world stuck with loving them. Children would either be left completely alone or not let alone at all.

Children would be taught in school the ideology of evolutionism or sociobiology. They would learn that they are no different in any fundamental way from the other animals, that people are nothing more than really clever chimps. They would also learn that those who in the past (such as Christians and Aristotelians) had had vain ideas about human distinctiveness also harbored gross superstitions and oppressive ideas about religion, morality, and politics. Science's "great demotion" of human beings to one species among many is the foundation of nonjudgmental human freedom, these students would be told, which is why they would now smile in disbelief when they heard someone say that one species is better than another. Only those even wiser than the natural scientists would understand the deeper truth missed by Marx, which is that as historical beings, humans used to be different from the other species, but are not anymore. Sociobiology, the deep thought would be, becomes true to the extent that communism does. Only when humans had become as at home in this world as the chimps, who surely are unrevolutionary and unalienated animals, would they also be communists.

The trouble would be that what people learn in school from the experts about the sociobiological view that we humans are clever animals and nothing more would not correspond with their personal experiences. They would remain strongly moved by anxiety, fear, love, and death, and they would know—more or less—that they are strange because they are open to the truth and chimps are not. Hearing that their strange experiences have no foundation, no reality, would just make them more alienated and obsessive—more anti-natural and unchimplike—than ever.

People would be mightily dissatisfied with the official evolutionary view that all members of all species share the same purposes: nature intends nothing more than for them all—including humans—to be born, spread their genes, raise their young, and then quickly step aside for their natural replacements. Individuals would be stuck with rebelling against blind and pitiless nature, against the seemingly cruel and random process that is so indifferent to the fate of particular individuals. They would even go so far as to ignore the good advice sociobiologists would give us about the connection between human happiness and our instincts to have children and do our natural duties to them and others close to us. If evolutionism really expressed the whole truth about nature, then the human judgment would have to be that nature is no good. And so people would regret that nature could not really be changed through history, and they would look for new ways to give ourselves a better deal. The ideology of sociobiology—like the ideology of communism—would have the unintended and perverse effect of intensifying obsessive individualism.

COMMUNISM AND BIOTECHNOLOGY

Alienated human beings living under the domination of the ideology of communism would lose hope in Marx's idea of historical transformation, and they would see no hope in evolutionism or sociobiology. Although they would also be deprived of the hope of revealed religion, they would still conclude that human beings are by nature alienated, and they would begin to long for the power to change that nature. Hope for that possibility would lie in biotechnology. Thus far, humans had been slaves to the natural evolution that determines our genetic makeup, but biotechnology would promise the power to give orders to their genes. Blind and pitiless natural evolution would be replaced with conscious and volitional evolution, which would be used to secure and perfect the human individual. This new evolutionary process would rightly be called "utopian eugenics," because it would allow humans finally to have the unprecedented power to make flawed, alienated human nature good.

Genetic therapy and regenerative medicine would promise to eradicate disease and extend individual life indefinitely. Death would no longer be viewed as an invincible necessity that gives definition to human life but as a disease to be cured. The promise of the ideology of biotechnology would be that human beings would be less death-haunted than ever before and so more ready than ever to live the free, "designer" life promised by Marx.

Biotechnology would certainly make each human life objectively more secure. But experience suggests that there is little connection between the fact of relative security and the human *perception* of security. Even under the regime of utopian eugenics, death—having come to seem less necessary and more accidental—would arouse more anxiety than ever. And people would be more impelled to plan incessantly to avoid that accident. The teaching of Pascal that people are, by nature, miserable accidents, which had always seemed to be unrealistically extreme, we would actually work to make more true. And we would provide more evidence for his claims that our true home must be somewhere else and that our greatness is intertwined with our misery.

Longer human lives would increase self-obsession in other ways. Individual lives would be less defined by children, and sex might have to be altogether detached from reproduction. We would be left with neither babies nor reliable sexual "partners" to help us get our minds off ourselves. Libertarians would assure people that the new eugenic regime would be the very opposite of tyranny, because individuals would be perfectly free to make biotechnological choices for themselves and their children. But the limit to freedom would be, as it is now, health and safety; personal choice would not be allowed to burden others with unnecessary risks. The old-fashioned way of having babies—two married people having unprotected sex and hoping and praying for the best—would surely be unnecessarily risky, so government would end up telling people how to have children and perhaps even how many to have. The state, in pursuit of risk management or eradication, would therefore intrude more and more into the most intimate details of people's lives. The more we would become obsessed with health and safety at the expense of love and virtue, the more we would be willing to surrender our freedom for security.

Biotechnology could not, then, any more than communism, ever really free us from death. But maybe it could free us from being strongly moved by that fact, and in that way make something like Marx's description of communism come true. Drugs like Prozac have already freed some individuals from anxiety while allowing them to remain thoughtful and productive. Maybe they are a prelude to a genuinely reliable psychopharmacology that can effect a change in our very natures. Rousseau said that the only genuinely good death would be an unconscious one, and it would not be hard to use biotechnology to abolish self-consciousness altogether—in some people, at least. But, as the example of Marx shows, we do not want to surrender our humanity altogether; we really want to *manage* our self-consciousness. We want to remain aware of and moved, but not too much, by love and death. The problem is that we do not understand self-consciousness at all, and how can we manage what we cannot understand? Our desire for designer moods is even less likely to be satisfied than our desire for designer babies. We are far more likely to unwittingly make ourselves more miserably disappointed in the intractability of our alienation.

The failure of the ideology of biotechnology to free us from being haunted by death while at the same time reducing the compensations we get for our mortality through our love of others and

God would eventually teach us that Marx was really wrong. No modern ideology can free us from religion—which will be around as long as human beings, unlike the other animals, are alienated by their natures. Nor can ideology free us from the state, because human beings will always remain free, proud, and perverse enough to require and demand to be governed. The resources human beings have been given to live well as self-conscious mortals are love, virtue, and spiritual life, and the main effect of modern ideology has been to deprive human beings of the words and self-understanding required to see this truth. Ideologies have kept us from seeing the truth about both our greatness and our misery, which is the truth about our dignity.

The Danger of Communism's Untruth

We have never been in danger of Marx's communist dream becoming real. The danger, rather, has always been that modern human beings will remain unnecessarily miserable—in one way too free, and in another too subject to tyranny—because they refuse to face up to the truth that they cannot really free themselves from their alienation through their own efforts. The next step—the genuinely postmodern step—is to realize that our alienation is good both because it is a clue to the truth about our being and because it is the precondition for the goods, the loves that we enjoy in this world. Much of our dignity comes from the fact that we are stuck with living morally demanding lives.

I know that in suggesting that contemporary American culture is like the communism Marx describes I have exaggerated a good deal. Many Americans, for example, remain authentically religious, and we have in this country a genuinely Christian counterculture. Many Americans also live fairly well in the present by loving their family and friends and not obsessing too much about the future. Many have a prudently minimal interest in diet and exercise only when it is fun. Studies even show that more Americans (although very few who think themselves sophisticated or in the know) are more obese than ever. (Not that overeating is less compulsive than overdieting.) We also should not forget that a good deal of our obsessiveness stems from the fact that we middle-class Americans are and will remain free beings who must work. As Tocqueville explained, those compelled to make money cannot help but love it, and the universal love of money is part of the equality and the prosperity that are genuinely American goods. And nothing I have said can explain why America was able to defeat the hard-communist ideology of Soviet totalitarianism or react so resolutely and so calmly to the crisis we call 9/11.

Even so, the attraction of soft-communist ideology is very much present among us, and it can be seen in the form of libertarianism—the promiscuous pro-choice ideology—that is infusing our intellectual life and both of our political parties. Because the miserable and perverse effects of our biotechnological pursuit of something like Marx's communism will not be as obvious for a while as the benefits that such technology will achieve for health, safety, and prosperity, we can expect that organized opposition to the ideological combination of libertarianism with biotechnology will grow slowly. And it will grow ambivalently, because being an "alienated individual" will always be part of our self-understanding—and a point of pride—in a high-tech time.

CHAPTER 2

POSTMODERN CONSERVATISM, CONSERVATIVE POSTMODERNISM

Astute thinkers from Hegel onward have claimed that we live at the end of the modern world. That does not mean the modern world is about to disappear: the world, in truth, is more modern than ever. So we must contest Hegel's assertion that the modern world is the end, the fulfillment, of history. The longings of human beings have neither been satisfied nor have they disappeared. Modern strivings continue to be fueled by a progressively more restless and anxious human discontent. But when the modern world is succeeded by another—as it eventually will be—human beings will continue to be human, beings with souls or capabilities and longings not shared by, and higher than those of, other animals.

What has distinguished the modern world, above all, is a particular definition of what it means to be a human being. Modern thought has held that a human being is a free individual and nothing more, but the modern "individual" is an abstraction, an invention of the human mind. The modern definition does not describe a real or complete human being. In fact, it was never even meant to be completely true, but rather to serve as a useful fiction in the pursuit of unprecedented freedom, justice, and prosperity.

Modern human beings—especially Americans—have used the idea of the individual to achieve those humane and liberating goals.

The modern autonomous individual is thought to be more free from social and political constraints, and less directed toward duty and the good by God and nature, than a real human being ever could be. Modern thought distinguishes individuals from the political animals—the citizens, statesmen, and philosophers—described by the Greek and Roman philosophers, as well as from the social, familial creatures described by Christian theologians. It liberates individuals from the philosopher's duty to know the truth about nature, from the citizen's selfless devotion to his country, from the creature's love and fear of God, and even from the loving responsibilities that are inseparable from family life.

Conservatives today oppose modern or liberal individualism both because its understanding of the human being is only partially true and because that definition can erode all that is good about distinctively human existence. The modern world has now ended only in the sense that we conservatives have now seen enough of it to judge it. Although we have much reason to be grateful for the wealth, health, freedom, and power that modern achievements have given us, we know that the individual's pursuits of security and happiness will remain always pursuits—and not possessions. So even as the modern world continues to develop, we can be free of its characteristic delusion, its utopianism. Our gratitude for modern material and political accomplishments is what makes us "postmodern" rather than "premodern"—or hopelessly nostalgic— conservatives. The postmodern world, we can reasonably hope, will incorporate modern achievements—personal, political, and economic—while dispensing with modern utopianism.

We can speak of modern strengths and its limitations from a

perspective "outside" modernity, and that perspective is the foundation of conservatism today. Conservatives can be—and are perhaps the only—genuinely postmodern thinkers. The reason we can see beyond the modern world is that its intention to transform human nature has failed. Its project of transforming the human person into an autonomous individual was and remains unrealistic; we can now see its limits because we remain more than individuals. The world created by modern individuals to make themselves fully at home turns out to have made human beings, in some ways, less at home than ever.

Conservative thought today is authentically postmodern, but it is obviously not postmodern as that term is usually understood. Most allegedly postmodern thought emphasizes the arbitrary character of all human authority, the freedom of each human being from all standards but his own will or creativity, and the death not only of God but of nature. But these putatively postmodern tenets are really hypermodern; they aim to "deconstruct" any residual modern faith in reason or nature in order to reveal such faith as incoherent and therefore incredible. Postmodernists shout that everything modern—in fact, everything human—is nothing but a construction.

Postmodernists in this usual sense sometimes do a good job of exposing liberal hypocrisy, but they can only do so in the name of completing the modern project of liberating the individual's subjective, willful, whimsical perspective from all external constraints. Conservative postmodernism, by acknowledging and affirming as good what we can really know about our natural possibilities and limitations, opposes itself to this sort of liberationist postmodernism—and to the modern premises it radicalizes.

THE MODERN VIEW OF LIBERTY

The primary intention of modern thought is not to understand nature, even human nature, but to guide action in order to transform nature in accordance with human desire. According to the modern philosophers, we have very little reason to be grateful for what we have been given by God and nature. Nature, according to modern scientists, chooses for life, not death—but not for my life in particular. For life's sake, nature intends each of us to be born, reproduce, raise our young, and quickly die. Both God and nature seem callously and cruelly indifferent to the lives of particular human individuals. So we individuals need to struggle as much as we can against the life of poverty, misery, and early death that nature intends for us.

Our lives, objectively speaking, are not really more contingent and doomed to death than those of the other animals. We have it better by nature, for example, than the bees and the ants, not to mention the fruit flies that live for only a few days. But the other animals are not conscious of, and so not animated by, awareness of their own deaths. We humans are the only self-conscious animals. Only human animals restlessly and anxiously rebel against death. Only humans are technological. We alone have the capability to resist with considerable success our natural fate: we will not go blindly to our deaths as so many bees and ants have done. We experience ourselves (to some extent) as free individuals, as (to some extent) ungoverned by instinct or the requirements of our social existence. We are, quite mysteriously, not only intelligent but free.

It makes sense for modern individuals to speak of a Creator, but not really to think of themselves as creatures. The possibility of creation exists, because of the mystery of human liberty. But the modern God did nothing but give human beings liberty. He is, for all practical purposes, neither *living* nor *giving* now. It makes no sense for us to think of ourselves as humbly grateful and loving (because loved) creatures. Because God might have been alive but now is dead—at least to us—we are stuck (maybe by Him) with fending for ourselves.

Surely modern thinkers should allow us to be grateful for at least our singular freedom. But grateful, they say, to whom? Human freedom is too mysterious to be regarded as natural, and even if it came from God, we cannot help but wish he had given us much more. How can we be grateful to a God who left us alone and shivering to provide for ourselves? We employ our freedom not to live according to nature, but to escape our natural constraints, to conquer nature. Our freedom does not simply inhere in our self-conscious individuality that is the source of our dissatisfaction with merely natural existence, but also in our technology—our ability to use our brains to give orders to nature. We might say—to avoid speciesism—that we are unsure whether the chimps and the dolphins are self-conscious. But we do know that they are untechnological, that they do not freely impose their wills on nature. There would be no "ecological crisis" if it were not for human beings, and nature would cheer if human beings were to disappear. Human freedom is what disorders nature. Or, to be properly modern, human freedom is what imposes human order on a nature that is hostile to individual human existence.

When we reflect on our freedom, we are inclined even to confuse ourselves with God. We easily lord it over the chimps and the dolphins, using them however we will. The technological success of modern thought is in a way supernatural. The very conception of ourselves as free or supernatural is what connects the modern individual to the Christian religion. Modernity is characterized by the individual's attempt to replace the God of the Bible with himself. The individual will not be happy until he or she is a personal god.

When the modern individual speaks truthfully about his self-consciousness, his freedom, and his mortality, he expresses his distorted debt to Christianity—a debt that he is very anxious, in his freedom, to deny. According to St. Augustine, human beings are pilgrims or aliens in this world; they know that their true home is somewhere else. Augustine observes that Christians are critics of pagan "natural theology." Christians know that they are not merely part of nature, that they are free beings with longings that cannot be satisfied by nature. Christians are also critics of "civil theology." They know that they are not merely citizens, reducible to parts of a political community. Only Christian theology recognizes and can account for human freedom, for why we personally and truthfully experience ourselves as more than natural or political beings. We were made in the image and likeness of the supernatural and suprapolitical God.

At its extreme, Augustinian Christianity was criticized by St. Thomas Aquinas for dwelling far too much on the human experience of alienation or homelessness. God, after all, created nature, and our natural enjoyments and fulfillments—although not completely satisfying—are still good. Human life would not, in fact, be nothing but restless misery without faith in God. Even if Aristotle was wrong, finally, to call us political animals, the pride human beings take in political accomplishments is a legitimate human pleasure that expresses at least part of the truth about human being. Even Christians cannot really claim that they merely use their political communities to achieve their true, nonpolitical goals. Being a Christian is compatible with experiencing oneself, if only to some extent, as a devoted citizen. Otherwise, good citizens would have every right to deny Christians any share in political rule. Augustine's account of the human creature surely abstracts, for polemical reasons, from our natural goods. A Christian at home with his homelessness because of his faith, according to St. Thomas and many Thomists, is actually more free than others are to enjoy the good things of this world for what they are.

The modern individual, from one view, is an Augustinian who does not believe in the personal and providential God of the Bible. Augustine used his considerable rhetorical eloquence to describe the human misery that undermines every natural good. He makes us aware, very aware, of our misery and contingency to show us that we can only be happy in our hope for the eternal life graciously offered to us by God. We have the best reasons to be grateful for grace. But we seem to have little reason to be grateful for nature without grace. The philosophers who argued otherwise, according to Augustine, were blinded by pride. The same pride that kept the philosophers from acknowledging their longing for God and the eternal life that only God can give caused them to construct fraudulent visions for human happiness on earth, such as the ways of life of the statesman and the philosopher.

The modern individual—or the philosophers who constructed him—might also be understood to be animated by the most insane form of pride the world has ever seen. The modern individual aims to create in this world—not through grace but through human work—what God promised in the next. But viewed in another way, the modern individual seems less proud than desperate. The individual agrees with the Christian view of human misery and contingency: he is totally persuaded by Augustine's "negative" rhetoric about human alienation. But he does not believe in the Christian God: Augustine's "positive" rhetoric about grace, providence, and salvation does not move him at all. And so he has no choice but to try to do for himself what the Christians believed God would do. The individual finds himself with a heavy—really, a horrible—burden. The modern individual is an alien, an absolutely contingent being who belongs nowhere in particular and who must build for himself his own place in the world.

Now the modern individual does see *some* good news in the Christian teaching about human freedom and alienation. The bad news is that there is no God, but that is the good news too. We are free from both God and nature to make of ourselves what we will. We are not merely parts of nature or parts of a city. We are not merely useful for the perpetuation of our species or our country. Like God himself, we exist for ourselves, and what He promised we have no reason to believe we cannot do for ourselves. Salvation remains personal; we are now personally or individually responsible for saving ourselves. We are, in a sense, mysteriously made or can make ourselves in the image of God. The effectual truth of grace—the real evidence for it—must be what we achieve through applied reason or technology.

ANTI-CHRISTIAN AUGUSTINIANS

But the modern individual has no particular view of what he should do with the comfort and freedom he wins from nature. He has accepted the negative teaching of St. Augustine that free beings are necessarily dissatisfied with their natural, miserable, or mortal existence, but without accepting his positive teaching, without any clear view of what their freedom from nature is for or what it should be like. The Christian vision of heaven—the constant, unimpeded love of God—has been replaced, in the characteristically modern imagination, by something like Marx's vision of communism, a world to come in which we can do whatever we want, whenever we want, without any constraint by or guidance from nature, other human beings, or God. In other words, a future full of love was replaced by one without any love at all. Before we allow our very reasonable prejudice against Marx to lessen the force of this conclusion, we should remember that the most consistent liberals and libertarians also hope that religion and the state will wither away, leaving each human individual with an indefinitely large menu of choices.

The individual was invented by early-modern thinkers who were anti-Christian but still Augustinian. Prominent among these was John Locke. In Locke's famous alternative to the biblical creation story, human beings are imagined to have existed in a state of nature in order to reveal what they would be like without the human construction of government. There they are free and equal individuals. They have no natural inclination to be citizens or even social beings, and they think for themselves alone. The foundation of government must therefore be consent: I must see how government serves my self-interest as an individual, how government makes me more secure and comfortable than I am without it. Because human beings invent government to serve their bodily needs, government should be understood as a particularly successful example of human freedom, of human technology. In consenting to be ruled, the individual never surrenders his self-conscious judgment about the ability of government to protect his rights. In his own mind, the individual never gives way to political devotion or genuine communal loyalty. He refuses to be a sucker, like a bee or an ant—or even like a human being blinded by love.

The individual is clearly an invention—an abstract, distorted, only partial human being—because Locke's state of nature is clearly something of a lie. As Rousseau famously observed, if we were really self-sufficient individuals by nature we would be so stupid as to be unconscious. Self-consciousness necessarily implies consciousness of and with others; it depends upon a language that could only develop among social, even political, animals. The human being is clearly a gregarious animal by nature—like the chimpanzee, but with a distinctive capability for far more complex and intensely social language. The natural individual Locke describes is, when we think about it, rather obviously impossible.

Yet it is a sign of human freedom that, as a human goal, the individual could be invented in order to free civilized people from their traditional, political, religious, and even familial dependence. Locke intended, as far as he could, to transform social, political, religious, and familial beings into individuals. Because nature was not really on his side, we can now say that Locke was engaged in an impossible mission. But it is also undeniable that he achieved some success, and that we Americans rightly regard much of that success as good.

Partly Lockean America

The American Constitution of 1787 is largely a Lockean construction. There, human beings are not defined in terms of race, class, gender, or religious belief. The Constitution does not acknowledge our people's dependence on God or the past. Americans are understood to consent to government as individuals. Blacks and whites, men and women, Jews, Christians, and Moslems—all human beings can be free and equal citizens of the United States. No citizen consents to our nation's government as a Christian or Jew or member of any other group: religion, gender, race, and communally- and class-based identities are all, from the standpoint of the national government of the United States, private and therefore inessential matters.

Blacks and women were degraded in some ways by American law for most of our history. But our Constitution surely created the framework by which all individuals would eventually be liberated from the inessential baggage of race, class, and gender. The core of the American form of justice—a real, if incomplete, form of justice—is the liberation of human beings from any arbitrary or oppressive qualities that define them as more than individuals. Our national Constitution is a construction—in the sense that we know it was invented by human beings—for a construction: the individual invented by Locke and other modern thinkers. It was an unprecedented victory for human liberty over all kinds of tyranny.

The American founding fathers certainly knew that human beings are more than individuals. They also knew that government must be limited. Thus, the most intimate and sacred aspects of being human are left relatively untouched by constitutional law. Human beings are free, in private, to consider themselves as parents, children, friends, and creatures with duties to their Creator, and our founders assumed that they would do so. They could consent as liberated individuals in public but love and be devoted to God, their families, and their friends in private. Unable or unwilling to become complete and perfect individuals, Americans would live double lives. As Alexis de Tocqueville explained, they would be restless and anxious pursuers of material prosperity during six days of the week, acting as if God is dead and therefore working incessantly to achieve self-sufficiency. And on Sunday they would do nothing but restfully contemplate God's goodness, certain that he provides.

Such double lives, although not easy, reflect both the incomplete truth of our individual existences and our equality under God.

By focusing on the Constitution of 1787, of course, we exaggerate America's modern and secular aspects. The first Americans were Puritans, and their view that American liberty is really intended to allow creatures to carry out their duties toward their Creator has always remained with us. The American people have always been, by modern standards, very religious. The Puritan virtues and vices were emphatically not those of Lockean individuals, and neither were the Christian virtues and vices Tocqueville found in America. The First Amendment to the Constitution is actually a correction to the Constitution that takes it in a Biblical, or at least anti-individualistic, direction. There the free exercise of religion is recognized as a positive good for doing our duties as creatures to our Creator. We too must not forget that the original intention was to leave almost all legislation concerning religion and morality to the states. This is yet another way in which Americans led double lives: state laws were less individualistic (and more tyrannical) than was federal law. Only in the 1940s, through the clever manipulation of the Bill of Rights and the Fourteenth Amendment by the Supreme Court, did the Madisonian or individualistic spirit of the unamended Constitution begin to be used to invalidate the minimalist moral and religious legislation of the states. Today the Supreme Court continues to reconstruct state law on an individualistic basis through its use of the single word "liberty" of the Fourteenth Amendment.

So despite our very modern Constitution, American lives have been only inconsistently modern. We might even say, as Tocqueville does, that it is that very inconsistency which has made modern liberty seem good. One aspect of this American paradox is that our political protection of individual rights attracted all sorts of premodern ways of life to our shores. Jews, Catholics, and various Protestant sects came to America not only to be individuals but to practice their faiths communally in peace and freedom. They wanted to maintain their traditions without political intrusion. Catholics, for example, cannot forget the extent to which their church—its faith and its institutions—flourished in America for a long time with a certain vigorous purity, free from the temptations and corruptions of political power. The writings of theologian John Courtney Murray, for one, demonstrate that the church as late as the 1950s stood ready to teach Americans the true meaning of human liberty. And then there is the telling fact that after World War II America had the largest and most vibrant Jewish community in the world. Reflection on what has happened to the Jews almost everywhere else allows us to see the humane nobility of the American devotion to individual rights. Jews in America could be full or free and equal citizens of a nation for the first time since the destruction of the Temple; they were no longer stuck with wandering the world as political aliens.

The English Catholic G. K. Chesterton, our most astute and friendly twentieth-century observer, explained that just as anyone can become a member of the Catholic Church simply by accepting her religious creed, anyone can become an American just by accepting our creed or dogma about inalienable rights or the proposition that all men are created equal. We have plenty of reason to be grateful for our singular political tradition of equality in liberty. And we note with Chesterton the paradox that the Americans—in some ways, as the philosopher Martin Heidegger claims, the most modern or displaced or homesick of people—are also all about creating an "asylum" or political "home for the homeless" everywhere. Chesterton, with Tocqueville, both describes and wonders at our divided soul. It is quite normal to be both very homeless and quite at home in our country, and surely that mixture reflects clearly an enduring truth about human nature. Deep down, suggests Chesterton (following Lincoln), our "romance of the citizen" is more in tune with reality than is the idea of the individual. And our Declaration of Independence, Chesterton and Lincoln add, is finally a statement about the way "all men" stand in relation to each other, the rest of earthly reality, and God.

But what Chesterton called "a nation with the soul of a church" may be at best ambiguously good in the long run for either souls or churches, and both of those are surely required for the perpetuation of the reality-laden dogma of our Declaration. Attempts to maintain premodern traditions (even the tradition of *natural* rights) in individualistic America have tended to fail. Children or grandchildren come to understand themselves primarily as individuals with rights, and so free not to be dominated by the authority of fathers, traditions, churches, or God. According to Tocqueville, the human mind hates inconsistency, and as such is almost irresistibly inclined to harmonize heaven and earth. The view that we are individuals for some purposes but not others is tough to accept indefinitely. So it is not surprising that Americans have come to understand themselves more consistently as individuals, attempting to apply the ideas of contract and consent to every part of their lives. We cannot forget, of course, the ambiguous but authentic counterexample of our tradition-less but not all that homeless evangelical Christians, and I give the case for them—and the future of orthodox religion in general in America—elsewhere in this book.

Still, we must also notice that marriage has come to be understood less as a sacrament and more as a contract between two individuals that may be dissolved at will. Sex has been dissociated from the hard responsibilities connected with procreation given us by God and nature; sex has become "safe sex," a contract between "consenting adults" who never lose their heads in passionate enjoyment or in love. From the point of view of the individual, sex cannot be safe—that is, it will always limit our freedom—if we ever stop calculating about it. Social arrangements reflecting real or imagined differences between men and women are now consistently and insistently regarded as oppressive—merely biological differences cannot be regarded as real limits to individual freedom. We are even coming to believe that limiting marriage to a contract between a man and a woman oppresses individuals.

We can even see religion is now often—although not always—regarded as a choice we make for our convenience. Sophisticated Americans tend to conclude that God would never command anything that would violate our rights. If he did, we would simply withdraw our consent to his rule. The orthodox belief is that, from God's view, the modern individual is the product of willful self-deception: it is a sinful lie for human beings to imagine themselves as self-sufficient as the individual claims to be. But the modern view is that the undeceived and autonomous individual must judge God: theology cannot be a rationalization for oppression. The individual, not God, is that for which everything exists. The modern individual believes that God cannot really provide him any security—although the individual may still, on occasion, hypocritically take advantage of the comfort that religious community provides.

The trend toward individualism in America remains incomplete and even ambivalent. Our foreign observers are still impressed by how many of us are able to think of ourselves as parents, citizens, and creatures, and by how many of us take seriously the future of our children, country, and churches. Human nature, in our country, continues to remind us that we are more than individuals. But even if our creeping individualism sometimes seems more intellectual than real, our future depends on our thinking corresponding with the way in which we really act.

The Individual's Pursuit of Happiness

Today, more than ever, we need to recall why it is good that we remain more than modern individuals. It is reasonable to believe that the individual Locke invented will never achieve the happiness he pursues. Such an alien could never be at home in this world. His life must remain an incessant pursuit that ends only in death. The mistake of modern utopianism is in reasoning that because the individual obsessively pursues bodily satisfaction, he will be happier to the extent that he achieves it. The individual does pursue bodily security and comfort, but the more he achieves it, the more dissatisfied he becomes. The more secure or free from contingency he is objectively, the more the individual experiences his existence as contingent and the more he is haunted by death. The more death is pushed back by modern technology, the more accidental it seems. The more accidental or less necessary death seems, the more terrible it seems.

Actual enjoyment, actual happiness, is even contrary to the modern individual's own view of his freedom. He is free because he can oppose himself to nature: so the moment he gives way to some natural enjoyment he surrenders his freedom.. We can even say, with Tocqueville, that the individual perversely takes pride in his inability really to enjoy. The individual is a materialist insofar as he rejects all nonmaterialistic human goals as illusions, but his disparagement of real human enjoyment makes him an equally extreme antimaterialist. We might say that his single-minded pursuit of material goals while being conscious of that pursuit's futility is undeniable evidence that he has a soul. No other animal could be so perversely screwed up, and Tocqueville's mind was subtle enough—Christian enough—to see the greatness in such misery. Nobody can deny that Americans today see both greatness and misery in their inability to relax enough to find time enough to enjoy all the good things they have acquired for themselves as individuals.

Contemporary therapeutic thought invites the modern individual to surrender his soul or his obsessions in the name of immediate enjoyment. Experts advise him to give up his singular freedom and become just one of the animals again. All he has to do is not be moved by what he knows to be true, by what he really knows about his own death and the nature that is out to kill him. The goal of therapy is to engender what Allan Bloom called a flatness of soul, a disposition to be unmoved by love or death and so to be no longer open to the truth. But the therapists' victories have been largely linguistic: Americans speak in their easygoing and amoral language more than ever before, but those soft and sort of whiny words do not correspond to their morally demanding lives. It has taken genuine postmodernists (and thus genuine conservatives) like Aleksandr Solzhenitsyn (and Mother Teresa of Calcutta) to both notice and have the courage to say that Americans are more lonely and death-obsessed than ever. Like Tocqueville, what Solzhenitsyn hears just beneath the surface in the lives of free, restless, enlightened, and prosperous Americans is the "howl" of existentialism.

People are more screwed up than ever, wrote Walker Percy, because they have been deprived of the language needed to express the longings of real human beings. But they are also screwed up because they have lost even the language of the individual. The modern individual, although abstracted from and so less than a real human being, is more than the being described by the therapeutic experts. Therapeutic language is particularly alienating because it is two steps removed from corresponding to the longings of real men and women. While the modern individual is moved by death but not by love, the entirely imaginary therapeutic being is moved by neither. The therapeutic remedy to the excesses of individualism is to get people to surrender all of their individuality; our "therapism" is really pantheism, as Tocqueville noticed, or a kind of self-indulgent self-surrender we might call American Buddhism.

But the truth is that, whatever they say, human beings remain moved by both love and death. The alleged therapeutic solution to the misery of individuality actually exaggerates the problem of modern disorientation—and we should notice that most, though not all, of what today goes by the name of communitarianism is therapeutic in intention. Our therapists produce pathetic human beings who can neither be good nor feel good. People today know they need help because, as the lapidary Canadian thinker George Grant observed, they know they have been deprived of something—but they usually get no help in figuring out what that is.

We live at the end of the modern world because we now see the consequences of the modern reduction of the real human being to an individual—its culmination in the failed therapeutic project of self-negation. What began as a well-intentioned and very effective fiction to limit government has redefined more and more of human life. If human beings really believe they are merely individuals, they perversely work to empty human life of the contents that make it worth living. A life defined only by work to avoid death, misery, and loneliness is, in fact, supremely miserable. That is why today our sophisticated individuals sometimes spend their time envying the other animals—at least they are content. Now, the individual rightly and really knows that the dog's life is not for him. But he often wrongly believes that his choice is between subhuman contentment and human unhappiness, and in his freedom he sometimes talks nostalgically about the former—the "simple life"—while still consistently choosing the latter.

The biotechnological revolution promises to make it possible for us modern individuals to build new weapons of unprecedented power in our war against nature. And the unprecedented health, longevity, and other indispensable means for human flourishing will deserve our gratitude. But the victories that will be won—like most of the victories won on behalf of the modern individual—will also probably be, in part, at the expense of the distinctively human goods: love, family, friends, country, virtue, art, spiritual life, and, most generally, living responsibly in light of what we really know about what we have been given. The biotechnological revolution is being driven largely by individualistic obsession, and we can limit and direct it only if we can recover the truth that we are more than individuals.

GRATEFUL POSTMODERNISM

Postmodernism rightly understood begins with the realization that we should, in fact, be grateful for what we have been given. We have been given not only self-conscious mortality and a mysterious freedom to negate nature, but all sorts of natural compensations for our distinctively human misery. Love is not an illusion, and we have been fitted by nature to know the truth. But both love of each other and our common love of the truth depend, as far as we can tell, upon the inevitability of death. As far as we can tell, self-consciousness—with all the virtues and distinctively human enjoyments it makes possible—depends upon our having corruptible bodies. The fact that despite all that nature has given us and all we do for ourselves we remain somewhat alienated might reasonably be seen as evidence that our true home lies elsewhere, and that it is in our nature to long for a personal God. As Thomas Aquinas said, what we know through revelation completes—but does not contradict—what we know through reason. Even if we are, for now, not ready to be grateful for the gift of faith, we can still reasonably believe that our homelessness is a price worth paying for all that we can know and love and do. Nor does the fact that we remain somewhat homeless mean that we are isolated individuals. Our homelessness—an inextricable part of our natural gift of language or speech—allows us to wonder together about the truth of all things, especially ourselves. Neither a completely autonomous individual nor a contented, clever chimp could ever be a poet or a philosopher.

It is no longer enough for Americans to accept being autonomous individuals most of the time and fully human creatures only in fleeting private moments. All of our institutions might be better understood in light of what we really know about human nature. We have religious liberty because human beings, by nature, are open to God, and because what we really know about nature points to the possibility that we are created. We have political liberty because we creatures (or at least beings open to the truth about our freedom) are more than citizens, but that liberty is compatible with political responsibility because we are, among other things, citizens. Postmodern conservatism is unreservedly in support of liberal, in the sense of limited and democratic, government. It certainly has a higher view than does liberal individualism of the capacity of the ordinary person to choose truth and virtue over security and comfort. And conservatives, in general, are loyal to their country and grateful for what they have been given by their political founders.

Conservatives today rightly attack so-called postmodernists for their attacks on truth, science, virtue, and God. But those attacks on our ability to perceive the truth and goodness of nature and human nature are actually modern in origin. The promiscuously ironic philosopher, Richard Rorty, once described himself as a postmodernist bourgeois liberal. That particular self-description turns out to be neither ironic nor oxymoronic. Rorty understands that postmodernism as it is usually understood does not really offer any challenge at all to the modern individual. Because postmodern conservatives aim to conserve the full truth about human and natural reality, they have no interest in conserving the modern and allegedly postmodern error of mistaking the autonomous individual for the whole, real human being. That is not to say, of course, that human beings are properly understood without both individuality and liberty.

CHAPTER 3

THE PROBLEM OF TECHNOLOGY

Technology is a problem because we cannot do without it, and our use of it clearly makes us both better and worse. Human beings are—among other things—technological or tool-making animals. We use our brains and our freedom to transform nature, and in doing so to transform ourselves. We also have a perverse capacity to make ourselves unhappy and a singular pride in our misery. We are both proud of and wish to free ourselves from the burdens of our technological success. So we find it almost impossible to judge how much and what kind of technology would be best for us. In principle, we should be free to accept or reject various technological developments. Technology, after all, is supposed to be a means by which we pursue whatever ends we choose. But, in truth, it might be our destiny to be moved along by impersonal and unlimited technological progress. After all, we do not have much evidence of significant numbers of human beings resisting technological changes for long periods of time. (The peaceful and admirable Amish, for example, represent a very small and only partial exception to this general rule.)

From a purely natural point of view, it is not clear why human beings are the only technological animals. Only we human beings can freely negate nature to satisfy our desires; only we human beings can create new and harder to satisfy needs through our technological success. Our technological acquisitions make us less happy than being deprived of such acquisitions—of, say, air conditioning—can make us miserable, not to mention whiny. We do not know why we, through our inventions, came to dominate the rest of nature. One of the best pieces of evidence of our fundamental difference from the chimps and the dolphins is we can so easily control them if that is what we want to do, but they cannot give orders to us. We do not know why we have the capability and the desire to threaten the very existence of all life on our planet. It is almost impossible to call what we have achieved through technological success—from a natural view—progress.

But from another point of view, technological change clearly *is* progress. It represents the increasing power of humans to control and manipulate nature. And societies that encourage or are open to such change generally overwhelm those that are not. That is why the modern West has exerted its control over the whole world, and why the Europeans almost eliminated the Native Americans in our country. But this control, of course, is quite ambiguous. Technology consists in the imposition of human will over nature; we comprehend nature insofar as we control it. But our control and our comprehension are always far from complete. Thus, for example, when we have dammed a river in order to produce power or end flooding, we have often discovered, to our surprise, that we have transformed a flourishing body of water into a dying one. We did not know enough to anticipate the destructive effects of our control, but that knowledge does not usually free us to remove the dam on which we have come to depend. We simply now know enough to damn and be very reluctant to build dams.

Another reason we are not free to relinquish control once we have achieved it is that we cannot dispose of technological knowledge once we have acquired it. Surely we regret, on balance, our invention of nuclear weapons. But it would be crazy for America to destroy its nuclear weapons or even to stop trying to produce better ones. The knowledge of how to build them is everywhere, and otherwise insignificant powers such as North Korea and even transnational terrorist groups are going to find it progressively more easy to use that knowledge. So whatever our desires, we are going to both become progressively more afraid and in need of nuclear weapons. In general, we are not free to reject military technology, and because so much of technology has military applications perhaps we are not even free to reject technological development as such. And it must be admitted that even nuclear weapons have unanticipated good consequences; the "balance of terror" they created surely has been indispensable in our avoiding (thus far) a World War III that would reduce much of Europe and Asia—and possibly America—to rubble.

It seems reasonable to speculate that we eventually will be freed from our Promethean excesses through a catastrophic high-tech war that will destroy most human life and most of the products of our technological development. But that speculation cannot free us Americans from our destiny of using high technology to do what we can to fend off that possibility. And it is very unlikely that such a war would bring technological progress to an end. Because the knowledge we acquired over time through technological thinking would probably remain with us, it would probably take surprisingly little time to rebuild the complex world we partially destroyed. And, yes, we would not hesitate to repeat our mistakes, in the mistaken belief that we had learned from experience.

The example of nuclear weapons reminds us that, whether or not it is escapable, the progress of technology is in many ways not an unalloyed human good. The change from a hunter-gatherer to an agricultural society, which lay behind the conflict between the Native Americans and the Europeans in America, and the later transformation of that agricultural society to an urbanized, machine-based one both caused huge amounts of human displacement and misery. Each change seemed like a fate worse than death to many. In truth, any rapid technological advance is always a cause of human disorientation; its initial effect is to cause at least almost as much misery as it alleviates. Such change seems to become on balance beneficial only after it becomes routinized, only after it assumes a place in a relatively settled way of life. Technological change might become an increasingly unambiguous evil as it becomes too rapid for we habit- and tradition-dependent beings to assimilate. Technology would become an unambiguous good only if its progress culminated in some sort of human perfection, if we were to become satisfied with some future level of technological development.

TECHNOLOGY AND
DEMOCRATIC LIBERATION: THEORY

Those who have described technological utopias, including Marx and others, assume that in the worlds they posit the need for further advance will have faded away because human scarcity will have been definitely overcome. The result is that human beings will be freed from the hard work and emotional disorientation caused by the fear of being left behind by technological progress. Work itself, in the precise sense, will have disappeared because machines will have become so advanced that people need not do much to keep them going. This vision is of a world in which technology has freed us all equally from natural necessity. Technology will have allowed us to exit the realm of necessity and enter the realm of freedom or leisure. We will finally be totally at home in the world; we will never have to do anything that smacks of alienation or compulsion.

In fact, the communism described by Marx looks the same as the democracy described by Socrates in the *Republic* (even though Socrates knew that the democratic regime he described would never exist anywhere except in a book). The liberation from alienation described by both Marx and Socrates includes liberation from dependence on or duties toward other members of society. In their utopias, every human being is on his own, able to design his life as he pleases. The young owe nothing to the old; citizens owe nothing to their cities; students owe nothing to their teachers (and vice versa); apparently children do not need to be raised or criminals kept in line. All humans are freed from their conformist dependence on habituation and tradition.

Some might say that a visit to Malibu or the Hamptons shows that this seemingly impossible life is really possible. We have all met people who have plenty of everything, are little plagued by anxiety, and do very little work. For our libertarians today, as Tyler Cowen explains, the "secret" history of the West culminates in a cosmopolitan world where each individual enjoys an unlimited "menu of choice" concerning whatever hobby will occupy his time. Cowen even presents some significant evidence that community, or our "irrational longing for the particular," only really has "aesthetic benefits."[1] But it is still very hard to see how the extreme displacement or rootlessness of cosmopolitanism will actually lead to the withering away of the state. "If the [cosmopolitanizing] process continues with the same degree of intensity," William Leach predicts, "we can only expect greater reliance on state power—more pris-

ons, more police, more attempts to manage or manipulate minds—
to compensate for the failure of Americans to remember and protect their places."[2]

TECHNOLOGY AND
DEMOCRATIC LIBERATION: PRACTICE

The modern liberation of technological progress from moral and
political controls has had democratic liberation as its goal. Its success, although far from complete, has been real. Most people are
free in the sense of having unprecedented material abundance, which
they may use as they please. This abundance, combined with real
advances in medical science and technology (doctors, on balance,
probably hurt more than they helped people prior to the twentieth
century), has kept more babies and children alive, freed us from
much disease, disabling pain, and physical suffering (think about
teeth, to begin with), and extended dramatically the length of the
average human life. More people than ever have been freed enough
from drudgery to pursue their natural capacities through education
and to decide for themselves where and how to live. Technology
certainly has been good for individual health, wealth, and freedom.

More of life is given over to personal choice for more people
than ever before. The personal mobility made possible by cars and
planes ought to amaze us; not so long ago, most people rarely jour-
neyed more than twenty miles from their homes. This was true
even in cities; those who lived, for example, in working-class neighborhoods in New York or Chicago were pretty much confined there
most of the time. And everything was available in the neighborhood because it was so hard to leave the neighborhood. But as
emotionally satisfying as the old neighborhoods surely were, Americans and in fact most people throughout the world have character-

istically chosen to leave them in pursuit of the new opportunity, mobility, and prosperity technological progress has made available.

Alan Ehrenhalt, in *Lost City*,[3] describes one particular ethnic, Catholic Chicago neighborhood where families were strong and parental authority respected, children were raised by the whole neighborhood, homes were arranged in a way that made personal or familial isolation all but impossible, mothers were moms (and not wage slaves), and authoritative spiritual roots were provided by the neighborhood Catholic parish (church and school). The neighborhood was a remarkably self-sufficient communal whole. There were places to work, shop, and bank, and these all respected persons and traditions and offered very personal service. As attractive as this picture is, there is no denying that the people living there didn't *choose* this community; they were *stuck* with it. There was no easy way to get downtown in order to shop or work elsewhere, and there was nowhere else these working-class Catholics could afford to live. With the coming of cheap cars, highways, suburbs, and new employment opportunities, the people from the neighborhood typically chose the liberation—including personal liberation and privacy (i.e., more square feet of living space and one's own room)—that suburban living offered.

This liberation from neighborhoods and fairly self-sufficient local economies has reduced, and is still reducing, the amount of real diversity in the world. During the last few decades in America, for example, locally owned stores and services and distinctive downtown shopping areas have been replaced by more or less indistinguishable "malls." The mall and Wal-Mart and Old Navy are always just a short drive away. From one view, this means that technological progress has reduced our country to an aesthetic wasteland; by making every place look and feel the same, suburbs and malls keep people from being able to experience themselves as being from any place in particular. Technology makes it increasingly difficult for human beings in many ways to be able to experience themselves as particular beings at all.

But from a more democratic view, a wide array of economically priced products are now conveniently available to everyone. Barnes & Noble may not be as good as the best old-fashioned locally owned bookstores, and the megachains may have forced those charming and quirky stores out of business, but each Barnes & Noble store is stocked with more good books and periodicals than any of us could ever read (not to mention the large and diverse collection of CDs), and taken together, those Barnes & Nobles serve far more customers than those old bookstores ever did. Plus, malls are usually very pleasant and very reliable places. They are certainly not cesspools of proletarian misery. The taste of the average American for gourmet coffee and other such food and drink has, in fact, been awakened by malls; McDonald's is on the decline in our country. Starbucks may be an abomination to someone with genuinely aristocratic tastes, but it has also succeeded in turning a vast number of people into snobs about caffeinated beverages.

We live today in the comfort of knowing that wherever we are in America (almost) we can go to the mall, a home away from home. Nobody may know your name there, but you can still reasonably expect to be treated well. The technological reduction in diversity represented by the mall is arguably the price to be paid for something like universal freedom in prosperity. And the aesthetic aversion to malls felt by some is arguably nothing but aristocratic nostalgia for a world in which most human beings were much more confined, for a world in which most people had little access at all to the good things the world has to offer. Yet in that limited world, surely, people had a greater appreciation for the goods given us by God, tradition, and nature; a properly moral and spiritual world may have to be a fairly static one.

It is certainly true that the prosperity produced by relatively unimpeded technological progress has had both good and bad aesthetic and ecological effects. One reason we work so hard toward historical preservation is that we recognize around us the remnants of a more artistically excellent time. We may not be able to re-create that excellence, but we can appreciate it: prosperous Americans today are educated enough to be at least an audience for beautiful deeds and noble leisure. They are sophisticated enough to read the classic books sold by Barnes & Noble, and they are aesthetically minded enough to be repulsed by suburban sprawl and to be moved to refurbish the old, crumbling beautiful buildings found in our cities. Consumers such as these have even caused mall architecture to become more stylish or "neotraditional." Not only that, the postindustrial environmental movement depends on technological success; it is led by people smart and rich enough to think of themselves as rising above merely material concerns. The rich and selfish capitalist countries have reduced the amount of pollution and so forth in the world in recent decades, while those who want to see really brutal environmental devastation have to go to the formerly communist countries or third-world cities where technological progress was slowed to a crawl by corrupt tyrants and ideological fanaticism. The impact of technological progress has arguably shifted; the world is becoming less rather than more of a wasteland in its most technologically advanced areas.

The most unnatural—and surely environmentally friendly— freedom offered us by television, computers, and the like is even more amazing. Through them we have immediate access to the whole world; what we can know and experience extends far beyond local and national boundaries. We can do all our shopping in front of a screen, without even having to waste time talking to another human being. (I enjoy going to the Lands' End website—where I can take care of all my clothing needs with quality, reasonably priced products and where I can enter my exact measurements to get tailored pants without having to be touched in any way by some salesperson. And I buy just about all my books on Amazon; my only complaint is its convenience: its low prices tempt me to buy more than I can afford.)

Our dependence on the Internet actually reveals technology's contradictory tendencies: It increases our openness to all the people of the world while freeing or isolating us from other, particular persons. It makes us skeptical of the pretensions of all real human communities; it has turned out to be an effective weapon against both tyranny and the family. And it surely increases our tolerance for human diversity while contributing to the reduction of that diversity. There are, of course, online "communities," too, and they do sometimes save the lonely and misunderstood (which perhaps describes most of us in this technological era) from some of their misery. But we also know that people who cannot tell the difference between virtual and real communities are pretty pathetic. Or maybe they're just flexible and free; "virtual" communities challenge us to consider to what extent human social life depends on physical proximity. Even the objection that virtual sex cannot lead to reproduction might fade if reproduction is separated from sex completely. This freedom also contributes in another way to America's technological domination. Being online allows more people than ever to work from their homes and live anywhere they like, and so they are bringing their demand for sophisticated, high-tech services to the most "backward" parts of our country.

OUR TECHNOLOGICAL REPUBLIC

The freedom at the mall or on the Internet that Americans now enjoy might be understood as the realization of the intention of our founders. America, the first nation devoted in its fundamental law to the promotion of technological development or invention, also gave the world the first form of government that was explicitly a form of technology, one aimed at freeing the individual from all forms of oppression. Our Constitution was understood by our leading founders as a human artifice consciously constructed to remedy our miserable natural condition. It was constructed to be an instrument for the individual's free pursuit of his own chosen way of life.

In this sense, Americans are not so much citizens as they are individuals. Government is, for the most part, a *mere* means for each individual's pursuit of his own ends; it exists through *my* consent to secure *my* rights. Americans typically ask what the government can do for them as individuals, not what they can do for it as citizens. The Constitution relies more on mechanisms invented by Montesquieu and others, such as the separation of powers and checks and balances, than it does on natural or cultivated virtue in order to protect individuals from the tyranny rooted in human nature itself. The experience of America seems to demonstrate that political technology can, in surprisingly large measure, free us from what seemed to be the necessity to exercise personal self-restraint if we were to live freely.

Partly due to the stunning progress in technology since the time of the founding, we now try to push personal liberation further than even the most "enlightened" founders had hoped. Today we understand the free pursuit of happiness under the Constitution to include mindless self-indulgence, stupefying diversions, almost unlimited sexual freedom, and even drug-induced euphoria. Today we say "there's nothing wrong with that" about activities that even Thomas Jefferson regarded as criminal. In our laidback non-judgmentalism, we really have come close to believing in the goodness and possibility of Socrates' democracy, and our libertarians now really believe that history is on their side, that the state is withering away. The founders believed that the political liberation made possible by the Constitution would be constrained by the discipline required to earn a living (usually farming), run a household, and raise a family, and that people would be ranked in local communities by the virtue and skill they exhibited in those necessary, difficult, and time-consuming endeavors. Ordinary life was necessarily much more demanding and so resistant to liberation in that relatively low-tech and dangerous time.

Our democracy is a combination of the political technology of the Constitution with the success of the technological project it unleashed. The result is that we believe it possible to apply what used to be regarded as the fairly narrow political principles of consent and egalitarianism to all areas of life. Women's liberation, for example, depends on both parts of America's technological combination. As Tocqueville reported, Americans used to believe that the necessary constraints of the division of labor compelled women to be more or less stuck at home.[4] We all now believe that such a narrow and alienating view of a woman's possibilities is unnecessary and unjust; women, like men, should be able to do whatever they want whenever they want. Marriage and parenting, almost everyone agrees, are lifestyle choices that should never define a whole life and are not more appropriate for women than they are for men.

From the beginning, our constitutional/technological principles pointed in the direction of the individual's liberation from material and emotional dependence on others. *Federalist* 10, for example, argued that America's "large republic" would moderate the tyrannical passion characteristic of all previous democratic or republican governments. Size and diversity—the distance of citizens from their representatives, for example—would promote psychological detachment. People would increasingly vote according to their interests and less according to their passionate attachments. And they would prefer the relatively impersonal and secure liberty protected by the national government to the comparatively unreliable and intrusive communal ties that animate local government. From this view, as Carey McWilliams explains, "All attachments are suspect, since the bonds of love and community limit liberty, tying individuals to particular persons, places, ideas, and institutions without regard to their usefulness."[5]

Tocqueville connects this technological or utilitarian view to the nature of democracy itself: Any view of truth or virtue—any view of science or theology—that aims higher than materialistic utility is really a claim of the few to rule over the many. So we can only achieve freedom by reducing all human relationships to "self-interest rightly understood."[6] Even in the most high-tech times we will still need the cooperation of others to achieve our personal goals. A free human being achieves that cooperation without the oppression of emotional dependence by applying the proper technique of human relations. The passion that sustains friendship is replaced by the calculating detachment of "networking." The history of America arguably centers on the gradual reconstruction of all human relationships according to that liberationist, techno-logical view. Democratic liberation requires that human beings not really be dependent on each other in any way.

ANTI-TECHNOLOGICAL THEORY

According to Martin Heidegger, technology is what defines all of modern life. In other words, our world is, in a way, a rational one. To us, what is "real" is what can be comprehended by reason; it is what can be calculated, predicted, or manipulated. Anything that cannot be objectively known—known as an object—by reason is not real. If something cannot be known as an object it is, as Socrates' democrats say, merely subjective or whimsical or weightless. So ours is a democratic age insofar as we accord no weight or reality to what used to be considered the hard-to-achieve and necessarily unequal manifestations of the human soul—piety, loyalty, com-munity, art, poetry, philosophy, and so forth. We also, as good democrats, do not accord any truth or virtue to anything that re-minds us of our finitude—of our mortality and contingency—or of the mystery of our very existence. Heidegger, more than Socrates, objects to the ugliness of the self-denial of technological democracy.

The tyranny of technological thinking is, for Heidegger, above all *nihilistic*; everything noble and beautiful that gives human life its seriousness or dignity is regarded in a technological age as, literally, nothing. The thought behind technological rationality is that we can only know what we can control. As Heidegger reminds us, the ancient science of Aristotle understood a cause as "that to which something is indebted." Aristotelian science sought to know what—nature, our political order—has caused us to be the way we are. But modern science denies that we really have or can know such debts. So modern—or technological—thinkers understand a cause as "that which produces an effect."[7] All we can know is what is effective, what we can control through reason for whatever we will. The modern view is that technological thinking frees us from the irrational illusion of indebtedness. It can be at the service of what we now call "free choice," because we neither have nor can have knowledge of those purposes or ends or limits which we may have been given. Unconstrained human choice or willfulness depends on a debt-negating, nihilistic foundation.

But Heidegger goes further by denying, quite undemocratically, that we can really freely use technology for whatever goal we please. He argues that what is really true (technology) can hardly be controlled by what is arbitrary and contingent, or by what is really nothing (each one of us). And thinking about how we can control technology does not free us from technological or control-oriented thinking. For this reason "democratic choice" is overwhelmed by the impulse of technological thinking to conquer nature, to kill God and the gods, to discredit tradition, and to rationalize or standardize all of human life. That impulse overwhelms or flattens out all the human qualities to which technology might be subordinated or which it might serve. Heidegger agrees with Marx that the technology-driven, urbanized, and progressively less diverse West seems to be the destiny of the whole planet or species. The result will be, according to Heidegger's best student, "the unity of the human race at the lowest level, the complete emptiness of life, the self-perpetuation of doctrine without rhyme nor reason, no leisure, no cultivation, no withdrawal; nothing but work and recreation; no individuals and no peoples, but instead 'lonely crowds.'"[8]

The danger is that human beings will have no existence at all that is not in one way or another regulated by applied reason or technology, reasoning that does not acknowledge the existence of anyone in particular. According to Socrates and Marx, technological progress is supposed to be the cause of a world in which human beings will enjoy an abundance of leisure. Freed from necessity, they will be freed to pursue any choice-worthy activity they please. But Heidegger shows us that in truth, technological thinking, by making leisure pointless, makes it impossible. There is no longer any foundation, any reality, to the idea of a genuinely inner or private life. That is why there now seems to be a therapy, a technique, to rationalize every human activity—for relaxation, for love, for grief. There is nothing that the expert technicians cannot tell us how to do.

There are many reasons, in fact, why technology, by itself, cannot make leisure possible. As Jacques Ellul points out, "it is simply not the case that the individual, left to his own, will devote himself to the education of his personality or a spiritual or cultural life."[9] Leisure depends for its growth on being planted in the soil of a non-democratic, non-technological education. As Socrates says, democracy is good for the philosopher insofar as nobody there has any objection to the philosopher's liberated thought, whereas in every other regime there is traditional or political or theological opposition to such liberation. But democracy is bad for genuinely liberated thought because it does not provide for the education that lies at the foundation of every serious human endeavor. Furthermore, genuine human liberation depends on the critical examination of serious moral opinions, but in a democracy nobody defends the truth or nobility of his opinions. As Allan Bloom famously complained, if students are laidback but dogmatic relativists on every question but the value of technological progress, then it is impossible to teach them anything more than how to be soulless, competent specialists.

Leisure is impossible for people who deny that human beings really should and can pursue truth, virtue, and God. It is impossible for those who do not believe that they can know the truth about their debts and responsibilities. Technology cannot free us from the boredom and anxiety that is the result of the uncultivated leisure that technology actually can give us. So we seek refuge in the diversion of what would otherwise seem to be unnecessary work. We invent necessity to free ourselves from nihilism; technology liberates us from meaningless leisure for meaningless work and the recreation that serves it.

TECHNOLOGY VS. SETTLED COMMUNITY

The farmer and essayist Wendell Berry explains that one of our primary dogmas or "conventional prejudices" today is the uncritical acceptance of the goodness of technological liberation. Our intellectuals, and therefore our education, mean to prejudice us "against old people, history, parental authority, religious faith, sexual discipline, manual work, rural people and rural life, anything that is local or small or inexpensive."[10] We are prejudiced against all that is required to acquire moral virtue, to what we must possess in order to subordinate technical means to human ends. We are prejudiced against "settled communities," against anything that has not been uprooted by the impersonal universalism of technological thinking. But it is only in the routinized and moralized context of such communities that any technology might be viewed as good, as not merely displacing or disorienting human beings for no particular purpose.[11] We are prejudiced against the prejudiced, traditional view of reality that allows human beings to be oriented enough to think and act reasonably well.

Berry agrees with Heidegger that laidback, relativistic egalitarianism is not the result of technological liberation. The truth is, "If we have equality and nothing else—no compassion, no magnanimity, no courtesy, no sense of mutual obligation and dependence, no imagination—then power and wealth will have their way; brutality will rule."[12] The democratic destruction of virtue paves the way, as Socrates says, for tyranny. Those who are best at manipulating others as objects will rule without restraint. Technological democracy tends to bring into existence a new sort of tyrannical ruling class; the clever, liberated, communally irresponsible meritocrats employ technology to impose a humanly destructive uniformity on those they rule. These meritocrats—who may well believe more strongly than any prior ruling class that they *deserve* to rule—are full of contempt for those they control. And they themselves don't realize the extent to which they are controlled by technological thinking, a way of thinking that has devalued all standards except wealth and power.

Democracy, in fact, though its tendency is to level human distinctions, cannot destroy those distinctions based on technological cleverness; it, in fact, liberates that cleverness from limits imposed by common decency. "Technology," Carey McWilliams explains, "is more than gadgets and machines; it is associated with a frame of mind, a preoccupation with getting results, a dangerous spirit that strains against limits and rules."[13] The first unreserved technologist—the first human being to identify the whole truth simply with what works—was Machiavelli. The most tyrannical doctrine ever invented, it turns out, is that there can be no real or weighty human objection to whatever technological success brings. Nobody, it turns out, is exempt from that amazingly impersonal tyranny. In our technological republic, it often seems that choices are automatically made in favor of greater efficiency. No one in particular—certainly no Machiavellian prince—is in charge, not even at the "local" level.

In America, according to Berry, members of every established community "sooner or later become 'redskins'—that is, they become the designated victims of an utterly ruthless, officially sanctioned and subsidized exploitation."[14] The example of the Indians or Native Americans is real evidence of how callously modern or technological democracy exterminates competing ways of life. But, as Tocqueville explains, Berry's claim for victimization is exaggerated because "indigenous" peoples—including the Indians—opened themselves to destruction by being corrupted by the modern temptations of unearned luxury and ease.[15] There is nothing weaker than a people who have developed modern tastes without the modern or "bourgeois" habits of technology-driven work. There is something romantic and paternalistic in the belief that America's largely agricultural population could have been protected from such corruption. Most of our farmers had neither the illiterate isolation of European peasants or the quite un-American and atypical religious and cultural resources of the Amish.

Heidegger and Berry, with some—but not enough—evidence, tend to view America as a sort of technological tyranny, a place where the unlimited pursuit of money and power that is the result of technological thinking has led the few to lay waste to the communal and moral world inhabited by the many. Technological progress, they maintain, tends to make true or communal democracy almost impossible, as even Tocqueville argued. (Technological progress, it is true, has given many Americans the time to get involved in public-spirited organizations, but that involvement seems to have peaked prior to most educated women entering the workforce in the name of liberation.) Berry compares the way of life of the Europeans who came to America—who were anxious and dissatisfied "road builders" from the beginning—to that of the indigenous Indians of our continent and the "Old World Peasants." The ways of life of the latter "had evolved slowly in accordance with their knowledge of their land, of their needs, of their own relation of dependence and responsibility to it." They lived according to "deep earthly wisdom of established peoples"; they "belonged deeply and intricately to their places."[16] They were dependent on and responsible to a certain small part of the earth. Because they had no desire to go any other place, they had no need for roads.

From the view of low-tech Indians and peasants, "We [Europeans] *still* have not, in any meaningful way, arrived in America." We "road builders" remain "*placeless* people." Berry explains that we characteristically "behave violently" toward the land and particular places because from the beginning we "belonged to no place."[17] We have regarded the land or nature as an alien or hostile force to be conquered, not as our home. For Berry, what we modern Americans regard as the natural human propensities for wandering and violence are not really so natural at all. Our anxious dissatisfaction can at least be checked by our natural capabilities to be bound by habit and familiarity.[18] As even Heidegger says, the existential view that we human beings have no natural place in the cosmos is not shared by people who have the experience of belonging "deeply and intricately" to a particular locale.

The same technology that has brought us liberation and mobility—which, in truth, are more wonderful and exhilarating and naturally fulfilling than Berry allows—also brings us, Berry rightly says, an experience of "strange loss and sorrow."[19] We do not have to be as anti-technological or as anti-American or as non-Christian as he is (Berry's affirmation of the natural world opposes itself to the anthropocentric tendency of Christian otherworldliness)[20] to agree that "[s]urely there should be a more indigenous life than we have."[21] Our fundamental human experiences and longings persist despite the technological denial of their existence, and surely we remain free enough to create a more settled world that can make more sense of them. The problem is that a more settled or indigenous world in our time cannot dispense with postindustrial technology. We can agree with some of the "agrarian" criticism of our nihilistic displacement without thinking for a moment that any significant number of Americans are really going back to the farm. They are, in fact, not even going back to the factory. But we have reason to hope that, for example, our Christian counterculture will find ways to promote deep and intricate communal belongings, even if these are not so rooted in the soil.

Berry's view is that human experience points to the individual's "inferiority" to the natural world, "his dependence" on it, and "its ability to thrive without him."[22] Knowing that "the human race is less important than I thought"—and that my particular existence is less important than I thought—frees my "mind" from its unnatural "urgings." I no longer desire to do "violence" to nature; I now "wish to be as peaceable as my land." I no longer "may decently hope" to be more than the little I really am by nature, but am ready to "die in my own time" just as the "forest" will.[23] The modern but still anti-technological and proto–New Age philosopher Rousseau said that we must be unconscious to live peacefully with nature. Berry holds that true self-consciousness without God can lead to that peaceful experience, which he compares to the bird's "serenity of living within order." Our minds, apparently, can affirm that we are more similar to than we are different from the birds.

Like Socrates and Rousseau, Berry believes that for human

beings, living well is learning well with death. But his own manner of accepting nature as "his source and his destiny" is closer to Socrates' than a peasant's or a noble Indian warrior's.[24] Certainly the technological frenzy—the anxious restlessness—that characterizes the modern world owes much to the idea that such natural serenity is not really possible for self-conscious beings. As Tocqueville says, what is new about American democracy is that restlessness has become common among ordinary people.

That human beings have to be some *place* to live and that technology erodes all particular human attachments is true. Beings with bodies have to be somewhere, and all human experience of the universal truth comes through reflection that occurs in the context of particular communities. But it is unclear to what extent that place has to literally be a piece of land; Indian communities, for example, were often really bands of wanderers. And to some extent so too are Christian communities and any others composed of human beings who believe that they are really pilgrims or wayfarers in this world. According to one of the very first modern thinkers, Blaise Pascal, human beings exist nowhere in particular. They are miserably contingent and displaced accidents. The truth, in fact, makes us so miserable that we spend most of our lives diverting ourselves from it.[25] The only real remedy for our natural misery, according to Pascal, is to believe in a God hidden from natural view. From this Pascalian vantage point, the disorientation we experience in our high-tech world actually brings us closer to the truth about what we are by nature than does the experience of rootedness characteristic of the Old World peasant.

For Berry, Pascal is simply wrong. We can live well according to nature if we are deeply rooted in a particular place; we are not wanderers by nature. And there is much human experience that supports such a belief. But Berry is not simply right; we are different from the birds because most of us self-conscious beings do not accept our deaths serenely. It seems natural for us to fight and to hope to overcome our natural, mortal limits, even noble. Longing for a personal God, winning our liberty by dying courageously, and resisting with technology the nature out to kill each one of us seem to be natural, authentic responses to what we are fitted by nature really to know. The truth, surely, lies somewhere between Berry and Pascal.

It seems clear that nature is in some ways our friend and in others our enemy, and so our judgments about the effects of technological progress are and should almost always be mixed. Our romantic idealization today of our species' past low tech harmony with nature—which is excellent therapy for the ways in which we are alienated from nature by our unprecedented dependence on technology—has been "made possible only by technology's liberation of people from the harsh realities of wresting sustenance from a recalcitrant and destructive natural world."[26] There is remarkably little evidence—even or especially from the Indians—that human beings ever experienced that harmony.[27]

But in the decisive sense Pascal still sides with Berry in his opposition to the promise of modern technology eventually to make us fully at home. Heidegger exaggerates the extent to which we have been changed by technological thinking; the deepest thought might be that technological progress finally makes no fundamental difference in our being at all. We are certainly not completely under the thrall of technological thinking; there is no technological remedy to the greatness and misery of being human. Indeed, in a sense our modern hopes and fears about technological progress are nothing but another diversion, perhaps the greatest of our time.

LIBERTARIANISM AND BIOTECHNOLOGY

So far, I have argued that both the hopes and the fears we have concerning technology today are exaggerated. The limit to both is human nature; technological progress cannot satisfy our deepest longings or make us at home in the world. Nor can it completely uproot us from our human attachments or produce beings without moral or spiritual lives. We remain social beings open to the truth, nobility, and God, beings who love and die, and it is a large exaggeration to say that technology has reduced our world to a wasteland completely inhospitable to beings such as ourselves. It is equally an exaggeration to say that technological progress has been good for moral and spiritual life, or to say that we are able to control adequately that progress on behalf of properly human purposes. The very idea of technological control takes part in a way of thinking that is incapable of making properly human distinctions. We should thank God that we are still required to live morally demanding lives, and that we seem unable to bring human nature or human self-consciousness under our control.

But what of biotechnology—our new capacity to give orders to our brains and genes? Does that mean that all bets are off? As we have seen in earlier chapters, the biotechnological project aims to reduce radically the places of contingency and vulnerability in our lives. Its goals are and will be to eliminate genetically based diseases and to extend our lives indefinitely through regenerative medicine. We will be able to consciously and willfully design better human beings, ones that are smarter, healthier, more productive, and happier. And above all else, the biotechnological project will be driven by the modern goal of keeping particular individuals—*me*—alive.[28]

Biotechnology threatens to overcome natural limits to the technological regulation of all of human life. Leon Kass, chair of

President Bush's Council on Bioethics, worries that Americans are now so dominated by technological thinking that, for example, they are not much bothered much by the potential consequences of undertaking embryonic stem-cell research, especially the consequences for human dignity of "coming to look upon nascent human life as a natural resource to be mined, exploited, commodified."[29] Similarly, the primary American objection to human cloning thus far has been that it is unsafe, not that it abolishes the distinction between procreating and manufacturing human beings. A world in which children are manufactured and sex and procreation are totally disconnected would surely be one without much love, one where one manufactured being would have little natural or real connection to other manufactured beings. The perfection of control would come at the expense of love. Only through contemplating the extreme possibilities biotechnology opens for us can we see with neon clarity how the excessive attention to perpetuating individual lives characteristic of the modern, technological project is destructive of the natural goods given to rational, social beings.

According to Heidegger, the source of the technological thinking that dominates our world may be traced to Plato. Heidegger's critique of Plato has never been clear to me, but Kass suggests something similar. In his earlier work, Kass connected human dignity only with living well or thoughtfully with death. Pascal also says that our dignity consists in thought. From this view, today's sophisticated Americans live most undignified lives, and the whole modern liberation of technology from higher human concerns is also revealed to be wanting. Our pursuit of happiness, Kass has been warning for a long time, has been undignified, and the principles of our technological republic do not provide us with the defense of dignity we now need.

Kass used to be more clear than he is now that Socrates is the model of dignity, and that Aristotle rightly taught that all of natural development culminated in that thoughtful dignity. But the problem is that if Socrates had been offered another seventy years through regenerative medicine right before his famous self-defense speech before the Athenians, he might well have flattered and not angered his judges. That is, if we identify our dignity simply with our minds, we might conclude that philosophers could well live undeluded about death and still welcome a much longer life. In other words, this understanding of dignity does not sufficiently appreciate what technology's assault on the virtues connected with marital and parental love does to the dignity of most human beings. Living well with death cannot be a complete account of human dignity, although it is a fundamental part of that account. "What humanity needs most of all in the face of evils is courage, the ability to stand against fear and pain and thoughts of nothingness," but the practice of the courage required of conscious but embodied beings requires the encouragement and usually love of others.[30]

So Kass now thinks that both ancient and modern philosophers, even the teleological Aristotle, have not adequately understood that "respect for a being created in God's image means respecting *everything* about him, not just his freedom or his reason but also his blood." The philosophers have not seen clearly enough "why it is not good for the man to be alone; why the remedy for man's aloneness is a sexual counterpart, not a dialectic partner (Eve, not Socrates)," and "why in the shame-filled discovery of sexual nakedness is humanity's first awe-filled awareness of the divine."[31] The philosophers have not given us a complete enough account of the relationship between the physical and psychic, or social and spiritual, dimensions of human, biological life, whereas the Bible presents human beings as whole persons made in the image of God and so as natural—but more than natural—beings.

There is no reason that philosophers cannot learn from the Bible at least what is certainly true: we are clearly more than minds or bodies or even a mixture of mind and body. Those "men from Missouri" who truly use their eyes to see will find plenty of evidence of human dignity all around them, in "the valiant efforts ordinary people make to meet necessity, to combat adversity and disappointment, to provide for their children, to care for their parents, to help their children, to serve their country."[32] They also should be able to see that "[t]o suffer, to endure, to trouble oneself for the sake of home, family, community and genuine friendship, is truly to live."[33] The challenges posed by biotechnology—which are only extreme versions of the challenges posed by modern technology generally—may lead us to rediscover the relationships among birth, sex, marriage and the family, openness to the truth and God, and death that constitute human dignity.

We also must return to Pascal for a reminder that the biotechnological project cannot turn us human beings from mysterious into manufactured beings. The effort to deny the reality of the fundamental unpredictability of human life that is intrinsic to technological thinking is ultimately futile. The good news is that technology may finally make us so unhappy that we will begin to effectively criticize its consequences with the whole human good in mind.

CHAPTER 4

THE LIMITS OF THE AMERICAN UTOPIAN IMAGINATION

America is *the* middle-class nation. That does not mean there is not great economic inequality in America. It does not even mean that there are not people who are not really middle class. Most of us cannot imagine ourselves as being either more or less than middle class, and all of us imagine that the existence of human beings who are more than middle class (aristocrats) or less (slaves, tenant farmers) provide evidence of monstrous injustice that is just plain un-American. Thus, for instance, most Americans think of the "underclass" as the product of un-American social policy. Liberals blame racism (a product of the aristocratic South) and conservatives blame welfare (which rewards people for not working), but both sides blame some form of discredited paternalism that keeps people from being treated as free and equal members of the middle class.

The good news about being members of the middle class is that we are all equally free. The bad news is that we all have to work. Now we tend to regard this middle-class view of being human as being both American and true, or consonant with human nature. Aristocrats, in their leisure, arrogantly and unjustly mistake themselves for gods. Slaves are treated as if they were naturally unfree, just like the other animals. Beings between the other animals and God, of course, are metaphysically middle class.

The classic criticism of middle-class life holds that it is boring, insipid, and unconcerned with human excellence. For our critics, America is simultaneously the most productive or workaholic and least civilized or less poetic of the world's nations. But the truth is that middle-class life is quite complex and quite unstable, not to mention wonderful. Surely the most wonderful thing in the universe is the being who is neither pure body nor pure mind, neither beast nor angel, and so caught in the middle. American instability—a reflection of human instability—is clear, for example, in our view of the truth. We are pragmatists. We believe that theory is for practice, that thinking, like everything else, ought to be directed toward making ourselves and the world better. For aristocrats, perhaps, freedom is achieved by transcending the vulgar world of work through pure, leisurely thought. But for us, we are free only to transform, and become free by transforming, the world and ourselves.

The best American pragmatists have realized that our work needs to be both inspired and inspirational, and so they have written poetically in order to ennoble—by revealing the spiritual dimension of—middle-class life. They have approached America, as Richard Rorty writes, as a nation of "romantic utopians trying to imagine a better future."[1] It is un-American, Rorty rightly claims, not to be able to imagine and work for the future "possibility of human happiness," a possibility that has not yet become real.[2] Rorty encourages us to hope and work for a softer and less competitive future, one which will be less workaholic, less self-obsessive, less cruel, more nice, and more egalitarian.

In truth, Rorty's project is only ambiguously middle class. He says that he writes, for now, as an American chauvinist, but his distant hope is that all that is distinctive about America will wither away. He seems to see nothing good or enduring in the free being who works. Rorty's Deweyan pragmatism, as Michael Barone has recently shown, is too "soft" to see the transcendence—what is not only productive but also good and noble—in our basically "hard" lives.[3] Our softness, Barone explains, doesn't point backward toward aristocratic excellence but forward to hapless dependence, to a world in which we would neither work nor be free. The right-wing, pro-capitalist pragmatist sees that it's not only noble but useful to celebrate the greatness and misery of middle-class life.

THE NEW WHITMAN

A better writer than Rorty for showing us the true greatness and misery of middle-class life is our most recent poet of pragmatism, David Brooks, who celebrates the facts that we members of the American middle class are stuck with both our freedom and our work, both of which have less to do with our bodily needs as animals than with our imaginary obsession with our transcendent futures. Brooks, the most conservative columnist at the *New York Times*, calls himself a "progressive conservative." He wants to conserve by ennobling our progressive, productive middle-class tradition. That tradition, he explains, is "built on an admiration for a certain sort of individual: the young, ambitious striver who works hard, makes something of himself, creates opportunities for others and goes on to advance America's unique mission in the world."[4] In other words, for Brooks the great tradition of the American middle class combines capitalism with messianic nationalism. It is the history of individuals who by fulfilling themselves serve their nation and the world.

Brooks's pragmatic poetry poses, for the most part, as comic sociology with serious moral and political undertones. His first book concerned a narrow slice of the upper middle class—the bourgeois bohemians, or Bobos, who, he claimed, were the Americans who served as role models for the rest of us. It was hard to tell whether in that book Brooks was describing, mocking, or ennobling the Bobo way of life.[5] Brooks's topic in his latest book, *On Paradise Drive*, is our middle class as a whole, and so he chooses to consider our suburbs. His approach in this book is far more ambitious and earnest than it has been in the past, and his writing deliberately and subtly blurs the distinction between poetry and prose, or the imaginary and the real world. Like any poet, he ignores, plays with, and exaggerates all kinds of facts. He also quotes often from authors in the American literary tradition in order to situate himself within that tradition. His most ambitious goal is to provide an edifying history of the American imagination, one that culminates with his own contribution. Despite his protestations about the limits of his literary ability and his constant reminders that he is trying to be funny, Brooks clearly means to be our new Walt Whitman.

Both the old and the new Whitman think that part of the greatness of democracy is that it fosters a way of life in which each person enjoys, and is compelled to maintain, his moral independence and fluid, always provisional sense of self. Yet both Whitmans believe that even this freedom, to be maintained, needs limits, and that we American citizens require poets who will help us understand why we should acknowledge our shared similarities and sympathize with our fellow citizens. The poet's role is to reveal to us why and how, despite our many divisions, we share a common greatness. Whitman found that greatness largely through his reflections on the common or "unionist" effort that was the Civil War. "The United States themselves," Whitman wrote, "are essentially the greatest poem."[6] Brooks, taking our national poetry one democratic step further, finds our greatness or transcendence in the achievements inspired by our common dreams or imaginings. The new Whitman finds our "national union" in the imagination that inspires the "social mobility" that—despite our many differences—we all share.[7]

Brooks ends his book by affirming with Whitman that "America is the Solution." He does not mean that it is the solution to the human problem of how to find love or happiness or even mere serenity in this life. As he observes at the book's opening, "If you were to judge from the literature of the past century, nobody is happy in suburbia" (5).[8] And Brooks, a literary man himself, seems to provide plenty of evidence to confirm that critical judgment. He says that suburban Americans deprive themselves of real happiness in the present by focusing on the imaginary "promise of total happiness" (270) that they will enjoy, as the result of their work, at some indefinite point in the future. Americans under this "Paradise Spell" are "more attached to the glorious future than to the temporary and unsatisfactory present" (263). We constantly distract ourselves from our present misery by losing ourselves in "mirages of the future" (273). These mirages, it seems, are the opiate of the middle class—an opiate mixed with speed. That imaginary stimulant is the source of our singularly energetic productivity.

The American imagination, Brooks shows, spins the pragmatists' knowledge of the utter contingency of each human life into good news, which is that all our problems are temporary. The insight that nothing is permanent, properly considered, can even serve as an antidote to "the tragic view of life that is supposedly the prerequisite for the probing and profound soul" (181). Sin and death—

the limits that we have been given that seem to frustrate all our plans for self-liberation—need not be part of our imaginary futures. That is why, according to Brooks, writers like Augustine mean little to Americans. The good news about our provisional or contingent existences is that even sin and death may be merely provisional too. Without that good news, we might, like some European, do nothing but whine incessantly about existing for a moment between two abysses. Pragmatism properly understood spares us miserable and unproductive existentialism.

We Americans, in our pragmatic way, put the individual's pursuit of happiness first, and so "whatever serves [our] self-journey toward happiness . . . must be godly and true." We call true whatever we think can make us happy, and we cast aside the theological or philosophic prejudice that connects bad moods with the truth about our sinful and mortal existence. God himself is nothing more than an image of one's own future perfection, and so the self on the way to perfection "becomes semidivinized" (276). The truth is whatever helps free me from my non-divine, contingent present; the truth is whatever helps me leave my present condition behind. "If there's an idea" Americans "don't like, they don't bother refuting it, they talk about something else, and the original idea dies from intention" (47). That insight originates with Santayana, but unlike Santayana, Rorty sees it as just plain good advice, and Brooks echoes Rorty in encouraging us to leave death, God, and even love behind by refusing to talk about them.

We Americans know, according to Rorty and Brooks and Whitman, that the imaginary cure to the problem of existentialism doesn't depend on a real solution. As Rorty explains, "Whitman thought that we Americans have the most poetical nature because we are the first thoroughgoing experiment in national self-creation:

the first nation-state with nobody but itself to please—not even God. . . . We redefine God as our future selves."[9] "It is not," in Brooks's words, "our duty to obey God's law . . . It's our duty to create and explore the self" (276). We are the most poetical people, our two Whitmans (Whitman and Brooks) and our two pragmatists (Rorty and Brooks) agree, because we believe ourselves to be purely the products of our own self-creation.

In *Bobos in Paradise*, Brooks seemed at times to align himself with such cultural critics as Allan Bloom and Francis Fukuyama— the whole "end of history" crowd. End of history thinkers wonder about the irony that we Americans have worked so hard to bring history or our idea of the future to an end. But now, like Rorty, Brooks wants to distinguish his hopeful view of Americans from fashionable European despair about the irredeemable flatness of American souls. Bloom and Fukuyama, Brooks and other pragma- tists argue with some justice, succumb too readily to alien thought. The contradiction that reveals that Americans have souls, Brooks notices, is that "we are utter failures when it comes to living the simple life, which we profess to desire" (274). American life is marked by the incessant pursuit of a future that is not only impossible but would also, workaholics that we are, make us miserable if we actu- ally achieved it. Our transcendence, our greatness, lies in being driven forward by mirages and in never really being happy. We think that something like the end of history is our goal, but that does not mean we will ever get there or be happy if we do.

American idealism, as Brooks presents it, seems to be an ex- treme version of the insoluble human tendency toward restless self- deception and self-diversion described so well by Pascal and Tocqueville. And so he suggests that existentialism far more than pragmatism is finally true. Finally, our country is "the solution to bourgeois flatness, to materialistic complacency, to mass-media shallowness, because America . . . arouses the most strenuous efforts" (279); we are constantly diverted from our true situation by losing ourselves in real work in the service of an imaginary mission impossible. Our salvation lies in the fact that we are so easily diverted from what we really know, which is that the simple life is not a real human possibility. Our salvation comes from the fact that we work hard and successfully to keep ourselves from seeing clearly that we cannot save ourselves.

THE TRANSCENDENT AMERICAN IMAGINATION

In *On Paradise Drive,* Brooks is at his most condescending in describing the various forms of inanity that characterize the American imagination. One especially prevalent suburban utopian vision revolves around golf, which he claims moves us far more than "war or literature or philosophy." The golfer who finally achieves the elusive state of "par" has achieved the "suburb's view of nirvana," "a state of harmony," "a mystical groove." And that is because "he has defeated his primary foe—anxiety" (40–41). American Buddhism—devoid as it is of real personal spiritual discipline—is understandable but silly. We have turned hard-won Buddhist serenity into yet another therapeutic diversion. Brooks's dripping irony is meant to emphasize that golf does not *really* release us from our anxiety for more than an afternoon. His description, in fact, deliberately deprives that sport of its genuine nobility, which has to do with the anxiety-inducing activities of keeping score, constant practice, and taking—and not taking—risks. There was nothing Zen-like, for example, in the recent Masters final-day showdown between Phil Mickelson and Tiger Woods. They were both sweating bullets down the stretch, and Tiger's primary foe was not anxiety but Phil. The pure and beautiful meritocratic high-stakes competition of golf is, in fact, something we would be more miserable or bored without.

The lameness of imaginatively idealized pseudo-Buddhist golf is one piece of evidence among many Brooks gives in *Paradise Drive* that there is no real possibility that middle-class Americans might reconcile the opposing goals of bourgeois productivity and bohemian self-fulfillment. His descriptions of that bourgeois bohemian reconciliation in *Bobos in Paradise* were wrong. He no longer believes in what Kay Hymowitz calls "ecstatic capitalism," or the coexistence of "playful exuberance . . . with a zealous work ethic."[10] The Bobos, playfully and happily achieving in abundance, think they are already in paradise, and Brooks depicted them as the most self-satisfied and conservative generation in history. Their imagination has no need of a utopian dimension. But now Brooks says that all, or almost all, Americans live in the future, because the present is anything but paradise.

He mentions almost in passing that he discovered a few genuine bohemians in the small "crunchy" zones of the suburbs, but these people constitute an insignificant minority. Those he had previously described as Bobos appear in *On Paradise Drive* as the inhabitants of the suburban "inner ring." Brainy, well-educated, and productive, these sophisticates are able to live in large, expensive, and tasteful houses near the city's artistic center. Like other middle-class suburbanites, they have "deep simplicity longings, visions of having enough money and space so they can finally rest. Yet you know they are wired for hard work, because they feel compelled to put offices in every room of the house. . . . The dream of perfect serenity and domestic bliss will just have to be transferred to the vacation home" (31). These inner-ringers, capable of little else but working hard, provide evidence in support of Brooks's generalization that the middle-class imagination—the imagination of free beings who work—derails every significant effort to establish a counterculture in America.

The American contradiction that unites the apparently disparate "cliques" that compose our suburbs is that, while we are the most future-oriented, time-bound people that has ever been, we are at the same time impelled by our imagination of "a new Eden," a place where "time does not exist" and we "will feel liberated from the burden of the future" (273). Just as the old Eden exists in the indefinite past, the new one exists in the indefinite future. We are constantly driven by our anticipation of a world to come that will include no anticipation. Our imagination of what will make us happy, then, does not consist of some sort of positive fulfillment— that is, of love or wisdom or union with God. If it did, we Americans would be separated by our different conceptions of what makes such fulfillments possible—our different conceptions of the human good. But we all share the illusory longing to be free from the burden of our freedom. The evidence that we are transcendent beings is that we are all driven by our longing to be rid of our transcendence.

The transcendent longings we all share, Brooks explains, are neither absurd, as the existentialist would say, nor natural, as Aristotle or Thomas Aquinas would say. They are quite distinctively *American*. Brooks has written, in his own way, a post-9/11, national greatness poem. Brooks shows us what it is about being an American that arouses the hostility and envy of the world, and he separates us from unnamed bourgeois nations in which human imaginings of future possibilities have all but withered away. Americans "have built a society that opens up opportunity and undermines security. . . . It is easier to get rich here, but more miserable to be poor here" (272–73). We have all the greatness and misery of a meritocratic people that has few safety nets. America—as the only imaginatively middle-class nation—works against every feature of the present—including any form of human permanence or security—with the imaginary future in mind. That is why our "Suburban Empire" now dominates the world as a not completely benevolent kind of wrecking ball.

Brooks's poetic mission is to restore a political sense of our common destiny as a people, to connect our individual imaginations with our country's historical imagination, to restore the vision of our founders that is echoed in our deep-souled poets Lincoln and Whitman, who held that Americans "were not only the chosen people, they were the *final* people, the children of prophecy. . . . Paradise would be realized on this new continent, and the redemption of all mankind would spread out from here" (256). For "early Americans, the United States was not merely a nation, it was an eschatology" (118). Our founders articulated a middle-class theology of liberation through achievement. Brooks gives us no reason to believe that this prophetic eschatology can actually become true, except as the imaginary ideal that consciously or unconsciously animates all Americans as Americans. So, in order to effectively drive our activity, our imaginings must remain vague about how and for whom paradise will eventually come.

Each individual achievement, "each [American] ascent," we should imagine, is connected to a "mission that will be realized only across generations and by institutions that transcend an individual lifetime" (182). For that reason, Brooks endorses a program of universal national service: "There should be at least one moment in life when people are encouraged to serve a cause larger than self-interest," and that cause should "cultivate a spirit of citizenship."[11] The blurring of the distinctions between our individual and historical destinies and between being a narcissistic individual and a devoted citizen lies at the foundation of our "optimistic faith" that the "essential goodness" of "the true inner self" will shine forth once we have removed every obstacle to free human work in this world (149). The two Whitmans agree that the goodness of the American self must somehow transcend the distinction between self-fulfilling individualism and selfless republicanism. The self-obsessed efforts of suburban individuals, after all, have made the most powerful contributions to our free and democratic nation's domination of the world.

It does not bother either of our Whitmans that the imaginary effort to suppress the difference between individual and historical destinies has sometimes made Americans rather fanatical. Our optimistic imagination is the source of "political causes that promise to purify the world," causing us to be "gripped sometimes by a zeal for purgative wars that will cleanse the world of some evil" (122). Only Americans could believe that they are fighting a war to end all wars, or that ridding the nation of alcohol or even slavery would really purify human life. The historical side of the American theological pursuit of achievement, like the personal side, is driven by mirages of paradise. It aims at the creation of a world without war, poverty, or disease, a world without flawed and anxious human life as we know it. Both sides of the American imagination flourish at the expense of particular persons, of being in love at home in the present, of erotic attachment to contingent mortal being, of a longing and love for a personal God other than oneself. Our restless, utopian imagination drives us away from family and friends and even our fellow citizens into an indefinite and impersonal future.

The core of Brooks's description of our suburbs is they have no sense of place or home, "no centers, no recognizable borders or boundaries." They are anthropologically unprecedented. Before them, "people always lived in some definable place" (4). Our detachment is both geographical and not just geographical. To live no place in particular in the universe, according to the great existentialist Pascal, is the unendurable experience of undiverted human beings. We are driven away from particular places and particular human beings toward no place in particular by our natures. But we Americans, according to Brooks, lack both a sense of place and a sense of "no place"; we manage to experience ourselves as neither at home nor radically homeless or without hope. We hope we are not destined to be homeless, but that is because our imagination keeps us from having a clear sense of what it would mean to be human beings at home. Our "Suburban Empire"—existing no place in particular between the city and the country—is working to make the whole world quite self-consciously middle-class—or full of beings who cannot really locate themselves anyplace in particular. From Pascal's view, Americans both serve the truth and divert themselves from the truth.

BEING HAPPY IN HOPE

The new Whitman hopes to move us to rethink the theological and philosophical criticism of the future-obsessed American that is a stock feature of our "anti-bourgeois" critics, a criticism made most powerfully, perhaps, by Alexis de Tocqueville: Tocqueville and like-minded thinkers have asserted, among other things, that we Americans pursue happiness but never achieve it, that we ridiculously pursue spiritual satisfaction through material pursuits. Brooks does not as much disagree with that view as redescribe it. To him, the

American perspective is a historical (but not really secular, in that it is not necessarily realistic or empirical) version of the Christian, eschatological view that people—otherwise miserable—can be made happy in the hope of things unseen. Brooks agrees with Rorty that we are bound together by a collective fantasy that is the common element in all our private fantasies, the fantasy that our national greatness has the capacity to bring history to an end.

But Brooks does not let us forget that our success—our productivity, our technology—is real. He sometimes appears to make a Machiavellian or capitalist argument for American superiority: What matters is that we employ the most effective means—including the manipulation of the imagination to produce productive drive—to material success. The proof of American greatness is the wealth and power generated by free beings who work, and the fact that we really are wealthy and powerful—and that our wealth and power have done ourselves and others much good—is part of Brooks's answer to our European critics, such as Martin Heidegger, who sneer that the truth is that we are empty nihilists. But reality is finally not the poet's standard at all. Brooks, like Rorty, like all imaginative pragmatists, does not quite buy the idea that there is a real or material world by which utopian visions should be measured. The truth, like everything else, does not exist independently of our wills. So Brooks writes that "Mentality matters and in the end, perhaps mentality is all that matters" (268). In other words, all that matters is how we Americans use our imaginations to think of ourselves. Our success is good only if put in the right imaginary context, which is why we will never be able to do without poets. Poetic technology ranks higher than technology in the more usual senses of the term.

That noble idea is what has separated American Transcendentalists from American materialists (Marxists and Lockeans) since the time of Emerson and Brownson. Like Brooks, Transcendentalists have always maintained that human beings are not moved so much by the harsh realities of material necessity as they are their minds or imaginations. That is why there is no point in asking whether we are *really* happy or simply deluded; if our thoughts and imaginations make us happy, then we really *are* happy.

That poetic conclusion, of course, is never completely convincing. We Americans are constantly at work—both productively and imaginatively—in response to our anxiety. That anxiety must therefore be fundamental, and it is what makes American life hard. Just because we Americans do not live well with love and death does not mean we are not moved by them. We pragmatic Americans, Brooks claims, have no idea how to talk about morality, regarding it as nothing more than another tool to maximize our freedom. And so we have nothing to say about courage or loyalty or gratitude. The professors at Princeton that Brooks describes view themselves as incompetent to form the character of their students, and their students imagine wrongly that they live in a time when character and virtue are essentially superfluous. But on Brooks's terms, nothing could be further from the truth; if he is right, they live in a time when people are more on their own than ever and so will need virtue more than ever. Even Brooks admits that the old WASP aristocrats—like all aristocrats a once endangered and now extinct species in America—were right to see that we pragmatic Americans are incapable of understanding, much less countering, the ways in which our "achievement ethics corrodes virtue" (179).

We must agree that there is truth in Brooks's observation that the profound experiences of soul that produced the tragic sensibility of a St. Augustine are contrary to American optimism and so often seem unreal to us. But it is also true that, at least some-times, we cannot help but know that those experiences are pro-found because they are true. Such experiences may chasten the self-deceptive imagination by revealing the invincible limits to human accomplishment, including the mysterious givenness of good and evil in each person's soul. We are tempted to conclude that the exis-tential subtext of Brooks's pragmatic poetry is that the greatness of Americans lies in their misery, in their inability to be grateful for what they have been given, to practice virtue of any real kind, to be in love in the present, or more generally ever to experience them-selves at home. But it is even more important to emphasize that both the edifying text and the critical subtext of Brooks's book achieve their force through exaggeration. And Brooks is honest enough to point to evidence that would modify his conclusions considerably: Some middle-class Americans really do act on their longing to be at home with their families in a particular place, and some really do believe in a personal, judgmental God who is other than and tran-scends themselves. That is, many middle-class Americans under-stand themselves, fundamentally, as much more than free beings who work.

THE EXURBS

From Brooks's view, the in some ways least characteristically Ameri-can suburbanites live in the suburbs' new outer-ring towns or "ex-urbs." People, he notices, move to these places not only to escape the culture of broken homes, crime, and drugs that they find closer to the city, but also from the social competition and cultural one-upmanship of the more pretentious Bobo suburbs. In these new towns, nobody is very rich or really poor, and employment tends to be more managerial or bottom-line and less professional or status-conscious in orientation. The denizens of the exurbs do value competition and achievement—they love sports, for example, but more than most Americans they are seeking community.

The exurbs are strange sorts of communities. They are without past or precedent, and people sometimes move to them without families, friends, or jobs, pursuing a dream of happiness. But their utopianism is rather singular, Brooks rightly says, because it is basically conservative. These exurbanites imagined an idealized or improved version of "1950s suburban America," and those imaginings were not far from the reality of what they made for themselves: "intact two-parent families, 2.3 kids, low crime, and a relatively flat divorce rate" (49). The exurban family is far less pathological than it is in the rest of the suburbs, while exurbanites are also less conformist and more thoughtful than people found in older, split-level/cul-de-sac suburban areas.

In the old cities, community was intertwined with poverty, lack of mobility, and inescapable moral repression. It is no wonder that Americans characteristically fled that life for the space and freedom of the suburbs. But in the new towns what is best for families and friendship is chosen by people who really have a choice. The choice has been made—to some extent—against the American grain by those who have experienced both the costs and the benefits of the progress of our moral freedom. Brooks sometimes implies that this choice has been too easy; exurban dwellers want all the benefits of freedom along with all the benefits of community. There is some truth to that criticism, but it is also contradicted by demographic facts. Healthy families always depend on the acceptance of considerable dutiful and loving constraint on choice.

Brooks, despite his poetic intention, provides impressive evidence that the exurbs reflect a maturing or humanizing of the middle-class imagination. The first people who moved to such towns clamored for homes near golf courses. But by 2000 their vision of perfection had changed. The demand for country clubs dropped, and the one for "walking paths, coffee shops, Kinko's, clubhouses, parks, and natural undeveloped land grew." In an age of perfectly climate-controlled indoor spaces, front porches have made quite an exurban comeback. The vision of timeless, tranquil solitude of suburban American Buddhism faded, replaced by the desire for diverse human connections in a location with "a sense of place." Stores, restaurants, and galleries designed by "themists" who cater to those desires (50–51) have opened overnight, promising that within their doors everyone will know your name and you will feel at home—bars with the look and feel of *Cheers* (which itself reproduces the look and feel of an Irish or English pub) and neighborhoods that appear as quaint and settled as Victorian villages.

Brooks, with his evidence, corrects libertarian Virginia Postrel's account of the meaning of contemporary aesthetics. She sees the middle class, having left the realm of economic necessity or scarcity, as now free to give expression to each person's special feeling for style. Each of us is free to show how "smart and pretty" we are, to exhibit our distinctive taste. Postrel's view is that we are all libertarians—that is, bourgeois bohemians—now.[12] But the exurbs are evidence that we also want to be freed from the restless experience of being nowhere in particular and of having constantly to reinvent ourselves to please people we do not even know. But the exurbs are actually evidence that *both* Brooks and Postrel are wrong: Our anxious longing is not to be free from families, friends, political responsibilities, and so forth; it is not for some serene new Eden without birth, time, and death.

The poet Brooks deliberately does not make conservative

utopianism very appealing; he does his best to make it boring and un-American. It undermines, after all, his poetic celebration of the essential homelessness of *all* middle-class Americans. Brooks even uses the tired line that all the exurbanites want is an "updated Mayberry." But such a place would be very interesting! Mayberry was fairly bizarre, with no intact two-parent families among the main characters. Those characters included only one kid (Opie), an underachieving single dad (Andy), a spinster (Aunt Bea), a single schoolmarm (Helen), a charming—almost bohemian—town drunk (Otis), and a variety of eccentric and ineffectual but not particularly bohemian unattached men (Barney, Floyd, Goober, Howard, and others). The show's deep teaching was that Mayberry had no future, and perhaps that was why it vaguely attracted harried American fake Buddhists.

No American today imagines living in Mayberry. But few can deny that Mayberry had some particularly attractive features; it was safe, unstratified, friendly, morally serious, and had a real sense of place. Those qualities, combined with some culture, achievement, and intact two-parent families, might be an appropriately human middle-class mixture. The exurbs might be evidence that this mixture is more possible than they realize who dismiss the longing for such a place as nothing but idealized nostalgia, a self-forgetting reaction against the anxious and exhilarating realities of our world of liberated self-fulfillment.

Brooks also criticizes the exurban conservatives for not being conservative at all, for not being as different from other middle-class Americans as it seems. They vote Republican to protect what they have as individuals or parents, but they do nothing to preserve the culture or decency of their country. They did not "stay and fight" against the growing decadence closer in to the city, but instead chose to stay on the fringe of cultural and political conflict. Rather than facing their problems, they chose to abandon them and move on (47). In this sense they are like their American fore-bears who abandoned the corruptions and confinements of civilization for the frontier, and certainly Brooks should have connected them better with the distinctively American capacity rapidly to build community and tradition out of nothing. But that observation is too simple: The exurbanites went to the frontier (of the sub-urbs, beyond which there is, so to speak, nothing) not primarily to escape civilization or to find opportunity. (They often work much closer to the city.) Unlike their ancestors, they aimed to escape—if only partially—the frontier of the American imagination Brooks describes in order to find civilization.

People in the exurbs tend to know little about each other's jobs, which are too technical and complicated to explain ("some-thing with cellphones" or "some sort of marketing"). They are ap-parently often niche-product people, although not the most suc-cessful or driven among them. They know each other through lei-sure-time activities, mostly connected with kids and sports (50). Sports, as Brooks later explains, may be the best way people in the suburbs have of teaching children about the connections among personal achievement, community, and nobility. Children's coaches (usually parents, of course) are often the most honorable and gen-erous people around. What they show and know about character ought to shame the Princeton professors who snigger and squirm at the idea of character education.

It's true that exurban utopianism is only very ambiguously conservative in origin. The "new-urbanist ethos," Brooks reminds us, "started in socially conscious communities like Portland, Or-egon." That seems, at first, to imply that it is bourgeois bohemian.

But the Bobos are not really that socially conscious; they care more about the rain forest than the real poor. Trees, unlike people, cannot help themselves. The original new urbanists were more like bohemian socialists, fighting against suburban sprawl with visions of old and beautiful urban communities without the old injustice and poverty. The new urbanists, Brooks admits, have had the nationwide effect of making lives "better and more community-oriented" (51), although he doesn't follow up at all on that observation. From the poet's view, they make America less American.

The original new urbanists cannot think highly of most exurbs. The people there lack social consciousness and are not big on diversity; they are the most Republican and probably least socialist of Americans. They care more about escaping America's pressing social problems than about taking a lead in solving them. They often have bad taste and are easily fooled by corporate-produced shoddy imitations of classic architecture. They do not even care that the restaurants and shops in their towns are rarely locally owned. (The food at Macaroni Grill, although good, only seems authentic to someone who has never been to a real Little Italy.) For entertainment they are too easily satisfied with the worst and most conventional versions of popular music from the recent past. (Today's bogus versions of the Marvelettes, Drifters, Rascals, and so forth draw big middle-aged, middle-class crowds in the exurbs.) It would seem that no indigenous music or art of any enduring excellence is likely to emerge from our new towns. We might also add that the moral quality of the exurbanites' child-rearing is uneven. Lots of exurban kids are corrupted by their parents' prosperity and middle-class ambivalence about their own authority, not to mention to the broader culture's moral indifference. The malls and patio parties are filled with girls dressed like what Brooks calls "preppy prostitutes."

And yet, in some ways the exurbs are nevertheless less corrupt than are the seemingly more authentic embodiments of the new urbanist vision. They are more affordable and less pretentious. They are not communities that look like America in all its diversity, but neither are they the most tastefully and expensively revitalized parts of our old cities. And the people who live in the exurbs really do have nothing against members of ethnic, racial, and religious minorities who are otherwise like them. They are good Americans in tending to believe that being middle class is more essential than any other human quality (except maybe believing in God), and so they think (like Brooks himself) that all the fuss over multiculturalism is counterproductive and silly. Furthermore, the corners the exurbanites cut are arguably inessential for the community possible in our time. Busy parents and children do not and probably should not waste time thinking about how to make their homes authentic works of art. The attempt to live aristocratically in a middle-class world, as Tocqueville says, usually leads to little more than snobbish dissatisfaction.

Many of the people on the exurban frontier, whether they know it or not, stand in rebellion alongside the left-wing bohemian new urbanists against capitalism's tendency to treat human beings only as isolated, self-fulfilling individuals rather than as parents, children, creatures, friends, and citizens. So they live, to some extent, in egalitarian rebellion against the extreme economic inequality of a pure meritocracy and against the elitism of the fake bohemian culture of aesthetic self-fulfillment promoted by our libertarian sophisticates. They are guilty as charged of indifference to the injustice and decadence of metropolitan areas as wholes, but maybe that is because they limit their concerns to what they can control. What can a man who sells cell phones do about the underclass? In response to the anxious sense of homelessness that characterizes the suburban middle class as a whole, they choose to do what they can to be at home. From the sociobiologist's perspective, the exurbs are some of the healthiest and most genuinely hopeful places in the prosperous and sophisticated Western world. There are few other places (such as wherever lots of Mormons live) where people are staying married, doing a decent job raising their kids, and, in fact, having more than enough kids to replace themselves.

Unconstrained by *Paradise Drive*'s poetic imperative, Brooks actually highlights the exurban difference in one of his columns. The exurbs contain a disproportionate number of "natalists" or people whose "personal identity is defined by parenthood" and who have three or more kids. Natalists "are more spiritually, emotionally, and physically involved in their homes than in other spheres of life, having concluded that parenthood is the most enriching and elevating thing they can do." Areas of our country that our sophisticated see "as sprawling materialistic wastelands," natalists see "as clean, orderly, and affordable places where they can nurture children." Because of the natalists, Brooks observes, the exurbs "stand out in all sorts of demographic and cultural categories," and so it turns out not to be clear at all that our suburbs can be understood as a whole. He still makes a fairly perfunctory effort to explain that the differences between the natalists and most Americans are "of degree, not kind."[13] Although it is true enough that most Americans understand themselves as partly family members and partly individuals, Brooks still cannot quite admit that large differences in emphasis are surely differences in kind.

THE EVANGELICALS

Brooks chooses not to integrate the exurbs properly into his poetry. Creating places or homes out of nothing is not, on balance, transcendent enough because it is too real. Our new Whitman is most moved when he sees his fellow Americans most clearly acting and imagining as dissatisfied individuals against what they have been given by God, nature, and tradition. That is what explains the strangest omission: In a book full of references to transcendence, eschatology, paradise, and Eden, there is no serious or sustained treatment of American Christianity. And that is not because Brooks somehow overlooks the fact that the suburbs have lots of people who call themselves Christians and go to church.

The new Whitman poetically proclaims the good news that American religion no longer has any distinctive content. He celebrates the "optimistic and easygoing" character of American faiths, which, to their credit "emphasize personal growth over any fixed creed." Our religion, like everything else, is all about "mobility" and "blurry boundaries." We believers "do not preach at one another, but partner with each other." The good news is that "orthodox" religion neither divides us nor makes us intolerant; our religious imagination can no longer be distinguished from the middle-class imagination that unites us.[14] Brooks only hints at the corresponding bad news: If he is right, our religion no longer offers us any respite from what he calls "the culture of contingency,"[15] from "the provisional life" of individuals constantly on the move (275).

From that view, Christians might notice that Brooks, despite his intention, comes close to practicing Christian apologetics. He suggests that only by allowing our imaginations to divert ourselves from what we really know about the contingency of our beings are we future-minded Americans made happy in hope. Our secularized or historicized eschatology is less reasonable than real Christianity; both we and Brooks know that we really cannot free ourselves from our anxiety by our own efforts. Brooks's transcendent account of what drives us might be viewed as evidence that we are more animated than ever by longings that only a personal, transcendent God could satisfy. But Brooks's actual intention is to inspire us with the thought that America has transformed Christianity, and nothing can or should be done about that fact. Like Whitman or Rorty or any other pragmatic American poet, he need not refute the claims of orthodox religion; all he need do is convince us that we have left them behind. Our longings, after all, are not natural, but American. They are not psychological necessities but historical or political products subject to change.

But Brooks does not shirk from mentioning certain facts that make his poetic impression questionable. A clear majority of Americans say that God is important in their lives, and an overwhelming majority believes in heaven. These two facts distinguish us at least as much as does our productivity from the bourgeois Europeans, and surely they moderate our drive for historical and self-perfection. Brooks also connects the genuineness of our religious beliefs with our spirit of volunteerism and our strong nonprofit sector. A close reader might conclude that he leaves us with the contradiction that America is at once the most Christian and the most post-Christian nation in the world. But he directs us away from dwelling on the thought that the pragmatic form of our eschatology might be dependent on the Christian form.

Most of the evidence presented by Brooks the poet calls into question the depth and authenticity of our belief. First is our singular propensity to switch religions. It is true—and disquieting to the orthodox—that we think of ourselves as almost as free to choose churches as cars. American Protestants often report that they are "church shopping," especially when they have moved somewhere new (the exurbs are crawling with church shoppers). But our switching can partly be accounted by the fact that we take conversion, or being "born again" (and sometimes again), so seriously. St. Paul was a famous switcher, but nobody doubts the sincerity and depth of his belief. American church-switching is therefore a tribute to our evangelical zeal—a zeal often celebrated by Brooks in a variety of secular contexts. After all, Christianity—because of the startling and unprecedented character of the news of salvation as described by biblical revelation—is only an ambiguously traditional religion. And it is no surprise that the least traditional versions of Christianity would flourish in America. Brooks notes in passing that 40 percent of Americans call themselves evangelical Christians. Surely one basic sign of the depth of Christian belief is the desire to evangelize, and most of the missionaries in the world are now American evangelicals.

Another time-honored strategy Brooks uses to disparage our Christianity is to connect it with the idiocy of rural Americans. Those with brains and ambition have moved—they have had to move—to the cities and suburbs. The sociologist observes that the "executives are congregated at the corporate headquarters in affluent areas, the local decisions are made by formulas, and small towns no longer have much of an upper class." Local brains no longer determine the fate of rural folks, and so they have no incentive not to be stupider than ever. So they "love QVC . . . and the Pro Bowlers Tour," and "high schools close the first day of hunting season" (67). Rural taste is so unrefined that there's no market for a meal that costs more than twenty dollars.

Sara Issenberg took the time to discover that most of Brooks's observations about rural life are either exaggerations or outright falsehoods.[16] It even turns out that the bulk of QVC's audience is composed of "suburban female baby boomers." But those exaggerations help the poet make a basic distinction between rural and suburban life: "In rural America, churches are everywhere; in suburban America, Thai restaurants are everywhere" (67). But the truth is that in many suburbs both restaurants and churches are everywhere, and lots of evangelicals enjoy Thai food. Brooks must know that the resurgence of evangelical enthusiasm in America—particularly in various kinds of "megachurches"—is much more a suburban than a rural phenomenon, that it is not at all the residue of fading rural fundamentalism.

In understanding the megachurch, Brooks says he is indebted to the "superb" (284) analyses of American religion provided by sociologist Alan Wolfe. Wolfe's major claim is that the American idea of nonjudgmental moral freedom has decisively transformed American religion in an individualistic direction. Our religion, like everything else, is part of our feel-good "culture of narcissism"; its focus is the individual's subjective "needs."[17] "Americans," Wolfe asserts, "are practicing their faith in ways so personal and individualistic that their practices blend seamlessly into the culture around them."[18] The alleged culture war between "orthodox" and "progressive" believers has fizzled as both sides have converged on individualism. Brooks understands Wolfe to say that "most Americans know very little for certain except what works for me is valid, and whatever works for you is probably valid too," and that therefore American churches have become less morally severe and more clearly in the business of providing comfortable illusions. There are, he adds, "many orthodox believers in America as rooted in absolute truth as a mountain is rooted in earth," but they are—like the genuine bohemians—an insignificant countercultural minority (277).

I suspect that Wolfe's analysis more than his own observations lies behind Brooks's mocking of the narcissism of the megachurch, which he employs in order to show that the exurbs lack real moral depth. He admits that the exurbanites are "loud and proud" about their religion (67), but what they say about religion is no more interesting than their prattling about traffic, sports, and Carnival cruises. To substantiate his point, Brooks describes "the seeker-sensitive Willow Creek–style megachurch, which has a 3,800-seat multimedia worship auditorium," and where someone "in the mood, can watch the service via video in the outdoor cafe in the parking lot, or if he's feeling traditional, he can watch the video in the faux-Gothic basement stone chapel" (51).

There *are* megachurches with such silly features, of course, and it is true enough that suburban evangelicals often fall far short of orthodox rigor. "Those who know even a little evangelical history," Mark Noll reminds us, "know how prone evangelicals have been to violate decorum, compromise integrity, upset intellectual balance, and abuse artistic good taste."[19] In those respects, evangelical religion has contributed to as much as it has been a counterweight to characteristic American excesses. Brooks could have gone on to make fun of the terrible music often promoted by evangelicals—so-called contemporary Christian (often the basis of a sort of karaoke night at church), praise music, and Christian rock. (As Hank says to Bobby on *King of the Hill*, "Son, you haven't made Christianity better, you've made rock and roll worse.") In evangelical literature touchy-feely psychology often fills the vacuum formerly occupied by theology, and evangelical self-help books are sometimes ridiculously mindless and upbeat.

But Brooks's description is still one-sided. Suburban evangelicals (I am now relying on my own observations) are routinely taught that pragmatism, relativism, and boundless moral freedom are anti-biblical. They really do believe that human beings are bound by the absolute truth of God's revelation, and that we have all been given very definite and sometimes demanding duties as parents, spouses, creatures, and citizens. The evangelical God is personal and loving, yes, but also at least somewhat judgmental. From the perspective of, say, an orthodox Jew or a traditionalist Catholic, it is fair to say that the evangelicals inhabit an unstable but real place between orthodoxy and individualism. Theirs may be a middle-class Christianity, but it is no mere rationalization for a narcissistic or even merely American imagination. The evangelicals see themselves as employing every American technique available—from communications technologies through popular music—in the service of the unchanging Word. Their antitraditional thought that the medium by which the Word is spread is inessential is surely naïve. Indifference to the medium is surely the cause of what Clifford Orwin, for one, has observed: "I've not come upon a single evangelical book that rose above mediocrity"; evangelical intellectuals have been unable to come up with a literary or artistic vision that reflects adequately the "impressive reproach" they give in their lives "to the gross defects of rampant secularism."[20] But a mediocre reproach via a decadent medium is often much better than nothing.

In his columns, Brooks—liberated from the poetic imperative—is even sometimes able to admit that what distinguishes an evangelical Christian from his fellow Americans is that "he does not believe that truth is plural." Nor does he believe that "truth is something humans are working toward." "Truth," instead, "has been revealed." The evangelicals believe we can all be at home with or because of the truth—the revealed or dogmatic truth—we can all share.[21] Our evangelicals, as so many of their books say, believe they are fortunate enough to possess an absolute truth that guides them through an otherwise relativistic world. To the extent that evangelicals fear and love according to the moral truth of revelation, Wolfe and *On Paradise Drive* are wrong.

Most telling is the foundation American evangelical churches provide for family life. The megachurch "campus" is often huge because it aims to be a "whole life" church, giving a Christian dimension to every feature of family life. Kids play on the sports teams in the church's gym. There are all sorts of theme-oriented activities for all ages: families take church-sponsored vacations and mission trips together. Christian bookstores—where one will find our country's bestselling books (and DVDs, etc.)—are filled with volumes giving accounts of what the Bible says about all aspects of human endeavor. In such books we can learn, for example, that the Bible is against mortgages and debt in general, in part because they get in the way of tithing but also because they get in the way of planning prudently for one's family's future. The exurban church—especially but not only in the South—is an important contributor to the relative health of family life; often the high birth rate, low divorce rate, and sense of community we find in the exurbs owe more to the new churches than the new towns.

Philip Longman has discovered, in fact, that American "[f]ertility correlates strongly with religious conviction. In the United States, fully 47 percent of those who attend church weekly say that their ideal family size is three or more children. By contrast, only 27 percent of those who seldom attend church want that many children." Birth rates among various ethnic groups "have either remained low or fallen dramatically" over the last fifteen years, and it appears that in the absence of our religious conservatives our birth rate would approximate that of rapidly aging France. Any sociobiological study would have to give "a strong evolutionary advantage" to families on the evangelical side of our cultural divide.[22]

It is still true, of course, that the evangelical imagination is as future-obsessed as the American one Brooks describes. It is often driven by the thought that human history is about to end, but that end has nothing to do with the efforts of free beings who work. The obsession is often with the Apocalypse, the Rapture, and the Second Coming, as well as one's own salvation through faith. The evangelical imagination so stirred by Mel Gibson's *The Passion* is, if nothing else, far more psychologically complex and less narcissistic than any part of the American imagination Brooks celebrates. Our intellectuals have a hard time believing that connecting intense, virtually unendurable personal suffering with human redemption could be anything but sadomasochistic. The evangelicals, of course, are finally more genuinely optimistic about human destiny than Brooks's Americans. And that genuine optimism about the future is part of what allows evangelical families to be in love with each other in the present, to be at home with the homelessness they cannot help but experience.

Suburban evangelicals are also usually very patriotic. It is easy, even in these tough times, to get them to cheer for our men and women in Iraq. They identify Christian America ("under God") with the *real* America, and they are the Americans most likely to believe that our country is a force for good in the world. Few of them agree with, say, theologian Stanley Hauerwas, who disparages patriotism as un-Christian and claims that we Christians in America should think of ourselves as "resident aliens."[23] Evangelicals are not so Augustinian because they don't think they live in a pagan or alien place.

The more secular and sophisticated Americans become today, the more they view patriotism as old-fashioned and unjust.
For the enlightened, patriotism should be replaced by cosmopolitanism. The American empire, from this view, is not the end of
history, but that end or perfection might be the consequence of the
withering away of all nations, especially ours. It is natural but out-
of-touch to blame Christianity for weaning us away from our political attachments. The City of God—which should include all
human beings—should alienate us some from the cities of man. But
for we Americans, there has always been a close connection between believing Christianity and genuine patriotism. That may be
because the Christian is more grateful than the American Brooks
describes for all he or she has been given. And for the Christian,
political cosmopolitanism—especially when mixed with historical
eschatology—appears as a heretical distortion of our true unity
under God.

Brooks's own vision of our nation's greatness, in fact, seems
to have no real place for patriotism, for our natural attachment to
our worldly home. The evangelicals—like most ordinary Americans—are attached to the American *nation*—not to some amor-
phous version of the imperial American future. They are not likely
to endorse Brooks's plan for universal national service, even as they
would support a draft for their nation's real defense needs. Evangelicals do not think that national service is the only or the best way
Americans should have for getting their minds off themselves.

Many believers who consider themselves good citizens have
nevertheless withdrawn quite consciously from the land of
nonjudgmental self-fulfillment Brooks describes, seeing it as a dangerous corruption of the real America. The megachurch sometimes
understands itself as a citadel-like defense against the sinful confu-

sion of excessive moral freedom. This self-understanding is also re-flected in the rapid and fascinating growth of homeschooling, an-other quite distinctively American phenomenon ignored by Brooks. "Ordinary evangelicals," Wolfe writes, "believe that abortion is wrong and homosexuality a sin, and many of them detest what their chil-dren learn in public schools as well as the way they learn it."[24] There is, of course, no gap between ordinary evangelicals and their lead-ers on such issues, and the ordinary evangelical is as well educated as his or her secular or religiously liberal counterpart.

This secessionist impulse of our evangelicals is, in part, the result of their intellectual weakness, their tendency not to read or write great books. Their Christian America is founded in the rev-elation of the Bible, not that realistic view of nature and human nature that all citizens can share in common. They believe that the only cure for our individualistic excesses is belief in the Bible's abso-lute truth. They perceive no middle space between that absolutism and secular relativism; the choice, they say, is between incompat-ible "worldviews." So the evangelicals in the megachurches wrongly believe that their fellow citizens cannot be improved by arguments based on what we know about human nature, but rather only through conversion. The weakness of the intellectual life of our evangelicals is one reason they are coming to believe they have no real contribution to make to the political life of our largely secular country. It is also the most important reason why Brooks and Wolfe are finally partly right to say that the evangelicals are unwittingly complicit in the individualism they criticize.

BROOKS AND MARRIAGE

Still, when it comes to connecting faith to family life, all Americans (including many with more orthodox beliefs) have much to learn from our uniquely American evangelical churches. Brooks himself once wrote, in probably his most famous column, that American marriage was "in crisis," because "marriage, which relies on a culture of fidelity, is now asked to survive in a culture of contingency." For us, the marriage bond, like every other human connection, "is now most likely to be seen as an easily cancelled contract." Brooks goes on to make a judgment completely absent from his book: "the culture of contingency . . . when it comes to intimate and sacred relations, is an abomination." In other words, here Brooks is not afraid to suggest, in the strongest terms, that an America without genuine religious belief distorts what is most important about our lives, causing confusion and degradation.

In his column, Brooks lectures conservatives that they "must make the important moral case for marriage" by employing, from his view, very un-American language. But he does not explain why they should expect much success in reviving the culture of fidelity today, especially if they were simultaneously to avoid religious divisiveness. He even asks them to include in their conservative case an argument for same-sex marriage. Why should homosexuals be forced to remain alone in the culture of contingency?[25] That question seems fair enough, except that any argument for same-sex marriage presupposes a very contingent understanding of that institution. Brooks may ask conservatives to do the impossible.

The old-fashioned, and relatively secular, view of marriage was that it was a license to have sex—a license that included the corresponding duties of sexual fidelity and raising children. Same-sex marriage was thought to be impossible, for many reasons. There is the obvious reason that it had nothing to do with children. But no case for same-sex marriage that I have read—including the relatively conservative, responsible, and moving ones by Jonathan

Rauch and Andrew Sullivan[26]—include the expectation of sexual fidelity within marriage or abstaining from sex until marriage. And they presuppose the easygoing divorce laws—especially for childless couples—that we have now. Gay marriage only makes sense to gays if marriage is understood, under the law, as a contract to be broken at will. The view is that marriage has become a duty-free system of entitlements, and in that case it should be made available to all Americans. There is certainly no denying that marriage has progressed in that direction.

The most thoughtful evangelicals (and others) oppose samesex marriage not out of any animosity toward homosexuals, but because they see clearly what the development of liberal individualism or "moral freedom" has done to all institutions based on fidelity. Marriage as it now exists—as a virtually toothless and nearly purposeless secular license—would do little to save homosexuals from the culture of contingency that disorients us all. But because this understanding of marriage as just another contract is an abomination, evangelicals believe that marital fidelity depends on a religious foundation. And when we look at marriage in America today, as Brooks says, we see contradictory extremes: Divorce may be more rampant here than in Europe, but we also take the responsibilities of marriage and family more seriously. We return to the thought that we are somehow the most post-Christian (or secular-eschatological) and Christian of nations. An adequate American poetry would show how our contradictory Christian and post-Christian kinds of thought and imagination manage to support each other. That we are caught between Christianity and post-Christianity—that we are not so much Christ-centered as Christ-haunted (in all our eschatological imaginings)—is another way of describing our middle-class existence.

I have praised American evangelicals for seeing themselves as more than individuals, as friends, parents, children, citizens, and creatures. I have agreed with Tocqueville that American religion is a powerful support for these countercultural inclinations. Most Americans are not evangelicals (or orthodox), and maybe half tend to confuse God with themselves. But my criticism of the new Whitman merely expresses what we all really know. Waller Newell, an obviously nonreligious writer, can still say today that "the five main ingredients of a satisfying life" are "love, courage, pride, family, and country."[27] That is because today we "have the same heartfelt yearnings for love, honor, and spiritual fulfillment as previous generations." In some cases, "these yearnings may be keener and deeper because they have been denied any constructive outlet."[28] The Americans Brooks describes have hard lives because they deny or distort the most profound and noble aspects of their natures. But thank God both our anxiety and our love continue to point us beyond ourselves. We cannot be nonjudgmental about the purposes that drive our efforts; our wealth and power have to serve human goods.

I have already suggested, of course, that Brooks does not do justice to Christian virtue, including humility. But in some respects the Americans he describes are altogether too humble. The only theologian our new Whitman quotes and praises is (the German!) Jurgen Moltmann, who contends that "[m]an has no subsistence in himself, but is always on the way towards something and realizes himself in light of some expected whole" (149). That is, we are now nothing, but we shall make ourselves everything. Because there is no otherworldly God to save us, our humility about our present condition spurs us on toward an incessant effort to save ourselves, to make ourselves whole.

Because Brooks distorts or exaggerates our humility, he also confuses us about pride. His poetry, from one view, concerns American pride, but he really challenges us to acknowledge that we take pride in our misery. Our anxious misery about the contingency of our being drives us forward, producing thoughts and achievements that are singularly free and singularly American. So we should be proud that we are emphatically not "last men" or the denizens of some Brave New World; all evidence points to the conclusion that we are free and transcendent beings. We should be proud of how driven we remain even in the midst of prosperity, that we are stuck—and not primarily by material necessity—with living in "the future tense." But how much pride can someone reasonably take in being stuck, in being unable to make one's mirages about paradise real?

Human pride, properly speaking, comes from the pleasurable consciousness of what we have accomplished. Brooks cannot help but also suggest that Americans must take pride in what they have accomplished in their tough jobs, with their homes and churches, in raising their children, and in serving their country. He says that Americans who flourish according to the narrow and often ridiculous standards of their particular cliques or niches hardly suffer from pride deficit; they, in fact, characteristically overrate themselves. Studies show that "90 percent of all Americans have way too much self-esteem" (73). Being proud of what we are counterbalances in many ways the anxiety we have about how much work the future is going to require of us. The successful American evangelical athlete and entrepreneur who credits all that he has done to God is never fully convincing.

Perhaps the deepest understanding of the middle-class character of human beings in the Western world—which includes, of course, our American world—is that it is caught between pride and humility. Pride, properly understood, ought to be taken in the great things we have done, and humility ought to come from the knowledge that we cannot help but have about the ineradicable contingency of our being, with all our flaws and sins. At times we cannot help but think that our greatness is almost divine; but at other times we see clearly the truth that we are infinitely removed from being God and remain dependent on him for our very being. Thank God, our pragmatism will never really free us from the greatness and misery of our middle-class existence.

Chapter 5

Compassionate Conservatism
and Biotechnology

Compassionate conservatism, according to Franklin Roosevelt, is an oxymoron. Conservatives, Roosevelt explained, hold that "individual initiative"—with some private philanthropy—is the best way of solving social problems. Liberals, in contrast, are in favor of using the cooperative efforts of government to alleviate the "cruel suffering" of the unfortunate among us. Compassion—the recognition of the cruelty of the suffering of others—is the basis of public cooperation. The lesson of the Depression was that none of us is immune from the possibility of economic misfortune, and the resulting suffering is so clearly cruel because it is undeserved. Any one of us might be impoverished by economic forces beyond our control.

Republicans, according to Roosevelt, were unable to learn from the Depression because they were in the thrall of the "comfortable superstition" of "individualism"; they did not appreciate how temporary and fragile all human success is. They could not imagine that they might be compelled to join the unfortunate at any time, and so they could not imagine how it is in the interest as well as the duty of us all to help the deserving poor, or rather to have government redistribute resources from the rich to the poor.[1]

The Republicans, since the time of FDR, have distinguished themselves by opposing public policy based on compassion. But lately the "compassion gap" that separates our two parties has been narrowing in strange and unexpected ways. A Democratic president signed a bill ending the federal government's responsibility for our main compassionate or redistributive public policy, welfare. He also said that the era of big government was over. The Democratic party, following the lead of Bill Clinton, has generally become less compassionate than libertarian. Democrats have surrendered many of their reservations about the free market, to the point that nobody still worries that we are slouching toward socialism. The Democratic party is now above all the party of unrestricted personal freedom and permissiveness; its members take fairly radical pro-choice stands on all the various social or cultural issues.

The Republicans have become more compassionate insofar as they have become less libertarian, less morally indifferent. On moral and cultural issues, they surely are now the more "statist" party, calling for government regulation when it comes to abortion, biotechnology, the family, and so forth. Much of that regulation is opposed to the cruel suffering caused by moral indifference, by the libertarian idea that we can all live "designer" lives free from the influence of, and dependence on, others. So some Republican activism now is animated by compassion for unborn and neglected children. But some is also animated by what biotechnology might do to the attachments and institutions that make human life worth living, to marriage, family, friendship, community, and the souls of particular persons.

Republicans are beginning to be moved by Tocqueville's thought, which he borrowed from Pascal, that even or especially prosperous and free Americans deserve our compassion. And the most astute Republicans even see that our creeping libertarianism—unchecked—will make us so deserving of compassion that the result will inevitably be an unprecedented and particularly intrusive form of statism, something much closer to the soft despotism Tocqueville feared than anything we have experienced thus far. The unfettered progress of "designer" biotechnology may well lead to a particularly intrusive form of big government.

Today's Republican compassion is based on a deeper version of Roosevelt's compassionate, liberal thought that all human beings are equally subject to fortune—equally contingent—in this world. Once again Republicans are much less optimistic than the Democrats that human reform can eradicate our human suffering, although the new Republicans agree with old-fashioned Democrats that public policy might be used to curb libertarian excesses that can unnecessarily intensify human misery. Republicans believe that compassion, and therefore government and religion, are not about to wither away.

Two Forms of American Individualism

That sophisticated Americans today might particularly need our compassion deserves some explaining. At first glance, there seems to be plenty of evidence for Tocqueville's view that democracy drifts toward apathetic individualism, and so toward a world where the free and the prosperous can neither feel nor need much compassion (*Democracy in America*, volume 2, part 2, chapter 2).[2] Allan Bloom and Richard Rorty—perhaps our two best philosophic critics in recent years—seem to agree on that. Sophisticated Americans are more nice or politely apathetic than ever before, and that means they are more unmoved by love and death than human beings ever have been. Bloom hated and Rorty basically likes what they think is happening. But they only disagree on values, not on facts.[3] Sophisticated Americans talk as if they live, as the social critics say, "after virtue" or "without good and evil."⁴

From this view, the movement from compassion to libertarianism of our Democrats would have not surprised Tocqueville. He thought modern democracies would be characterized by compassion; people would become similar enough that they would readily feel each other's pain. But he added that compassion—a very diluted or generalized form of love—would ordinarily not rouse up citizens enough to lead them to aid one another. Compassion, instead, would have a tendency to level remaining human distinctions, to make government and society more egalitarian (DA, 2,3,1). Democratic compassion is felt mainly for the cruel suffering imposed on people by inegalitarian oppression or moralism, and it can even extend to the "specieist" cruelty caused by privileging human over non-human beings.

So today's Democrats remain easily moved by stories of racism and homophobia. But they also believe that all that is required to alleviate such cruelty is for people to become more tolerant and accepting. There is no need for activism based on love; all one need do is not hate. The main thing indiscriminate or generalized compassion does is dissolve the passionate exclusivity of both strong love and strong hate (DA, 2,3,1). Such compassion is progressively more difficult to distinguish from moral indifference, which is why Tocqueville can say that the deepest sentimental tendency of democracy is toward the apathetic indifference he calls individualism (DA, 2,2,2–4).

But Tocqueville also reminds us that Americans will probably and should never completely free themselves from their religious beginning (DA, 2,1,1), and if we look more closely we can see a puritanical streak in sophisticated Americans today. They are moral fanatics—or quite unlibertarian—when it comes to health and safety. They are, as the libertarians say, not only "moralists," but "prohibitionists."[5] They increasingly demand that government throw its weight behind the view that almost all sex be safe sex, or disconnected from birth and death, from all risk. And they are no longer pro-choice when it comes to seatbelts or helmets; diving boards have disappeared from the land. They demand that government protect us from the dangers of second-hand smoke, even at the expense of the liberty to smoke. They are just awakening to what government can do to protect us from the empty-calorie culture of death of the fast food industry and trans-fatty Oreo cookies.

The one area in which sophisticated Americans do not even claim to be laidback or nonjudgmental in their personal lives is health and exercise. Even or especially the most "postmodern" among us—those who say modern science is merely a dogma of domination—exercise in a most disciplined, scientific way. Our obsession with health does sometimes cross that line between modern science and medieval superstition. We probably all know of someone who, having recently read a best-seller and learned those with their blood type and only their blood type are fitted by nature to eat bloody red meat, has abruptly abandoned his or her vegetarianism.[6] Now knowing that there is no safe haven for Type Os in vegetables, he or she throws away the tofu and hustles over to Outback, revealing that vegetarianism is so often not a moral choice at all.

So we can say that we can see evidence of two quite different kinds of individualism in America today. Tocquevillian or apathetic individualism corresponds roughly to what we say about our souls. And Lockean or aggressive and obsessive individualism corresponds roughly to what we say and especially do with respect to our bodies. The American example today does not confirm Tocqueville's prediction that people in a democracy would gradually surrender any concern about the details of their lives, their futures (DA, 2,2,16; 2,4,6). The decay of institutions and attachments—such as religion, local community, and the family—that helped Americans get their minds off themselves and extend their hearts to others has not really produced apathetic indifference. It has produced self-obsession, an obsessive concern with one's own future as an individual. Sophisticated Americans are living longer and having fewer children because they have been working hard on their own behalf, even at the expense of their natural replacements. We see ourselves less and less as social or political or familial animals and more and more as free individuals.[7]

OUR INDEFINITE RESTLESSNESS

Tocqueville himself did not actually believe that the Americans of his time were wallowing in apathetic individualism. Both then and now we have resisted that democratic tendency quite well. He saw Americans not as passive but as the most restless people the world had ever seen; their incessant action guided by "two principal ideas"— "indefinite perfectibility" and "the doctrine of interest well understood."[8] The latter doctrine, taught by American moralists, is a doctrine about human freedom: Free human beings calculate constantly about their material self-interest; once they stop pursuing enjoyment and actually enjoy they are no longer free. Even or especially all our connections with other human beings should be based on calculation and consent; once you lose your head in love or friendship you have submitted, in effect, to the rule of another.

Living completely according to that doctrine would be the choice for free human misery over aristocratic illusion and subhuman contentment. But Tocqueville also notices that the Americans often "do not do themselves justice" with their "philosophy." The truth is that they sometimes, like all people, give way "to the disinterested and unreflective sparks that are natural to man" (DA, 2,2,8). They are not only better but happier than they say, and they seem to use their doctrine, in part, as a form of boasting to hide the extent to which love governs their relations with others and God.[9] Now, it is true that the heartless moral doctrine of interest explains the action of sophisticated Americans better in our time than it did in his. For us, much of our friendship has been transformed into "networking," and the most intimate moments of our lives are governed more than ever by calculation and consent. And in this respect human life is harder or less enjoyable than ever, and so particularly worthy of compassion. Sophisticated Americans today exhibit in an extreme way what Pascal describes as an unhappy feature of the human condition as such: "we never actually live, but hope to live, and since we are always planning how to be happy, it is inevitable that we should never be so" (fr. 80).[10]

Tocqueville was astonished by the unprecedented American example of a whole people restless in the midst of prosperity. He thought that Americans were so obsessed with time—or managing time—that they had no real leisure. To the Americans, time spent in unconscious or unplanned enjoyment was wasted time, and that opinion had caused people to have gotten less "serene" and "playful" as they had made themselves more free and prosperous (DA, 2,2,13). All this effort has today produced unprecedented human freedom from poverty and physical suffering, and so from one view it has made human beings less deserving of compassion than ever before.

But Tocqueville's description reminds us of the restlessness described by Pascal, of the human being's constant pursuit of diversions to get his mind off his misery without God, "off the natural unhappiness of our feeble mortal condition" (frs. 132–39). The fact that our restlessness increases as we get more free and prosperous suggests that it has no merely physical or material cause; it is evidence of the real existence of the soul. The American most of all wants to divert himself from the boredom and anxiety that arises even or especially "amid enjoyment of the senses." From this view, Pascal would say, what Tocqueville describes as "the singular melancholy" of the Americans that causes them to be overcome sometimes with "a disgust for life" especially deserves our compassion (DA, 2,2,13). They restlessly disappoint themselves constantly and wear themselves out in pursuit of the "true happiness" that will allow them to rest, which they always but wrongly believe is just around the corner (fr. 136).

Today our Lockean individualists or libertarians, we can say with some exaggeration, are constantly at work trying to secure their futures against the blind and pitiless nature that is out to kill them, and they are also constantly at work diverting themselves from what they really know about the futility of their efforts. As our bourgeois bohemians say, they want to make their whole lives— every moment—a work of art, leaving nothing to chance. They have abolished what they believe to be the alienating distinction between work and play by turning play into a kind of work. The last thing they seem to want, as Pascal explains, "is . . . the easy peaceful life that allows us to think of our unhappy condition"; they prefer, instead, "the agitation that takes our minds off it and diverts us" (fr. 173). Our lives may be objectively more secure but we experience them as more contingent or accidental than ever, and so, as both Pascal and Locke would observe, our lives are more anxious and uneasy than ever.

INDEFINITE PERFECTIBILITY

Tocqueville reports that the Americans he observed took their minds off the limits of individual effort by allowing themselves to be inspired by the idea of the indefinite perfectibility of man (DA, 2,1,8). This idea is a rebellion against the traditional and aristocratic view that human nature has definition, that our freedom is bound by limits we cannot overcome. In the traditional view, we are stuck with disease and death, even injustice and oppression. We cannot cure ourselves of the misery of our mortality. But because we can definitely distinguish between man and God, we can hope for divine redemption.

Much of the aristocratic and Christian idea of virtue called for the proud and humble acceptance of what we cannot change. The clear definition of being human—the basic experience of human limitation—contained, for Christians, the human experience of contingency with necessity and faith. The Pascalian view that we exist nowhere in particular in an infinite universe for no particular reason never animated aristocratic society. Because human beings thought they were defined by nature and God (not to mention by family and class), they thought they knew their place in the world, and that focusing of their love enlarged their hearts toward others and lessened their self-obsession (DA, 2,2,2). Because they were redeemed at least by love, they did not think of human beings in general as pitiful accidents worthy of compassion more than anything else.

The modern, democratic view is that the Christian and aristocratic emphasis on human limitation was, above all, an illusion justifying oppression. We should doubt and work against all claims for divine and natural limitation, the modern democrats teach us, since nobody can say in advance of such efforts how free our species might become. With such a view as our foundation, human perfectibility seems the only appropriate goal. We therefore point ourselves toward a vague future in which we will have freed ourselves from the oppressive miseries of the present. The pride we take in what the species will eventually accomplish, Pascal would explain, diverts us from how little any particular individual can do in democratic times (fr. 71). Tocqueville, although he was astonished by what had been accomplished by this "confused glimpse" of "immense greatness," also observed that this ideal of human perfection must remain "always fugitive" and sometimes "beyond measure" (DA, 2,1,8).

INDEFINITE DEATH

The first inspirational proposal of the idea of our indefinite perfect-ibility came from the French Enlightenment theorist and revolu-tionary, Condorcet: "Would it be . . . absurd to suppose . . . that the day will come when death will be due only to extraordinary accidents or to the decay of vital forces, and that ultimately the average lifespan between birth and decay will have *no assignable value?* Certainly man will not become immortal, but will not the interval between the first breath that he draws and the time when in the natural course of events . . . he expires, increase indefinitely?"[11] (Em-phasis added.)

Notice, first of all, that Condorcet has no Christian or aristo-cratic illusions about human immortality. He believes death to be an ineradicable natural fact, one that, finally, imposes a limit on indefinite human progress. But he still believes that "the average span of human life" will eventually have "no assignable value," that it will be long enough that we literally will not be able to count the days. To deprive life's length of its "assignable value" would surely mark the culmination of modern progress, since it would essentially deprive death of its power over us. We would be free from our anxious sense of contingency, completely at home in the world. A stock criticism of Marx is that even under communism there would still be scarcity—scarcity of time. But Condorcet hold opens the promise that even this kind of scarcity will wither away.

So it is easy to see why our libertarians view biotechnology as a compassionate way to bring compassion to an end. Condorcet was necessarily vague about how "[t]he improvement of medical practice" would lead to "the end of infectious and hereditary diseases" and so forth.[12] But today, biotechnology really does promise to make our lifespans indefinite. It may well be that all genetically based diseases (and genetic susceptibilities to disease) can be cured, which is to say, most or perhaps even all diseases. Regenerative medicine may obtain the capacity to rejuvenate every bodily organ. The idea of the indefinite perfectibility of our species is therefore more plausible today than ever, and biotechnology is what will bring it about.[13]

The fall of communism gave us the bad news that Marx was wrong to think that history could save us from our alienation. At the same time, sociobiology seemed to say that we were stuck with being controlled by a blind and pitiless evolutionary process, that we could not save ourselves as individuals from nature. Biotechnology promises to replace natural evolution with conscious and volitional evolution, thus inaugurating a new birth of indefinite human progress away from blind and pitiless natural domination. We will be able to gradually—even if never completely—free ourselves from the strange and cruel contingency that is our lot as conscious natural beings. Instead, we will become conscious, willful beings who give orders to our genes, our natures.[14]

THE STRUGGLE AGAINST ACCIDENTS

But would the biotechnological achievement of indefinite longevity really free human beings from being defined by their contingency and mortality? Is there any real evidence that biotechnology can produce anything other than an intensification of our Lockean individualism? Condorcet predicted that we would ordinarily no longer be affected by death; the exception would be "extraordinary accidents." In other words, we can look forward both to an ordinary, death-free world and an "extraordinary" or accidental world in which death intrudes. Death, no longer experienced as a necessity for and by us all, will become only an accident to be avoided. Our experience will be that nobody need die any more, yet it will still be possible for a healthy person to, say, be blown up into a million pieces in an accidental explosion.

Under the future biotechnological regime, it would seem at first that life would become more ordinary, or less concerned with accidents, than ever. What Pascal calls human greatness and misery—the results of our anxious contingency—would disappear. But paradoxically, the near-disappearance of death as a necessity would actually make us more obsessed with accidents than ever. Sophisticated Americans already obsess over their children's safety, overorganizing their lives to free them from risk, including even the risk of playing unsupervised with other children. There are even now so few deaths in childhood that no sophisticated American thinks any longer of the death of a child as a necessity (or God's will), but only as a terrible accident that might somehow have been avoided. That is why it is becoming increasingly irresponsible not to plan incessantly to keep children's lives "ordinary" or predictable. And that planning now begins with the fetus in the womb and in some cases with the embryo to be implanted; everything must be done to keep genetic flaws or accidents that lead to death from seeing the light of day.

Another reason our elites worry more than ever about children is, as we have seen, that they have become rarer than ever. From one view, people today have just one or two kids so that they can plan adequately for the future and secure their children properly from the various risks of life. But from another view that prudence leaves parents more open to chance than ever—should something go wrong, there aren't any spares.

Of course, parents today love their children when they choose to have them. But they obsess over their children because they understand them too completely as individuals to be protected from nature, and not as natural gifts to be loved with all their imperfections and limitations. They are in some measure victims of the paradox Leon Kass finds at the heart of the progress of medical science: "The greater our medical successes, the more unacceptable is failure, and the more intolerable and frightening is death."[15]

We can anticipate that this trend will continue: Childhood will continue to become objectively safer, and parents will be more anxious nonetheless. If the average lifespan is extended to, say, 200 years, then the number of children to be born may have to be severely restricted. If people stop dying, there will be no need and no room for replacements. Perhaps libertarians are right that there will be no need for such a public policy because enlightened individuals will soon enough choose on their own to have virtually no children. But perhaps they are wrong, for libertarians are also anticipating that the parents of the future will have the unprecedented pleasure of using genetic enhancements to design their children as they please.

Limits to how parents might design their children will be set by health and safety concerns. Individual parents will doubtless usually make safe choices voluntarily. But we will not allow obsessive or perverse parents to choose deafness for their children or even less than the highest possible IQs. Deafness and stupidity will be undeniable and avoidable risk factors. We can also anticipate that having babies the old-fashioned way—two married people having unprotected sex and then hoping and praying for the best—will become illegal. That natural approach will also involve unacceptable risks.

Already it is difficult for women to avoid the genetic testing of their unborn babies. That negligence—even if it originates out of love—seems increasingly irresponsible. How could love produce unnecessary suffering? Bioethicists tell women that it is an act of love to make sure genetically defective babies are not born. A baby, apparently, is not lovable enough to live unless it is free from defects, and we have to admit that correctible defects are hard to love. Nonetheless, we have also to admit that the result will be an increasingly anxious focus on the contingency of imperfect human existence, and less of a focus on the fact that all that we find lovable lies at least in part beyond our calculation and control.[16]

The law will be used to ensure that babies are as perfect or risk-free as babies can be at any particular time. We certainly will not be able to allow Catholics or Mormons to have hordes of unenhanced little monsters; such stupid and disease-ridden kids would be nothing but a burden on society and a danger to us all. And we can anticipate government working even harder to stamp out unsafe sex, even invading, in Justice Douglas's memorable phrase, "the sacred precincts of marital bedrooms."[17] The present limit to our libertarianism—obsession about health and safety—will lead to a progressively more intrusive statism.

Biotechnology, combined with our present libertarianism, points to our surrender of our freedom to choose in the most intimate parts of our lives. Indeed, we might almost say that this is the route by which Lockean individualism culminates in the soft or apathetic despotism Tocqueville feared. As Harvey Mansfield and Delba Winthrop have observed, Tocqueville's democratic despotism "apparently mean[s] well to its subjects. The people are not exploited for the use and pleasure of a tyrant, but on the contrary they are made safer, healthier, and in regard to safety and health, wiser."[18] The soft-despotic government of the future will teach us to want wholly predictable, rational—and so ordinary—risk-free lives. It will gently lead us, Tocqueville feared, to cede control over ourselves—genuine self-government—because we finally prefer security to liberty, or because we find anxious liberty unendurable (DA, 2,4,6–7). And yet, despite Tocqueville's insightful analysis, it is difficult to see how any public policy can lead us to surrender our personal anxiety or to believe that we, and others, do not deserve compassion. It seems more likely that we will remain all too aware that government cannot give us the risk-free, laidback existence for which we think we long. As Marx would say, the persistence of the state will be evidence that human beings are still alienated.

THE REAL FUTURE OF VIRTUE

The ideal of the indefinite perfection of man is, most radically, not reasonable at all. And Tocqueville says that the democratic tendency is to unmask all illusory human ideals; they are all, somehow or another, rationalizations for oppression. That is even true, as the twentieth century showed us with the ideology of communism and the twenty-first will demonstrate with the ideology of biotechnology, of the idea of man's indefinite perfectibility. That is, the democratic poetic imagination culminates not with that vague idea of human perfection but with "a glimpse of the soul itself." The truth, as Tocqueville paraphrases Pascal, is that "man comes from nothing, traverses time, and is going to disappear forever in the bosom of God. One sees him only for a moment wandering, lost, between the limits of the two abysses." Pascal teaches the truth about the invincible limits that bound the existence of the human wanderer. And our time-bound contingency is the true source of our "infinite greatness and pettiness," which deserves "at once pity, admiration, scorn, and terror" (DA, 2,1,17). It is when our vague, Promethean hopes of indefinite perfectibility are exposed for what they are that the true ground of our pity or compassion is exposed. For Pascal, the indefinite extension of life would really change nothing at all. A thousand years is still nothing in the light of eternity, and our greatness and misery would still lie in our truthful awareness of that fact (fr. 200). Each of us would still be stuck, perhaps more than ever, with considering how contingent our own lives are, existing as they do nowhere in particular in an infinite universe—that is, stuck with being moved to anxiety and wonder about a reality that eludes our comprehension and control (fr. 68).

The achievement of indefinite longevity will show us that Tocqueville was right to say that the fundamental modern or democratic experience is the disorientation that comes with the perception of "limitless independence" (DA, 2,1,2; 2,1,5). Biotechnological success will not make our lives less morally demanding, but it will make virtue and spiritual life more difficult to acquire. As individuals, we will become increasingly detached from the natural fulfillment that comes from being parents; life will be more child-free than ever. We will have fewer natural responsibilities to save us from boredom and anxiety, and so our diversions will too often be merely diversions. The compassion we now feel for a rich and healthy old person with nothing to occupy his time but recreation will be deserved by larger and larger numbers of people. And the main reason for our compassion will be that we will recognize the difficulty that such a person must have in finding the resources for living a virtuous and purposeful life.

The practice of virtue is relatively easy if each human life is defined by its relatively short span of time. We readily sacrifice and die for our children when we view them as our natural replacements; their living beyond us is the only way we have of extending our own limited natural being. (Although the problem is, contrary to Kass, that we individuals do not regard children as a completely adequate compensation for our mortality. If they were, we would reject the pursuit of indefinite longevity out of hand.)[19] We can seek immortal glory only if we see clearly that we are really mortal, and that therefore immortal glory is the best deal we can get. Otherwise we might agree with Woody Allen, who said, "I don't want to achieve immortality through my work. I want to achieve it through not dying."[20]

Tocqueville thought that democracy might be the enemy of virtue because people would become too materialistic and hyperskeptical in the face of claims that human accomplishment could stand the test of time. But it turns out that biotechnology may make us even more skeptical about our mortality, with even worse results for personal excellence. A Socrates busily and obsessively pursuing an indefinitely long life right up until the moment of his rather ridiculous accidental death (much like Francis Bacon really did) might, in fact, deserve our compassion.[21] Risk of one's own life or the lives of others for virtually any reason may make little or no sense if people's "lives could potentially stretch out ahead of them indefinitely," and "clinging desperately to the life biotechnology offers" has the potential to strip even philosophers of their claims for nobility and happiness.[22]

MOOD MANAGEMENT

But there still may be an effective biotechnological alternative to practicing virtue—mood control, which might allow us to feel good without being good or even having good luck. Our willful rebellion against death as individuals is, if Condorcet is right, not directed so much against the biological fact of mortality but against the fearful and anxious misery it causes us while we are still alive. So even if biotechnology cannot really push death back far enough to free us from our time-bound existence, it seems, at first, that we might readily take a pill, have a nanobot implanted, or submit to genetic therapy in order to free ourselves from our distinctively human, moody misery. Biotechnologically provided "virtual" freedom surely would be more satisfying than any form of "real" freedom human beings will experience in the biotechnological future. And the objection that "virtual" reality is not reality at all is not, despite the success of the *Matrix*, all that convincing, at least at first, to us American democratic individualists.

Tocqueville says that democrats have a technological view of truth. They regard philosophy and science as means for producing material comfort. Conscious and willful mood control should therefore privilege comfort over truth. Or, as Rorty explains, we can call true whatever makes us comfortable. That view is supported by evolutionary biology, which shows us that we are not fitted by nature to know the truth anyway. Moods are nothing but chemical reactions. It makes no sense, then, to say that one chemical reaction—which could be the product of a pill just as easily, or more easily, than it is the doing of a good deed or reading a great book—opens us to truth more readily than another.

In other words, there is no reason to agree with morbid philosophers and poets that bad moods are more truthful than good moods. Tocqueville would not have been plagued by Pascalian moments had he been properly medicated. Pascal himself would have been a happy and productive mathematician and, as Tocqueville reports, not have thought himself to death. Our standards of mood control, it seems, should be happiness and productivity. The libertarian Jacob Sullum is right to wonder whether we have any real reason to prefer getting to the "root causes" of our unhappiness over a "shallower approach" that might achieve our goals just as effectively.[23]

We already know that in the best cases people who take Prozac report that their very being has been changed. They say they are more happy and productive, less anxious and less subject to mood swings. They do not sacrifice their self-consciousness, and they are more able to enjoy the good things of life. In the future, we can expect the development of much better drugs that will allow us to design our moods more predictably and reliably. We can imagine, for example, producing moods just alienated enough to stimulate artistic creativity but not suicide, substance abuse, or even lateness for work.[24]

THE COMPLEX IMPERFECTION
OF THE SCIENCE OF HAPPINESS

Aesthetic pleasure is not the most basic reason why we cannot be happy or un-anxious all the time. There is surely a tension between our pill-induced happiness and our material productivity, between the "virtual" and the "real" dimensions of the biotechnological project. If we can live too well with death, then we will not work hard as individuals to push death back. We will no longer be anxious consumers of what biotechnology has to offer; we will no longer desire regenerative medicine. The capacity of biotechnology to produce indefinite progress toward a genuinely risk-free life depends on the anxious individual not really being satisfied at any point in the process.

If mood control works too well, then we might, for example, be quite indifferent to and so make no effort to divert the asteroid soon to pulverize our planet. Bad moods, both common sense and studies indicate, are indispensable for our species' perpetuation and flourishing.[25] But, the experts say, our moods do not have to be as bad as those evolution has given us; without chemical enhancement, our moods now fit beings who lived when nature endangered us far more than it does now.[26]

We might respond to the experts that the more we have detached ourselves from our natural home, the more our well being has come to depend on our own effort. Bad moods are needed to protect free individuals even more than mere members of species. And so it might be only natural that our anxiety would increase as conscious and volitional evolution succeeds, because from a natural view human beings are more on their own than ever. What would be the most natural or reasonable response to a world where even our moods depend upon our conscious planning?

Beings who work hard to use biotechnology to control their moods surely deserve our compassion, because they really believe they could not stand to be moved by what they really know. Perhaps they will not often experience the misery but they will also miss out on the extreme happiness and joy that uncontrolled human beings used to have. The science of mood control will remain very imperfect; we must remain moved strongly in some way by the mysterious contingency of being human in order to be moved to manage our moods. The other animals seem happy enough with the moods evolution gave them.

Stephen Braun, author of a fascinating book on mastering the mysteries of mood, thought he was needlessly unhappy because he experienced at times unexpectedly and uncontrollably a melancholic disgust for life in the midst of prosperity. And so he spent years seeking out "some psychological or pharmacological inculcation" against the "maddening irregularity" of his moody "microbursts."[27] He claims that by taking a single antidepressant he finally acquired for himself the happiness that is possible for a human being. He can now enjoy ordinary life without being dangerously insensitive to the inevitable swings of fortune. When bad things happen, he feels bad, but not too bad.

Braun reports that "[a]lmost miraculously, a single small white pill taken every day seems to have balanced my mood machinery such that I can look my fate squarely in the eye—hold my mortality and the existential uncertainties of life firmly in mind—and not flinch, quail, or despair."[28] He has come to terms with his contingency and mortality without denial or despair. A pill has given him easily what the philosophers of old thought they had achieved quite imperfectly and with great exertion of their minds. Quite mechanically, he achieved self-conscious serenity. He seems not to be miserable without God.

But Braun has only achieved a tolerable amount of happiness, not the excess of happiness un-mood-balanced beings sometimes have. As Martin Heidegger might say, because Braun has suppressed his anxiety, it cannot turn into wonder. He may have the serenity of the philosophers, but without their joy of discovery or "insight." Braun has freed himself from being moved by what he thinks he knows; there is no "rational meaning," no point to his momentary existence.[29] He seems really to believe that there are no natural compensations for experiencing deeply the truth about ourselves; he misses the moody connection—what Allan Bloom called the twinship—between love and death.

It does not take much thought to see that Braun still deserves our compassion, that he has not really protected his experiences of ordinary life from "extraordinary" intrusion. He is, in his way, an extreme and dogmatic follower of Pascal. Francis Fukuyama with considerable justice worries that we are "unwilling to take a clear stand on drugs solely on the basis that they are bad for the soul," but that does not mean that our pursuit of some materialistic or biotechnological science of happiness can really put the soul out of business.[30] Our precise worry should be about that which is bad and good for the soul and will persist despite our best efforts.

That is not to say that mood control, like reproductive control, will not produce tyrannical—if not perfectly tyrannical—results even or especially if officially left to individual choice. Shyness, Carl Elliott reports, has already become "social phobia" or "social anxiety disorder"; it has been "medicalized" into a disabling disorder that puts an unjust burden on society.[31] But according to Walker Percy in *Lost in the Cosmos*,[32] shy people are particularly shy because they are particularly aware of what they do not know about themselves. They are shy because they are particularly moved by part of the truth about being human. Because drugs are now available to help them overcome their anxiety, they have no excuse not to suppress what they really know about their anxiety in order to be effective. If we believe that moods are merely collections of chemicals to be altered at will, employees will have no reason that will hold up in court to tell their employers that they would rather choose against the moods that make them most happy and productive. Even we professors have no reason not to get ourselves to the drug store to get what is required to perfect our student evaluations. Libertarian Ronald Bailey doubts that mood control will be any threat to our autonomy, noting that it would not be any more compulsory for a job than higher education.[33] But that is the point: We may be nearing the time when both a diploma and a pill will be required to get one of the scarce positions in teaching.

Percy feared that in a therapeutic and biotechnological world we would no longer have a right to our anxiety. But despite the inevitable and increasingly intrusive efforts to deny us that right, we will still become more anxious and in some ways more angry than ever. Our anger will be directed, whether we know it or not, against attempts to deprive us of part of the truth we have been given as human beings. That sort of anger, of course, is already everywhere just beneath the surface in sophisticated, relativistic America, and the beings who have it surely deserve our compassion.

COMPASSION AND OUR BIOTECHNOLOGICAL FUTURE

One of our fundamental human experiences, as Tocqueville describes in his own case, is of dizzying disorientation. We really are "displaced persons" or, in the words of Percy, "lost in the cosmos." Tocqueville remembered that his "insatiable curiosity" culminated in a "universal doubt" that filled him with the "blackest melancholy" and "a disgust for life." When he was in such objectively "ridiculous" moods, he wrote, he "was very worthy of pity."[34] Passion for other human beings and for the greatness of political life delivered him from that moody agitation, but he never forgot that to be human is in some measure to be an anxious, displaced wanderer, as Pascal had said. According to Pascal, "I can feel nothing but compassion for those who sincerely lament their doubt, who regard it as the ultimate misfortune" (fr. 427), and from that view—

our misery without God—even Tocqueville himself deserved compassion more than anything.

So there is something true that impels us toward conscious and volitional evolution, and what is achieved on behalf of the human individual by that evolution certainly can have good uses. As Pascal says, man has the advantage over the universe because he alone "knows that he is dying," and that particularly human truth is the foundation of his ability freely to attempt to subject nature to his will (fr. 200). The technological conquest of nature is both a diversion and much more than a diversion. It may, as Pierre Manent suggests, teach us that neither nature nor history can provide a completely adequate account of the human being.[35] And the human greatness and misery our wandering away from nature produces should certainly be a source not only of anxiety and pity but also of wonder.[36] The indestructible strangeness and potential for good and evil of the human being should, in fact, be the main cause for wonder. If human life actually were defined only by the individual's anxious experience we would deserve little but compassion, and we could not even enjoy all that has been achieved by the individual.

But the very example of Tocqueville reminds us that that experience is far from expressing the whole truth about our being. Even for Pascal, the appreciation of the "wretchedness of human existence was matched by his admiration for human grandeur."[37] Other moods—such as pride, fear, wonder, humility, and gratitude—also point to parts of the truth about ourselves. The danger is that biotechnology in the service of the anxious, obsessive individual at the expense of the complexity—what Tocqueville sees as the paradoxes and contradictions—of the real human soul will undermine further the many compensations that nature and God have given us for our distinctively human misery. So far, human life has been worthy of much more than compassion; no human being, thank God, has really been only or even mainly an individual. As Leon Kass says, our pursuit of indefinite longevity is bad to the extent that it "threatens . . . human happiness by distracting us from the goals toward which our souls naturally point."[38]

Tocqueville's fear (a fear that has also been felt by Kass, Fukuyama, and Aldous Huxley, among others) that we would become subhuman, indifferent slaves to petty contentment by surrendering concern for our futures to schoolmaster-despots is, I think, ultimately ill founded. Tocqueville's imagination of the future surely describes us in some respects: "I see an innumerable crowd of like and equal men who revolve on themselves without repose, procuring the small and vulgar pleasures with which they fill their souls. Each of them, withdrawn and apart, is like a stranger to the destiny of others." But that self-absorption has not led to the emergence of "an immense tutelary power" which has removed from us "the trouble of thinking and the care of living" (DA, 2,4,6). We see, in fact, both self-obsessive and libertarian tendencies in America today, and even the new statism that I think will characterize our future will not produce thoughtless and carefree beings.

So Tocqueville was probably wrong to think that our future choice is going to be between "servitude or freedom," because we are going to remain free even as we become more dependent on technology than ever. That dependence—the product of conscious and volitional evolution—is, of course, evidence of our freedom. And our choice is not likely going to be between "prosperity or misery," because we will very likely have unprecedented and closely connected forms of both (DA, 2,4,6). The good news is that we are going to retain the greatness and misery characteristic of human liberty; the bad news is we probably won't be very happy. I think that is the good and bad news Tocqueville delivers to his aristocratic audience about the Americans he observed, and I think Tocqueville's error is in imagining that democratic apathetic withdrawal might eventually overwhelm American restless self-obsession.

My view here is, I think, genuinely Tocquevillian in the sense that it is neither utopian nor fatalistic. Tocqueville's comprehensive comparison of the advantages and disadvantages of aristocracy and democracy shows us that in some basic way things are always getting better and worse. Various forms of human partisanship reveal part and obscure part of the truth about ourselves; only God can see things as they really are without distortion (DA, 2,1,3). The human excesses to be countered by the whole truth about being human and so a fulfilling and sustainable view of human liberty change from time to time (DA, 2,2,15).

Tocqueville says that had he lived during the oppressive injustice and poverty characteristic of aristocracy, he would have, without reservation, encouraged people to seek prosperity and develop technology (DA, 2,2,15). But now we Tocquevillian conservatives ask, with compassion, what this or that biotechnological advance will do to family, friendship, love, communal life, and virtue, what it will do to that which allows us to live well with suffering and death. Our obsessive and impossible pursuit of a risk-free world with no uncomfortable moods will make us in some ways more miserable and undignified than ever before. And we conservatives must therefore maintain, in compassion, that there are no biotechnological substitutes for the cultivation of one's soul. As Tocqueville says, we can deny and distort but not destroy the needs of our souls, and that is because those needs "are not born of a caprice of [man's] will; they have their immovable foundation in his nature; they exist despite his efforts" (DA, 2,2,12).

Tocqueville observes that the natural human reaction to a too single-minded obsession with material well-being is a fierce spirituality (DA, 2,2,12). Surely we see the markings of such a countercultural reaction in America today, the counterpart to a similar reaction that developed, Tocqueville reminds us, at a time when the sophisticated world was in the thrall of a mixture of Roman "delights" and Greek "Epicurean philosophy" (DA, 2,2,12). Even so, there is no reason for friends of human dignity and religious believers to oppose biotechnological progress fanatically, although they should oppose its tyrannical impulses resolutely. No matter what human beings do, there will still be dignity in living well with our invincible limitations, and we shouldn't worry about dignified action getting too easy. Furthermore, religion—like the state—will not wither away.

New ways of maximizing health and safety will probably produce statist intrusions on religious liberty, but the biotechnological failure to eradicate human misery or the mystery of self-consciousness will make the case for God stronger and more attractive than ever. The truth is that we will remain in some measure "incomprehensible to ourselves" (fr. 131; DA, 2,1,17). Biotechnology will not really provide the compassionate redemption for which we long.

Chapter 6

The Caregiving Society

In his stirring second inaugural address on "America's ideal of freedom," President Bush called upon us to build "an ownership society." "By making every citizen an agent of his or her destiny," he declared, we "will give our fellow Americans greater freedom from want and fear." With that vision in mind, he proposed to reform Social Security by bringing it under the control of each individual agent. Certainly, as individuals live longer, children become scarcer, and the baby boomers retire, some reform is needed. And surely there is a large potential upside to making today's workers active investors in their own retirements and in deploying today's assets in the entrepreneurial economy.

But there is also something deeply inadequate about viewing old age in terms of the individual "ownership" of one's destiny. The aging society, after all, will confront us with the realities of human neediness. Freedom from "want and fear," to the extent such freedom is humanly attainable, will require the old accepting the inevitability of their growing dependence on others, and it will require others who willingly accept the burden of caring for their elders, even at the expense of their own independence. The ownership society only makes sense if it prepares us to be *care-givers* and *care-receivers*, and if it does not encourage us to see ourselves as unencumbered individuals.

The president seemed to understand this human reality. He reminded the nation that "America's idea of freedom . . . is ennobled by service and mercy, and a heart for the weak. Liberty for all does not mean independence from one another." But he did not explain how our dependence on others should limit the vision of the self-reliant, middle-class American. Nor did he show how our mutual neediness should limit the idea of self-ownership in our formulation of public policy. We may well have a crisis today because aging citizens look too quickly to the government and not to themselves in securing their financial futures. But we have another, surely more intractable crisis, as the individual's need for care increases in a society where the ties of family and fidelity have often weakened and the supply of voluntary caregivers has diminished. No government program, insurance policy, or personal savings account could possibly replace what Americans have done for one another without compensation.

This potential crisis in long-term care is due in part to the last century's great advances in medicine. People are living longer and longer, but often at the price of living with severe infirmities—bodily or mental—that render them incapable of taking care of themselves for long periods of old age. At the same time, fewer and fewer people are available to serve as voluntary caregivers: today's baby boomers had fewer children than their parents; these grown children are more geographically dispersed; and family bonds are increasingly complicated by the high rate of divorce. And there is no reason to believe that there will be enough professional caregivers to fill these gaps. The cost of decent professional care is increasingly daunting, and fewer and fewer of us will be able to provide it ourselves or pay others to provide it well for those we love.

But this crisis does not arise simply from demographic shifts or shortages of manpower and money. It is, at bottom, a crisis of culture, a crisis about "caring," a product of our society's opinions on freedom, dependence, and care. It confronts us with one of the peculiar ironies of our time: The more we understand ourselves as independent of others (i.e., as in pursuit of our own self-interest and self-preservation), the more dependent we ultimately become on others (i.e., the more in need we are of the care that all human beings rely upon, especially in their old age). Our spirit of ownership and the realities of our dependence inevitably come into conflict, and this conflict is not easily resolved.

THE ILLUSION OF INDEPENDENCE

Self-reliance, of course, is a great American virtue. America is a middle-class nation, and it continues to become more middle-class. This does not mean that we are all equal economically, or that we are all equal when it comes to intelligence and virtue. It means that we all work because we have to work, and that we are all free. We believe that all human beings have an equal right to work and no right to expect the fruits of other people's labors. And we believe that freedom means not being dependent on others or constrained by others. We are against all forms of servitude and dependence, and we often see no real difference between paternalism and despotism. Even the rights and responsibilities of parents are quite limited and temporary; our children are raised to be free and independent, to achieve on their own, to go their own way.

More than ever, we experience ourselves *simply* as individuals, distinguished by our freedom from what nature has given us. We are freer to escape the constraints of bodily limitation, of gender, senescence, and decline—or at least to live for an extended period of time as if we could do so. The world exists, the individual thinks, for me. In the beginning, there I was, and after me there is nothing.

But this view of ourselves as individuals remains far from complete. Despite our pretensions, we remain in many ways dependent beings. Nature eventually erodes those freedoms that depend on an active body and a flourishing mind. And there is no way we can get all the care we need merely through calculated, contractual relations with others. Perhaps the economy can be reduced largely to such consensual relationships. But it will always remain true, as the French political philosopher Chantal Delsol observes in *Icarus Fallen*, that "the amount of vigilance, care, friendship, and patience that must be given any person, if he is not to be driven insane or to despair, is almost literally incredible." "Nothing today," she adds, "is more depreciated than caregiving activities that go . . . unremunerated."[1]

The individual often thinks of the caregiving life as unproductive or wasted, and he usually cannot imagine himself as a care-needing being. Caregiving and care-receiving are commonly viewed with contempt, because freedom for us means giving and receiving as little of it as possible. The happiness bestowed through caregiving does not appear to the individual to be real, and the virtue of caregiving often seems too ordinary. Our goal is not to care for those who are suffering and dying, but to reduce and eventually eliminate the amount of suffering and dying in the world. Our goal is not to help others live well with natural disability and decline, but to conquer all disability and decline.

In this view, physicians and nurses are in some measure both producers and caregivers. They aim at eradicating suffering and pushing back death mainly through the method of cure. Curing is often, of course, the most effective way of caring, and it generates the feeling of accomplishment we associate with production. But once curing becomes impossible, and all that remains is the need for care, the patient is typically handed over to those who do the work of merely caring: keeping company with the patient, meeting the seemingly ordinary needs of those who are beyond medical help, sustaining those who will soon be unsustainable. Not without reason, we often rank curing over caring; we revere doctors and give little thought to those who change bedpans; we view activities based on the thoughtful acceptance of our natural limits as being below those which attempt to overcome those limits; we seek solutions first and foremost and see everything else as signs of defeat.

The views of the caregiver and the producer are, in reality, both partly right. It is a tough question whether the saintly solicitude of the Sisters of Mercy or the physicians who introduced the latest medical technology into their hospitals did more to reduce the amount of suffering and to increase the amount of happiness in the world. But they clearly worked best in combination. Surely the most admirable American type is some mixture of productive individual and loving caregiver. At our best, we combine technique with recognition of the permanent limits of technique. But this combination of innovative engineering and perennial wisdom is a rare human achievement.

THE NEW DIVISION OF LABOR

Not so long ago, the individualistic, "productive" activities were characteristic of men, and unpaid caregiving was reserved for women (and all those with a religious vocation). This division of labor seemed to slight both the intellectual capabilities and the freedom of women, and today we believe that either a man or a woman can simultaneously have a career and be devoted to caring faithfully for others. The traditional roles of the ambitious man and the devoted mother are arguably combined in today's micromanaging, achievement-oriented parents.

But the old division of labor is giving way to a new one. We have turned more and more caregiving over to salaried employees, making it a species of production. Caregivers have become *workers*—social workers, healthcare workers, daycare workers, and so forth. When caregiving is combined with technical expertise—as in the case of nurses and some social workers—salaries rise to a solidly middle-class level. But when caregiving is seen merely as the unproductive maintenance of ordinary (including profoundly disabled) lives and so requiring no special technical competencies, compensation is stuck near subsistence. And the overall effect of turning caregivers into workers is to lower their communal standing and to reduce still further the honor we accord to *unpaid* caregiving.

We may dream of turning all caregivers into wage-earners—so that all we as individuals owe them is money for their services. But in reality, our free economy would collapse under that burden. Our medical system depends on most of the chronically ill being cared for voluntarily by women—a burden that will grow more crucial and more difficult as the baby boomers retire. Even in our individualistic times, as the Senate Special Committee on Aging reported in 2002, "family caregivers are the cornerstone of our long-term care system . . . , providing 80 percent of all long-term care in this country," with women providing "75 percent of all caregiving for family members."[2] Replacing "these unpaid family caregivers" with "paid home care providers" would cost hundreds of billions of dollars.[3] And despite our society's gender-neutral ideal, "the modern technological extension of the life span has put pressures most directly on women rather than on men."[4]

There is some truth in the gross caricature that the ambitiously productive men who made history ruled over the largely invisible caregivers, who left little record of their activities and even less of their happiness. But in more Christian and aristocratic times, there was also much greater awareness that production and caregiving are both *valuable* and *incommensurable*. Caregiving need not be paid, it was thought, because its value is intrinsic, and women were able to work without personal wages and public recognition because they knew that everyone understood the singular and indispensable importance of what they did. "Between child-rearing and prayer," as Delsol says, "there is but a step; between selling and prayer, there is an abyss." The lives of women (both wives and nuns) were thought to be both more ordinary and more spiritual than those of men. That is because "the women of yesterday knew no middle ground . . . between the banalities of daily life and the most profound wisdom."[5]

That "middling" way of life—the way of life of the productive individual, who produces the means of human happiness but knows little about the sources of human happiness—was the way of life of men. For much of our country's history, as Tocqueville noticed, American women were both less and more than middle-class American men, and he presented the true philosophers as allying with American priests and American women against the misanthropic excesses of individualistic American men.[6] But today, we *all* think of ourselves as middle-class—as free beings who work. So we tend to devalue everything below and everything above the realm of production. Below production are our invincible natural needs and limitations; above it are the invincible spiritual dimensions of our lives. Caregiving is not something we do merely out of social instinct. It requires an awareness of the relationship between human limits and human love, and a faith that attentive devotion to the frail and incompetent is a worthy and fulfilling human activity, even if its worldly rewards are not often obvious.

THE YOUNG AND THE OLD

Caring for the old is distinct from caring for the young, and the decline of caregiving is most apparent in the way we stand before our elders. Raising children combines nurturing and ambition; indeed, raising children can be the most satisfying project of all. Their lives progress, as we believe history and technology progress, toward wonderful and indefinite futures. But to look at the old is to be reminded unambiguously of necessity, of our limitations, of what we human beings cannot do for ourselves. There is no place for the old, for example, in David Brooks's books about our achievement-driven meritocracy, just as there is no place for caregiving for anyone but our own children.[7]

Yet caring for—being attentive to—those in their declining years is a crucial source of human wisdom. "Aging, like illness and death," writes Thomas Cole in *The Journey of Life*, "reveals the most fundamental conflict of the human condition: the tension between infinite ambitions, dreams, and desires on the one hand, and vulnerable, limited, decaying physical existence on the other—the tragic and ineradicable conflict between spirit and body."[8] This conflict is distinct to human beings—a mark of both our misery and our greatness. We alone among the animals have longings that transcend the pleasures and limitations of our biological existence, and that truth is the same for all of us. While nurturing the young may have the aid of natural instinct, caring for the old requires transcending mere instinct and meeting biological decline with more-than-biological love.

Today, being old increasingly defines who we are as a nation, while the vigor and freedom of youth is more than ever what we desire. Our enlightened prudence about healthy living and our achievements in medical technology keep more of us alive well beyond our reproductive and parenting years. Evolution might suggest that the elderly individual should die in the interest of the species or the next generation, and yet we are freer than ever to refuse to be replaced. We work infinitely harder than any other species at keeping particular individuals around, pursuing longevity through technological ingenuity, and as we have had occasion to note elsewhere, we are also getting older as a society because more individuals are making the choice not to reproduce, or not to reproduce much. The good news, as Boston University professor Robert Hudson explains, is that "for the first time in history" we have "large numbers of older people whose existence is centrally defined neither by work nor by illness."[9] The prospect of a lengthy retirement seems to present us with a new kind of freedom. The bad news is that the freedom of old age always gives way to the neediness of old age, a neediness that grows as people live longer. We increasingly need a selfless kind of caregiving that we are increasingly less able to give. We live in a world in which the Sisters of Mercy have just about disappeared. They too have grown old without replacing themselves, and the few young sisters that remain are increasingly burdened by the old.[10]

As we grow old, we are also becoming more repulsed by the natural effects of aging. In our individualistic meritocracy, people are often judged by how "smart and pretty" they are, and nobody is obliged to like or support or care for anybody else.[11] Aging is generally bad for both our brains and our looks, and so to avoid failure and loneliness we try harder than ever to fend off and mask its effects. Any technology that keeps us looking young has an immediate and huge market. We are repulsed by the sight of old age, in part, because the appearance of the old brings death to mind. But we seem to fear dependence as much as death, and we know that the downside of living in a meritocracy is that the love of others is hardly guaranteed.

For those used to thinking of themselves as free individuals, dependence is especially humiliating; we know too well that nobody really owes us a living. That is why we now often say that we would rather be dead than lose our autonomy, and we readily sign legal directives making that clear. But the choice for death that we make when we are healthy does not necessarily predict what we would choose when death is actually "imminent."[12] Precisely because we live our lives believing the self is the measure of all things, we shudder at the prospect of the self's oblivion, and cling to every living moment as if being itself depended on our individual existence.

Some worry that the prolongation of life may turn society into "something like a giant nursing home."[13] And this prospect has provoked a certain backlash in the name of productivity. "Longer years of life," observes Audrey Chapman, "decrease the relative period in which people are contributing economically during their lifetimes and increase the period of dependency."[14] A harsher way of expressing this observation is that insofar as we value productivity, we must devalue the old. Productivity and creativity, on balance, are characteristics of the young. People retire for many reasons, but most often because they have become short on the desire and the ability required to keep up. What happens to basketball and baseball players in their thirties eventually happens to most of us in our sixties and seventies. Retirement sometimes offers new possibilities, such as aiding and encouraging the lives that will replace our own.

We know that the elderly "make substantial unpaid contributions" by providing care for grandchildren or long-term care for disabled siblings or spouses.[15] But we also readily distinguish that caregiving from their former productivity.

The wisdom traditionally associated with age has to do with our limitations, with being chastened by experience. For achievement-oriented individuals, that alleged wisdom mainly gets in the way of progress; the prudence of the old is therefore interpreted as inflexibility, an inability to imagine new and better futures. We have a hard time thinking about *the point* of being old, although we readily choose it over being dead. The old are supposedly free to experience life without the burdens of work and parenting, and yet the limits imposed by age itself always loom large. Their realm of freedom, they know too well, is contingent and temporary.

Of course, it is just as American, as Carl Elliott observes in *Better Than Well*, to criticize "the cultural attitudes" that make anti-aging enhancements necessary as it is to have such attitudes in the first place. But "there is an air of futility," he says, about all such criticism. The spiritual objection to worrying enough about wrinkles to get Botox injections is trumped by the very tangible benefits accrued by looking wrinkle-free.[16] We cannot say that the choice is merely an aesthetic preference, because the choice to look young is also a choice for productivity. Various anti-aging enhancements may one day be regarded as reasonable conditions for employment. The choice against being as smart and pretty as technology allows is a choice for needless dependence on nature, and there is no obvious reason why employers or anyone else should honor such a perverse choice.

It may be objected that choosing youth-and-vigor-enhancing technology shows how dependent we are on how we look in the eyes of others. This objection makes good sense, and we have no trouble making it. But it finally limps because we lack a standard higher than productivity from which we could defend some other choice. We will do what we can to remain productive and independent for as long as possible. We will continue to devalue caregiving and caregivers, hoping to live as much as possible without them.

BETWEEN FAITH AND EUTHANASIA

The contribution of biotechnology to lengthening human life will merely reinforce these longstanding individualistic trends and successes. No vaguely death-accepting policy has any chance of success, especially as the electorate continues to age. The only possible exception is the future embrace of euthanasia, a policy that is not *death-accepting* but *death-imposing.* As Daniel Callahan observed nearly two decades ago, "Only a full-scale change in habits, thinking, and attitudes would . . . make it morally and socially possible" for any "proposal to limit health care for the aged" to succeed.[17] But such a transformation seems unlikely. And if it were to occur, we would have reason to fear that it would be based not in *caregiving love* but *care-denying utilitarianism,* because the latter would be more characteristic of the excesses of the individual. We are thus stuck between two unrealistic views of the autonomy of the individual. The first is that the self can be autonomous forever; the second is that only the autonomous deserve to live at all.

The ironic result of our increasingly individualistic habits, thinking, and attitudes is that we are stuck more than ever with giving and receiving care. More people are dying of Alzheimer's disease, an approximately decade-long process of decline toward complete dementia—or, more precisely, the total regression to infancy. Caring for a child is full of the joy of seeing natural promise fulfilled; caring for someone with Alzheimer's consists of watching a being gradually emptied of his or her distinctively human content, a slow and initially very conscious surrender of all independence. The explosion of Alzheimer's is one way in which we are victims of our own technological success; old and very old people suffer and die from this disease because nothing else did them in earlier. Because the incidence of Alzheimer's increases with age, the number of victims will only increase further as we extend the length of life. Virtually any other form of debilitation and death would be less of a physical and psychological burden on caregivers. And even if we figure out a way to cure or prevent Alzheimer's (a prospect that seems not to be on the *immediate* horizon), more people than ever will live long enough to experience some form of senility or dementia and the long-term care it requires.

The burden of caregiving often falls on a single child or an elderly spouse—and more and more on rather elderly children. As Francis Fukuyama explains, we have "created a novel situation in which individuals approaching retirement age today find their own choices constrained by the fact that they still have an elderly parent alive and dependent on them for care."[18] The result is that the caregiving family member must sacrifice very sizeable amounts of time or income or both at a point when a life devoted to unpaid caregiving may well seem like a wasted one. This burden increases all the time, and it is a testimony to the good natures of American women that they still so often accept it, are ennobled by it, and find happiness in it. But the young (or youngest retirees) cannot help but grow more resentful that their otherwise free existence is more limited by the requirements of the old (or very old). "Young people," Chapman observes, "may question whether their futures should be mortgaged to care for those who are not making productive contributions to society."[19]

"The caregiver for the severely demented," write Richard J. Martin and Stephen J. Post, "must be a person of faith. . . . He or she must have some trust that caring is a source of meaning in life," and such a faith is what the individual as individual often lacks. But few of us are individualistic enough (or nihilistic enough) to affirm faith's "only serious alternative, the destruction of the radically infirm."[20] From a caregiving perspective, we are stuck—in a middle-class way—between faith and the negation of faith, either of which would make our lives in many ways easier. We reject the turn to euthanasia as a way of getting rid of the infirm, but we do not believe that caring for those whose lives are seemingly pointless is the best way to spend our productive years. Our anxious disorientation about what we are supposed to do provides plenty of evidence that we are more than merely individuals. This anxiety makes us miserable and opens us to the possibility of faith.

More often than we like to admit, middle-class persons with Alzheimer's find themselves without any reliable voluntary caregiver. The result is dangerous and needlessly disorienting for a while, culminating in relatively early institutionalization. The institutional workers given the allegedly merely "custodial" task of taking care of those in decline are often inadequately trained and inattentive to the consequences of changes in their patients' capabilities and moods. Such work is both underestimated and underappreciated. Its satisfactions are both intellectual and emotional, and those who think of themselves as merely individuals stand most in need of its lessons.[21] Alzheimer's victims need, most of all, to be at home with large families or attended to by the Sisters of Mercy (or their equivalent), but both alternatives have become rare in our individualistic time.

Surely there is little worse in the human experience than having Alzheimer's and being alone. But the currents of our time push us almost inescapably in this lonely direction: Lives moved by a veneration of independence threaten to leave us unprepared for dependence, and thus increase the burdens and challenges of long-term care. The inability to think clearly about caregiving—or to provide as well as we should for a basic human need—may be one of the prices to be paid for all the undeniable and wonderful technological successes that characterize our time.

LOVE AND OWNERSHIP

Perhaps the "ownership society," if it comes, will make matters marginally better. Rather than envisioning the social contract as an arrangement between the individual and the state, it might free individuals to see their wealth as rooted in families, as a nest egg for the young, the old, and the middle-aged to provide for one another. Perhaps ownership will promote not only self-reliance but love, even when love requires accepting the loss of freedom that comes with giving and receiving care.

But this is more a hope than a prediction, and it may be that our apparent willingness to reform Social Security—a policy issue that can be framed in terms of today's workers—is mirrored by our great reluctance to confront the problem of long-term care—an issue that confronts us squarely with tomorrow's needy elders. Perhaps we falsely believe that individualistic solutions to the problem of caring for the old are really possible. Or perhaps we simply know that long-term care is a problem we cannot solve, and that all we can do now is to reject those solutions that encourage independence and productivity by denying life to those with no worldly use, no power, and no voice.

CHAPTER 7

THE RISE AND FALL OF SOCIOBIOLOGY

Three views of the relationship between human beings and nature have been hugely influential in recent decades: those promoted by social constructionism, sociobiology, and biotechnology. Each contains a good deal of truth, and each is still a potent force. But like all popularized science, these grand theoretical approaches gain clarity by distorting reality. Each presents part of the truth about being human by disfiguring the whole.

   Social constructionism is the belief that human nature does not matter or exist, and that most of what we believe about human nature is actually the product of human institutions and cultures, and therefore changeable. *Sociobiology* is the belief that human beings have real natures and natural purposes, but natures and purposes that are fully intelligible through evolution and not really different from those of the other animals. *Biotechnology* is not so much a belief as it is a project, one that involves using our knowledge of human biology to improve human life and perhaps remake human nature. It thus presumes at least some measure of discontent with what we are now, as well as the existence of an objective biological nature (or "system") that it can reliably manipulate.

Each of these views is actually ideological rather than scientific, more a program for human reform than a truthful account of the way things are. Each is also a form of reductionism, that is, each reduces human beings to less than we really are. In what follows, I focus on the rise and fall of sociobiology: what sociobiology says and what it means; how it is true and how it is false; and how it fits with the views that human nature can be created out of nothing (social constructionism) or reshaped into whatever we desire (biotechnology).

THE DEATH OF SOCIAL CONSTRUCTIONISM

The social constructionists agree with the sociobiologists that we are fundamentally social beings; they disagree about how and why this is so. The sociobiologists say that our sociality is a natural or programmed trait; we are gregarious like the chimps are gregarious; everything about us can be explained through evolutionary biology. The "natural law," in fact, is the same for all animals: We are born, spread our genes, raise our young, and die. The species that accomplish these goals flourish; those that fail by not adapting to their changing environments disappear. Contrary to our pretensions, there is no God or Nature that cares about particular human beings—or particular chimps or particular ants. Nature chooses for life, and in doing so chooses against each particular life. Nature wants each of us to be replaced by a new, better, or more adaptable being as soon as we have completed our simple and fundamentally physical tasks.

The social constructionists, by contrast, say that we create (or inherit) social and moral life according to our preferences (if we are strong) or slave-like condition (if we are weak). In either case, what we make of ourselves owes little or nothing to nature. There is no "natural law" worth heeding, because we alone among the species have a mysterious but real capability to be other than natural beings. Rather, we make ourselves into social or historical beings over time; everything distinctively human is the product of our free or unnatural social construction.

The most influential manifestations of social constructionism in our time have been Marxism and feminism. According to the Marxists, we create ourselves through our mode of production. There is no human nature but only historical human types: feudal human beings, capitalist human beings, and socialist human beings. Once we become aware that our prevailing idea of God or nature is just an ideology imposed on us by the ruling class, we can revolt against all historical oppression. We can create a world where we all live freely and equally while doing very little work. We can finally socially construct a world without the socially constructed domination of some human beings by others. This new world will be populated by a "new man"—a new human type—who has never existed before.

Radical feminism works in a similar way: We have no experience of natural men or natural women; even the sex act is socially constructed and so not really sex at all. We don't have natural purposes but "gender" roles, and those roles have been determined by those who have wielded social power—namely, the patriarchy. To the extent that we dispel the illusion that masculinity and femininity are "natural," we are free to construct a new way of life—one that allows men and women to share in all the privileges and duties of society and that frees men and women from their illusory dependence on each other. To be a free human individual is to realize that biology in no way shapes one's destiny.

The utopias of the social constructionists are characteristically based on the premise that the human responsibilities connected with birth, love, and death have no real foundation. They have been constructed by human beings and so can be deconstructed by human beings. But surely a world full of individuals unmoved by love and death—unmoved by some perception of the truth about their natures—would be full of beings who are less than we are now, however happier or more "free" they might imagine themselves to be. And while social constructionism is right to see that human beings are distinct from the other animals, it errs in believing that our distinct quality is total freedom from nature.

Over the last decade or so, it has become fashionable to say that social constructionism is dead. Communism, the great dissidents Václav Havel and Aleksandr Solzhenitsyn rightly told us, was defeated by human nature. Private property, for example, seems to be rooted in the limitations nature places on our powers of knowing and loving. We naturally prefer our kin and close friends to human beings in general, and in many biological ways our natural selfishness makes good sense. We prefer those who share and help us spread our genes. We cannot live as if we had no bodies, or as if we did not live in a particular place with particular people.

Like communism, feminism also seems to be on the way out. On one level, this is because feminism has mostly won: almost everyone now believes that the truth about nature points to equal rights and equal opportunity for both men and women. But in a more fundamental sense feminism has almost completely lost. Most women do not really believe that they can be happy by liberating themselves altogether from their natural desires for both men and children. They do not believe that being a woman simply means being duped by society's oppressive construction of gender roles.

But the fact that the utopias promised by the social constructionists are not in our futures is not unambiguously good news. We capitalistic, bourgeois animals are working harder than ever to

avoid dying in a way that other nonhuman animals never do, perhaps because we are haunted by death in a way that human beings
never have been before. Surely we are too self-obsessed really to be
happy, and the hope for a remedy to that self-obsession is what
really attracted many intellectuals to Marxism. The life of the contemporary "post-feminist" woman also looks rather hard and often
miserable. She is free to leave the home and enter the workplace,
but this freedom is now seen by most women as an "economic
necessity." As Marx predicted, most of our women have become
"wage slaves" just like men, while men are not reliably doing their
part at home and with the children.

More evidence of the untruth of social constructionism has
come from the new sciences of evolutionary biology and evolutionary psychology. The idea that the human mind is simply a "blank
slate" has been totally discredited. Human beings do not simply
create themselves out of nothing. We are much more hardwired or
programmed by nature in certain directions—toward being men and
women, living in particular families and communities, and developing language with a certain kind of grammar—than the social constructionists imagined. We have animal natures, which are not fundamentally different from the other animals in being determined to
some degree by our evolutionary genetic inheritance. This is the
partial truth of sociobiology, if not the whole truth about being
human. It aims to provide self-help for the misery that social constructionism has caused us by helping us see that as natural beings
we have nothing to worry about.

THE DARWINIAN LULLABY

In his sociobiological book *The Great Disruption* (1999), Francis
Fukuyama celebrated the return of Americans to more natural lives

after the failure of the disastrous social constructionist projects of the 1960s. Human beings are returning to family, local community, and church in response to their natural social needs, especially those connected with children. And the free market and private property are back in fashion, too. Fukuyama and others (notably Steven Pinker in *The Blank Slate* (2003)) explain that evolutionary naturalism is no threat to human morality. It is, in fact, the source of a truly conservative defense of family, moral limits, social duties, and personal responsibility. We have no real need to work as obsessed individualists or radical feminists or religious fundamentalists to transform our miserable condition. Sociobiology sets us free from such self-destructive fantasies by showing us that our being is both quite natural and quite good.

The most ambitious effort to unite political philosophy and evolutionary biology into a conservative ideology may be found in Larry Arnhart's *Darwinian Natural Right* (1998). Arnhart's conclusion is that "even if the natural world was not made for us, we were made for it, because we are adapted to live in it." The continued existence of our species is evidence that we are fit to be natural beings and that "we have not been thrown into nature from some place far away." Christians, Marxists, and existentialists say in different ways that we are "aliens," but they are all wrong. We are the products of natural evolution and nothing else; there is nowhere else that we have been or could possibly be. Nature "is our home."

Arnhart claims that there is little new about sociobiology; his view is that the scientific naturalisms of Aristotle, Thomas Aquinas, David Hume, and Charles Darwin are all pretty much the same. There is no fundamental contradiction between recent biological discoveries and the scientific thought of those who reflected rationally in the past about man as a natural being. Those who oppose Darwinism in our time must be "motivated by moral, religious, and political concerns," because their intellectual case is obviously so weak. But such moral, religious, and political ideologies are out of step with the truth about our natures. Misguided creationists and intelligent design theorists, Arnhart argues, should understand that sociobiology is compatible with a free, conservative, pro-family outlook on politics and culture ("Conservatives, Darwin, and Design: An Exchange," *First Things,* November 2003). By abandoning the mix of perversity and fantasy that causes us to choose against our natural inclinations, we can realize our true happiness as animals.

Human beings, Arnhart notices in *Darwinian Natural Right* (1998), are different from the other animals. They possess language, which gives them the ability to reflect upon and rank their desires. They also have acquired a "natural moral sense" that inclines them to perform the social duties required for the species to flourish. But this "uniquely human morality is rooted in natural inclinations (such as sexual mating and parental care) shared with other animals." We have distinctively human natural means to pursue the same biological or physical *ends* as the other animals. And even our means—"such as symbolic speech, practical deliberation, and conceptual thought—are elaborations of powers shared in some form with other animals." Our differences are only ones of complexity.

For the sociobiologists, human social behaviors came into existence as unintended and unconscious results of various natural threats to our species. At a certain point in evolution, human beings came to see adaptive behaviors "as meaningful and moral." And yet, human morality seems to encompass more than what is "best for the species as a whole," and its purposes do not seem to be simply or predominantly "adaptive." We think that moral action is good for its own sake, and we cannot see any morality in nature's lack of concern for particular human individuals. Only human beings, such as some Christians and Kantians, could decide that nature is not always on the side of meaning and morality. Only human beings, such as Thomas Aquinas and Aristotle, could claim that human beings by nature have different and higher purposes than the other animals. And only human beings can make themselves miserable by thinking or imagining that they are more than they really are.

Arnhart's solution to our misery is a kind of biological enlightenment, a method not at all needed to save the chimps or dolphins from themselves. The self-help he provides is to show that those who say we are more than natural beings and that we have more than natural longings are wrong. The Augustinian or existentialist tradition is false and the Aristotelian or naturalist tradition is true: "While pagan philosophers like Aristotle think that human beings as mortal animals can be happy, Augustine insists that human beings can never truly be happy as long as they are mortal, because their deepest natural desires can only be satisfied through an immortal union with the creator."

Arnhart does admit, in a muted way, that the distinction between pagan naturalism and Christian alienation is too sharp. Aristotle, he notes, also observes that human beings "can know only momentary and incomplete satisfaction of . . . [their] social and rational desires." Our self-conscious mortality—not shared with the other animals—gets in the way of our happiness; it frustrates the full satisfaction of our "deepest natural desires." For this reason, Aristotle acknowledges that we cannot help but long for immortality, if often in ways that are "unreasonable" because they "ignore the eternal limits of our nature."

Reasonable or not, these human longings persist. The self-help method promoted by Arnhart is to use sociobiology to discourage them. We should be happy as animals because we can be happy no other way. By reducing our longing for distinctively human happiness or completion, Arnhart hopes to reduce our distinctively human misery. In his hands, Darwinian evolutionism becomes a lullaby aiming to soothe certain misguided human experiences to sleep.

But Aristotle himself would not have seen such a lullaby as reasonable or effective. For him, human beings are the only animals that desire to be more than simply animals. This desire must be accounted for and satisfied, not explained away as some form of chimp aggressiveness. As Richard F. Hassing explains in his review of Arnhart in *Interpretation* (2000), Aristotle sets man "apart from nature in a way that is uniquely problematic." The greatness and misery of being human is that we can be much better and much worse than the other animals. But we are not capable of being just like them. We are too proud, too self-conscious, and too rational. We are the only Darwinian creatures that know we are Darwinian creatures, and who wish to be something more. Arnhart's belief is that "our earthly happiness is securely founded in our nature as mortal animals endowed by a moral sense that serves our natural desires." But only human beings are fully aware of their contingent and temporary existence; they are the only animals that know there is no natural security for their existence.

The ancient philosophers, unlike the modern sociobiologists, understood this. The view of Socrates and no doubt Aristotle was that philosophy is, in great measure, learning how to die. This is a lesson only human beings have to learn through great and thoughtful effort. The other animals "know" it instinctually or unconsciously.

We have been given duties by nature as animals, but we perform them quite unreliably because we have been given the additional duty of living well with our insecure and temporary natural existence. Everything that human beings do is infused by what we alone among the animals know about ourselves. Human love and human death cannot be reduced to anything like the experience of other animals. And thus it is unlikely that a moral sense linking us to the other animals can serve as the foundation for what human individuals alone have to do.

Whether he realizes it or not, Arnhart presents us with an ideology that aims to make us, for our own good, into something less than we really are; he attempts to make us happy by saying that the human being is just another animal. But his account is too obviously reductionistic to be effective. It blandly claims that the desire for knowledge, the experience of love, and the need for redemption are simply complex animal experiences, not hints of our difference but odd manifestations of our sameness. In the end, however, we cannot simply obliterate the human longings described so well by Aristotle, Augustine, and Heidegger by saying that they make no sense in a purely evolutionary framework. Sociobiology cannot provide enough evidence to convince us that we should rest content with our natural being. The lullaby cannot finally put us to sleep.

THE HOPEFUL MYTH

Despite Arnhart's deep knowledge of philosophy, he does not seem nearly as self-conscious about sociobiology's function or its inadequacy as its brilliant and famous founder, Edward O. Wilson. Wilson admits to preaching the scientific myth of evolution as a replacement for traditional religion. He has ironically and rightly been called a scientific evangelist. Even more than Arnhart, he regards the fundamental human alternatives as dogmatic creationism and evolutionary materialism.

Wilson's first full-scale and best sociobiological polemic, *On Human Nature* (1978), forecasted the demise of the era of sociobiology before almost anyone else even knew that this era had begun. He boldly asserted that "the intellect was not constructed to understand atoms or even to understand itself but to promote the survival of human genes," and he noted with favor "the growing awareness that [religious] beliefs are really enabling mechanisms for survival." Morality, too, is just another "technique by which human genetic material has been and will be kept intact."

But it is also true, Wilson observed, that "man's destiny is to know, if only because societies with knowledge culturally dominate societies that lack it." Knowledge is the foundation for the domination of some human beings over others; those who do not have it do not survive. But knowledge can do more than promote survival; it can allow human beings to free themselves, to some extent, from their unconscious natural determination. By coming to understand "the elements of biological human nature," we will gain "some measure of intellectual independence" from natural forces. By knowing how we are like the other animals, we can win a measure of "real freedom" or conscious control over our natures that the other animals can never possess.

Before scientists discovered the truth about sociobiology, we were blindly controlled by evolutionary forces we did not understand. Religion, morality, and philosophy were only illusory adaptive mechanisms. But once we discovered the truth of sociobiology—the truth that we are no different than other natural animals—its truth began to become less true. The evolution of our species—

unlike all the other animals—must now become, to some extent, conscious and willful.

Wilson presents this new understanding of our biological natures as an unstable middle point between complete genetic determination and complete freedom from such determination. He knows that the era of sociobiology will be followed rather quickly by the era of biotechnology. Soon enough, knowledge that can only ambiguously be called "self-knowledge" will allow us to alter our "hard biological substructure," our genetic composition, and thus our human nature. By determining what our genes *are*, we will be able to change what natural evolution *means us to be*.

Wilson acknowledges that we cannot know in advance to what extent we can change human nature or negate the truth of sociobiology. Even in the age of biotechnology, sociobiology might remain more true than false. In our efforts to change "the very essence of humanity," we may discover that "there is something already present in our nature" that limits or even thwarts our will. Or we may not. We cannot tell in advance how free we are capable of being—perhaps because sociobiology itself cannot account for the willful freedom from nature that is uniquely characteristic of our species. Where there is no explanation there can be no prediction.

For example, Wilson complains in *Promethean Fire* (written with Charles J. Lumsden, 1983) that human beings react to death "bizarrely," without really giving a sociobiological explanation or even wondering why this is so. But he does admit that "the anguish of death alone" may well be sufficient to keep "belief in a personal moral God" alive in spite of all scientific evidence. He would oppose scientists helping chimps acquire a sense of "personal death" unless the chimps could somehow know death without our fear, and he aims for us to keep that sense without being strongly moved by it.

Wilson seems both to affirm and deny the fact that we human beings are distinguished by both death and religion. Like Arnhart, he
clearly wants to employ myth to *make* us more like the chimps, to
make our lives less unreasonably determined by death and religion.
And in this respect, sociobiology means to be a form of social constructionism. He concludes *Promethean Fire* by admitting that "the
planned manipulation of values" may be a "distasteful exercise," but
it is the way "to a stable and wholly benevolent world."

Wilson seems to understand in *On Human Nature* both the
truth of our mortal anguish and the problem it creates for sociobiology. "While explaining the biological sources of religious emotional strength," he writes, evolutionary biology "is unable in its
present form to draw on them, because the evolutionary epic denies immortality to the individual and divine privilege to society,
and it suggests only an existential meaning for the human species."
But the human individual still hungers for meaning and immortality, and that individual is moved very little by the quasi-immortal-
ity of the "evolutionary epic." All the great existentialists—from St.
Augustine to Walker Percy and beyond—have focused on the experience and fate of the individual, and we are much more moved by
epic personal struggles than by evolution. There is, to my knowledge, no great literature on "species existentialism." Because "scientists cannot in all honesty serve as priests," Wilson observes, they
cannot lie to human beings in order to move them the way priests do.

But then Wilson goes on to show why scientists, like all other
mythmakers, must lie. "Men, it appears, would rather believe than
know," he observes. Once we know what really moves human beings, "noble" lying on behalf of scientific truth is necessary. The
mythmakers of scientific naturalism must use what they know about
evolutionary biology to make a "precise and deliberately affective

appeal to the deepest needs of human nature"—including the need for personal immortality and existential meaning. The true scientific myth must actually be "Promethean"; its strength must come from giving people "blind hopes" that all they long for can be achieved through scientific progress and liberation. The original Prometheus, Wilson remembers, "caused mortals to cease foreseeing doom." Blind hopes can cure or at least deaden the symptoms of that specifically human "sickness" of foresight.

Wilson is pretty certain that our deepest needs cannot be satisfied through biotechnological progress, and that sociobiology by itself shows that they cannot (or perhaps need not) be satisfied at all. Sociobiology might balk at the absurdity of the longings that stand at the foundation of individual existentialism, but it cannot dispense with or explain them. It cannot explain why our species cannot live well without blind hopes, even as it claims to show that the hopes we place in social constructionism and religious belief are untrue. It makes the individual human life seem so hopeless that we cannot help but focus our hopes on biotechnology, even while acknowledging the limits of biotechnology to remake human nature.

Wilson's later books seem to some extent to repudiate this flirtation with Promethean mythmaking, if not to abandon mythmaking altogether. But the "Ionian enchantment" of his magisterial and stunningly comprehensive *Consilience* (1998), or the belief in the materialistic unity of all knowledge, limps as an ideology or myth because it only inspires the mind. Wilson's new hope and expectation is that human beings will be conservative in their use of biotechnology, and that they will keep much of their natural home intact, including qualities given to them as particular animals by evolution. His concern is properly sociobiological: the danger of biotechnology is that human beings might destroy the happiness they enjoy as natural animals and make themselves much more homeless than they are now.

In his more recent work, Wilson has focused increasingly on the dangers of destroying the good of natural diversity. In *The Future of Life* (2003), he appeals to our natural "biophilia" as the foundation for a "culture of permanence" and against promiscuous natural devastation. He even heightens our sense of biological responsibility by overstating, at least on sociobiological grounds, the difference between human beings and the other species: "If the rest of the world is the body, we are the mind."

But in the end, there remains an undeniable tension between Wilson's calls for moderation and his view that the purpose of scientific knowledge is to give human beings a level of control over nature—including human nature—not enjoyed by the other animals. Biophilia is surely not sufficient compensation for our dissatisfaction with the sociobiological account of our meaningless, temporary, and contingent existence as individuals. And it is unlikely to halt or limit our desperate turn to biotechnology in pursuit of the happiness that nature by itself does not seem to give us.

The Era of Biotechnology

While it is important to see the limitations and ultimate falsehood of sociobiology, it would be wrong to ignore or disregard its partial truth. We remain in some measure at home in the world as natural animals, and our enjoyments as parents, children, friends, and community members have a natural foundation in social instinct. Both communism and radical feminism were indeed defeated by human nature, though the time and place of communism's surrender also had much to do with human *persons* making human *decisions* that shaped the course of human *history*. And for those in the know about nature—such as Arnhart or Fukuyama in *The Great Disruption* (1999)—it is not surprising to see revived interest in "family values" or the emergence of all sorts of new moral communities. Nor is it surprising to see the growing strength of property rights and the free market throughout the world. The "social capital" we need to live well as human beings is partially embedded in our nature, not just in our "culture."

But the view that all of human life can be explained by evolutionary naturalism makes human beings seem far more at home in nature than we really are. It makes us believe that the natural world should fully satisfy us. By denying our alienation as self-conscious mortals, it makes our experiences of individual longing and anxiety seem groundless or absurd. By trying to make us feel too much at home in the world, sociobiology has the perverse effect of making human individuals feel less at home than ever before.

The central problem is that human beings cannot be satisfied with a teaching about nature that says we are here simply to spread our genes and be replaced. From the individual's point of view, as Nicholas Wade puts it in his excellent *Life Script* (2001), evolution is a "blind and pitiless process." Even those who wonder at the power and creativity of evolution have to come to terms with its complete indifference to us as individuals. But one point of human distinction is our ability to use scientific knowledge to bring nature under human control. Human technology is not fundamentally an elaboration of primate tool-making, because the chimps show no signs of being death-obsessed control freaks. Our technology is rather something distinctly human; it is a response to the dilemmas and possibilities of being the only moral, rational, and death-haunted animal.

At its best, sociobiology might produce human beings with a serene resignation or stoicism about our inevitable fate. But the

Promethean teaching of modern science is that resignation is ridiculous if we can use knowledge to win our freedom. Without scientific knowledge, we blindly adapt as evolution intends. With scientific knowledge and modern technology, we can perhaps defeat nature in the name of the individual. We can take evolution into our own hands, and the individual can willfully and effectively choose his own life over what is best for the species.

Wilson is correct when he says that the truth of sociobiology is an unstable middle position between unscientific ignorance and biotechnological willfulness. Sociobiology is true until we know it is true. Once we understand how human nature "works," we stand armed and ready to try to change or improve it. Perhaps that is why right after publishing a book celebrating nature's victory, Fukuyama wrote another book, called *Our Posthuman Future* (2002), speculating about the end of our merely natural existence as human beings. And perhaps that is why witty new defenses of sociobiology against social constructionism, such as Pinker's *The Blank Slate*, seem out of date even before they are published. Biotechnology, after all, is a new and far more plausible form of social constructionism. All bets are off about what human beings are and how we will act if we can actually change our natures.

Perhaps feminists will use biotechnology to eradicate the natural differences between men and women. Perhaps society will use biotechnology to make men less aggressive. Perhaps psychiatrists and psychologists will use biotechnology to make everyone happy (or at least so unaware of reality that they are no longer sad). Perhaps the Chinese (who have a very different view of what should be socially constructed) will use genetic technology to create a race of strong, spirited, and fearless warriors. Or perhaps the new biotechnology will aid the creation of new forms of tyranny, producing a world that really is full of natural (or genetically engineered) masters and slaves. However it is used, biotechnology would be a means to construct an existence that is "naturally" different from the way we are now. The fact that the technology for achieving such things may be far off or never exist does not mean that experimenting with it (on ourselves or on our offspring) will be benign. Marxism, after all, was a fantasy that failed, but not without dire consequences in the real world.

Arnhart has speculated that the development of biotechnology might be directed by the natural moral sense that we have received through evolution ("Human Nature Is Here to Stay," *New Atlantis*, Summer 2003). But it is unclear how much human behavior in our time—or in any time—can be explained through the evolutionary idea of human nature. The most highly sophisticated individuals in the most prosperous nations seem to be consciously thwarting natural evolution by choosing not to produce their natural replacements. They may act or at least talk like laidback animals untroubled by death, but they pursue health and safety in the most scientific and disciplined way. They are rather fanatical about lengthening their own lives and fending off death indefinitely; they consciously prefer themselves to their species.

Sociobiologists should criticize these hypermodern individualists for neglecting their natural sources of happiness and obsessing about staying around long after their natural purposes (spreading their genes) have been fulfilled. But modern individuals seem more death-haunted than ever before precisely because they believe that something like sociobiology is true. They obsess about their bodies because they do not believe they have souls.

THE TRUTH ABOUT HUMAN NATURE

It is too early to know for certain to what extent the latest advances in biotechnology will achieve their immortalizing promises. But the dominant tendency of the biotechnology project, whether successful or not in achieving its own aims, will be an intensification of the modern preference for the individual over the species. The activities of raising children and having families will have more marginal roles in our lengthening lives; and genetic enhancement, embryo screening, and human cloning may well make the few replacements we have more manufactured than natural.

But in the end, biotechnology is not likely to satisfy the human longings that inspire it. What we need instead is a richer, more truthful account of human nature, one that comprehends the excellences and passions, the joys and miseries, of being the only animal who knows, loves, and thinks about death. Human beings are both social and natural, but we are not only social and natural. We have demanding responsibilities and thus a dignity not given to the other animals.

Human beings may have become human through an evolutionary process, but at some point in that process there must have been an "ontological leap" that made us more than simply clever animals by nature. We are the beings with genuinely complex language and speech; we have been given the capability to seek and partially understand the truth about our souls and perhaps the truth about God. This capability alters the way we experience everything, including our enjoyments and miseries as animals. Birds do it, bees do it, and we do it, but human sex is quite different from winged sex; it can be exalted or degraded in a way that animal sex can never be.

A more truthful understanding of human nature would connect what we know from contemporary biology with the human experiences of alienation, anxiety, love, nobility, and wonder. We need, as Leon Kass once put it, a "more natural science" that accounts both for the heterogeneity of nature and the heterogeneity of natural human purposes, but which knows, recognizes, and learns from its own limitations. Sociobiologists, who have benefitted us greatly by reflecting on the social meaning of evolution, would do us an even greater service if they stopped teaching that a materialist understanding of evolution explains everything about our behavior, especially when the facts suggest otherwise. But Arnhart is right that human nature is here to stay.

We are, in part, natural beings, but we alone among the animals are in some ways alienated from the natural world in which we live. But our alienation is, in truth, the consequence of what is unique about human nature. Fundamentalist creationism and rigidly atheistic evolutionism are both pretty implausible. We should instead face up to the truth about human nature, which might make us more at home with our homelessness and more open to the distinctly human joys, such as love, and the distinctly human responsibilities, such as caring for a dying parent or mourning a dead child. It would give us a genuine standard by which to accept or reject the various biotechnological possibilities that will rapidly be presented to us. And it would show why we should not put our deepest hopes in either history or science.

CHAPTER 8

THE UTOPIAN EUGENICS OF OUR TIME

W e live in a time when eugenics has replaced socialism at the center of utopian speculation. Utopias, for us, are not merely literary devices. They are programs for changing the world. "Utopian," for us, means "unprecedented," and much of our world is the unprecedented result of action to make utopias reality. We have reason and evidence to believe that the future will continue to be different from and better than the past. We do not yet believe that the only limits to what we might do are the limits of our imaginations, but we are progressing toward the acceptance of that idea. We are less clear than ever about what the real limits are to what we might think and do to make our lives better.

For instance, we may soon be able to change our natures. "Human nature" no longer describes a necessary principle of human limitation. Perhaps for the first time ever, we have to consider seriously whether what distinguishes us (so far) as human beings by nature is good and so worth preserving. Or perhaps we may be able to choose to fix our flawed natures through biotechnological eugenics and make them truly good. Whether either of these choices will be possible is still a matter of speculation, but it is very plausible speculation. There are reasonable foundations for hope and fear.

The good news is that we may well end up making neither choice. We hope that biotechnological eugenics will free us from the defects that make us miserable, but it is likely to make us more miserable. We fear that eugenic transformation will deprive us of our distinctively human features—our greatness and misery— by making us too happy or content. But the impulse that drives us to eugenics—the obsession to be free from fear and anxiety through calculation and control—will continue to heighten as biotechnology succeeds. The progress of biotechnology will make us more anxious and restless—less able really to enjoy; we will remain and in a way continue to become even more distinctively human. We will probably move further than ever from the wretched contentment of Nietzsche's last man or the subhuman contentment of Rousseau's natural man. Our future will probably not be "posthuman" in the sense that we will become either beasts or gods.[1]

Biotechnological progress, in fact, is more likely to be a continuation or enhancement of the bourgeois tendencies characteristic of modern American life than it is some sort of eugenic antidote for them. It is most probable that we will be unable either gratefully to accept what we have been given by nature or to make our natures truly good. This good news for human distinctiveness may well be terrible news for human happiness. That is why it *will* remain possible, if highly unlikely, that we will surrender what distinguishes us as human beings because it makes us unendurably miserable. If the "last man" comes (and I doubt he will), it will be not because bourgeois life is too easy but because it is too hard.

THE FAILURE OF HISTORY

What I just wrote seems to contradict what the great anticommunist dissidents Václav Havel and Aleksandr Solzhenitsyn said we learned or ought to have learned from the fall of communism. Communist ideology was defeated by human nature. Being and human being, Havel said, successfully and inevitably resisted human manipulation. The premise of Communist ideology is that human beings are not natural but historical beings. Human reality is socially constructed in the image of the prevailing form of the division of labor. Once we realize that human beings make themselves, then we are free to make a reality in which human misery disappears, so that government and religion simply wither away. We can create, so the feminists still say, an androgynous, egalitarian, nonrepressive, and nonoppressive society.

Marxism is flawed in many ways, but most of all by a fatal contradiction. Marx says that the human being is a historical being. He also says that the human perfection that is communism is the end of history. But if history ends, then the distinctively human being would also disappear. Marx claims that what distinguishes human beings is the social production of needs and the means to satisfy them through the division of labor, and that all other forms of human consciousness such as philosophy and art are merely reflections of human production. At the end of history, he says, the division of labor will disappear. But, then, on what foundation could the other distinctively human qualities or activities continue?[2]

Marx's optimism about our human future was the result of the inferiority of his thought to that of Rousseau, the first thinker to distinguish systematically between subhuman nature and human history. Rousseau says that prior even to the division of labor, human beings distinguished themselves by governing themselves by time and awareness of death, meaning each human being's own death. Human beings, accidentally and unfortunately, make themselves the only beings full of the misery that comes with the self-conscious awareness of one's own contingency and mortality. Historical beings become progressively more aware that their accidental existence as particular or self-conscious individuals cannot really be fitted into a natural world indifferent—or, rather, hostile—to their existence. And so human misery cannot be reduced to the result of economic exploitation. Economic exploitation, in fact, must largely be explained by distinctively human social passions that elude materialistic or natural forms of explanation.

For Rousseau, the end of history would have to be the end of all distinctively human qualities. We would become stupid animals content with the present and unmoved by the past or future, much less by contingency and mortality. The end of history would be good for our species; it would make eugenics unnecessary (and, of course, impossible) because what we had been given by nature (as opposed to history) would already be perfectly good. The end of history, if it comes, would be the result of our growing awareness that historical existence is a misfortune that has made us more restlessly miserable than anything else.

Thus, the Communists were both fanatics and failures because they were engaged in mission impossible. There cannot be a posthistorical world of human beings. Not only that, we know that the qualities that distinguish human beings cannot be eradicated through historical or political transformation. Francis Fukuyama once tried to convince us that history came to an end with communism's fall and the definitive global victory of liberal democracy. But he had to compromise his case by showing that the political regime of liberal democracy was satisfying to the three parts of the Socratic or distinctively human soul. Fukuyama never even tried to make the case that all distinctively human desire had withered away; he would have had to show, after all, that human beings no longer had any political or religious passion. Marx had already been right to say (against Hegel) that the problem of human misery cannot have a political solution.[3] It is true that brilliant social critics, from Philip Rieff to Alan Bloom to Richard Rorty, have claimed that the human capabilities to be moved by love and death, and so good and evil, are fading and that we are well on our way to becoming clever animals and nothing more.[4] But surely those who read their books cannot really believe them. Everyone knows that distinctively human thought, desire, and action remain with us, always, for better and worse.

SOCIOBIOLOGY

The idea of history or social construction—the idea that we freely create our distinctively human, social world over time—produces two contradictory and unrealistic conclusions. We might become like the other animals again, although we really do not know how to surrender our self-consciousness. Or we might free ourselves from natural reality altogether, although we really do not know how to overcome all of our bodily constraints. Both forms of social constructionism aim to free human beings from the realities of human suffering and death, but neither has a plausible path to success. Given social constructionism's unrealistic aspirations, it is no wonder that the idea of "human nature" would make a comeback.

Both the fall of communism and the advances in our knowledge of nature have caused the era of social constructionism to be displaced by the era of sociobiology.[5] It turns out that we are much more like the other animals than we thought, in the sense that we too are largely determined by nature. Our distinctively human qualities are also natural; as animals or natural beings, we are much more complex than we thought. We evolved from less complex forms of natural life. And we have learned from contemporary biology that the qualities our species has acquired through evolution can be best understood in terms of the requirements of the survival and physical flourishing of a certain kind of animal. The goal of sociobiology is to explain all that we do biologically or physically. Sociobiology frees us from the characteristically human illusion that we are more than natural (in the Darwinian sense) beings. We are smarter than but qualitatively no different from the other animals. All the social animals are given natural desires that correspond to the ways they pursue the biological goal that all life shares. We have distinctive natural capabilities but no special natural purpose or place.

As we have seen, partisans of sociobiology, such as the Fukuyama of *The Great Disruption*, have celebrated America's return to nature after the disastrous social constructionist projects of the 1960s. Human beings are returning to family, community, and church in response to their natural social needs, especially those connected with raising children. The free market and private property are once again flourishing and in fashion; socialism is contrary to our natural preference for our own.[6] But this return to nature is not to Aristotelian or Thomistic natural right, in the sociobiological account. Human beings do not really, by nature, desire to know the truth about God, the sociobiologists maintain. They are not moved by their awareness of time, death, and contingency toward goals radically different from those of the other animals. The truth, the sociobiologists say, is that human beings are at home in nature. Thinkers such as Pascal and Nietzsche who thought we longed to be somehow "redeemed" from this world, who thought that human beings experienced themselves most truthfully as homeless or alienated, were deluded.[7] It is hard to tell whether the true teaching of sociobiology is that we *are* or that we *ought* to be at home in this world.

The sociobiologists say that in the era of sociobiology marriage will no longer be understood to have a sacred or transcendent dimension. Church will merely be for comfort and community and not to learn about in order to know and love God. The corresponding reduction in human love will be more in line with the biological requirements of the animal. The sociobiological imagination inflames human eros much less than do the historical or philosophical or religious imaginations. It deprives love of the illusion of eternity in the service of both truth and well-being.

Sociobiologists tend to sputter when trying to explain why such an illusion once existed. The capacity to be seduced by illusion, E. O. Wilson contends, turned out to be an evolutionary advantage for our species.[8] But that makes it hard to understand why he spends so much time trying to dispel illusion. Perhaps because, as we saw in the previous chapter, he would like to provide a substitute illusion: "Preferring a search for objective reality over revelation is another way of satisfying religious hunger."[9] Belief in "the gods," thinks Wilson, can be replaced by belief in "biology" (or really the integration of physics and biology). We can be totally at home in the world, he promises, if philosophy—that is, speculation about the unknown—is replaced by unified and comprehensive science. For then the mystery of the human being will turn out not to be a mystery at all. The truth is that we are well integrated into the cosmos; there is nothing really different or displaced about us. But then, why does no other species need the self-help that Wilson's "consilience" might provide?

Thoughtful defenders of the sociobiological or evolutionary view, such as Carl Sagan, agree with the existentialists that individual lives have no natural significance.[10] If we have a point of pride as a species, it is in our discovery of how puny, insignificant, and alone we are. Evolution, so to speak, cares not at all for individuals, but only about genes and species. Nature selects for life, not death. But it does not select for the lives of particular human beings. Individuals must be disposed of soon after they reproduce so that life as such might flourish. Death, from this view, is the price we pay for sex, for producing new life. The individual's perverse and futile effort to choose against his own death by choosing against sex or at least reproduction is a choice against the only way that the species and life itself can flourish indefinitely, if not eternally.

Sagan suggests that we turn our attention away from the individual—our insignificant, disposable selves—to the species as a whole. We now know that there is nothing we can do to save ourselves, but we might devote ourselves to fending off the species' eventual destruction. So far, we human beings have depended on this planet for our survival. That is a pretty precarious situation. An asteroid might end life here any time, and we should not be deceived about how reliable the sun has been so far. It is unlikely that the planet will become uninhabitable in any of our lifetimes, but we should think about the species' future, not just our own or even our children's. Our effort should therefore be devoted to populating other planets, ensuring our species' survival should any particular planet become unfit for life. Making conscious the purpose—the perpetuation of the species—nature unconsciously gave us all, according to Sagan, solves the problem of human meaning in our time.

But Sagan's suggestion, of course, does not really help us

much. Our devotion to the species is necessarily unconscious, and it is actually unnatural to make it conscious. Even the sociobiologists tell us that we consciously prefer ourselves and our own. We cannot effectively devote ourselves to all human beings now living, much less to those to be born at some distant time in the future. Nature wants us to reproduce, spread our genes, raise our young, and die. That is what is best for the species.[11] But human beings—except, perhaps, compulsive sperm donors—are not consciously concerned with gene-spreading.[12] Few of us would choose a shorter life just to make sure that our genes live on. We love and would die for our children, but everyone knows that that is not the same thing. We would also die for our spouses and our friends and even our fellow citizens, people who do not even carry our genes. Not only might we also die for God, but we long for what nature does not grant us—personal immortality. Because we cannot help but have "non-Darwinian values," we can and often do choose both longevity and death—among many other things—over fecundity.[13] And so sociobiology, even at this elementary level, is no guide for how we should act. Sagan's suggestion that we devote ourselves to the species is actually more arbitrary than devoting ourselves to our country. The latter is more connected to a natural need shared by members of our species.

Sociobiology, precisely because it has little or nothing to say about the individual's fear or anxiety in the face of his own death, can only, contrary to its intention, heighten his sense of contingency. Human experience does not disappear just because the experts deny that it exists. Sociobiology is certainly no antidote to existentialism; it makes the individual who clings to his existence seem more absurd than ever before. It only seems to be conservative or traditionalist in its affirmation of the naturalness of social institutions, sexual differences, and so forth. It does not convince us that we do or should experience our natural existence as good. Nicholas Wade correctly states the core sociobiological conclusion: "Evolution shaped humans and human nature, yet it is a blind and pitiless process."[14] What is good about being the plaything of such a process, one that is so coldly indifferent to me?

Sociobiology's failure as a program for human self-help can be seen in its kinship to the idea that history has ended. The sociobiologist claims that there is no qualitative distinction that separates humans from other animals and that all accounts of human freedom from nature are illusions. The end-of-history theorist should say that sociobiology becomes true as history ends, for then we become just one of the animals or wholly a part of nature again. The sociobiologist errs only in thinking that his account was always true. As long as the human was a historical being, the sociobiologist was wrong. The return to nature occurs—the great disruption is over—with the end of history.

Yet we know that sociobiology is not completely true for the same reason we know that history has not ended. Human beings are still moved to thought, perversity, and misery by love and death; they are still anxious in the face of the contingency of their very being, and they cannot experience themselves, as the other animals do, as completely at home in nature or this world. The truth is largely the opposite of what sociobiologists and end-of-history theorists think: Rich, smart, and free Americans may be more anxious and death-haunted—or less at home in the world—than any of their predecessors. At the very least, they are the most bourgeois human beings ever. Unlike the other animals, they are obsessed with health and safety, and they plan incessantly to minimize chance or contingency in their lives. They even have difficulty loving their children in the present, because they are so concerned with protecting them and planning for their futures.

The Greatness and Misery of the Bourgeois Bohemian

This view seems to contradict the observation made by sociologist Alan Wolfe and others that Americans have become promiscuous nonjudgmentalists, that even middle-class Americans have absorbed the sixties "do your own thing" ethic.[15] And as we have seen, David Brooks and others have shown that our elite has managed to reconcile anti-establishment bohemianism with the pursuit of wealth and productivity.[16] At first glance, it seems that the bourgeois bohemian is the result of a ridiculous and superficial reconciliation of a tension that gives modern society its human vitality. But the Bobo, on closer inspection, is much more bourgeois than bohemian.

Bobos certainly find no solace in what they learn in school about evolution's intending them to be replaced quickly for the species' sake. They do not want to think of themselves as insignificant parts of an accidental process. But they find themselves unable to believe in a God who can really redeem them. I must disagree with Brooks's suggestion that Bobo lives are marked by nothing but the contemptible pursuit of diversions meant to keep them from ever considering questions about the nature and destiny of mankind. The Bobos really do know and in some measure live in the light of the truth, that nature is hostile to their particular existences. Their diversions do not work particularly well. There is an air of desperation about their calculation and their inability to achieve serene self-denial.

The Bobos are unwilling and unable to take solace in the thought that nature cannot be defeated. If evolution is true, it must, if possible, be conquered by human will on behalf of individual lives. Those who are against cruelty and for human dignity cannot rest content with nature as it is now. We cannot be nonjudgmental about nature!

THE ERA OF BIOTECHNOLOGY

The Bobos live at war with the nature that wants to kill them and their own. Their diet, exercise, hard work, and money have already extended human life by an extra decade. But they are still all too aware of the limitations of even their best efforts. That is why they will welcome the move from the sociobiological to the biotechnological era. The era of sociobiology lasted only for a moment. It was based on understanding, not changing, what nature or evolution had given us. But now we know that human beings can change their natures—that is, can modify their genetic inheritances. At this point we are confined mostly to speculation about how much can actually be changed through genetic engineering. But it seems clear that, to some extent at least, we will someday be able to free ourselves from the genetic lottery that cruelly condemns some to disease, misery, stupidity, physical deformity, and early death and rewards others unfairly with brains, strength, health, happiness, and longevity. The misery of the Bobos is evidence that what we have been given by nature is somehow defective and that the nature described by evolutionary biology is not worth defending.

We have left the period of unconscious evolution, when nature required us to sacrifice ourselves blindly for our species. We are entering the period of conscious or engineered evolution; we will change our natures with the benefit of the individual in mind. Rather than be determined by our genes, we will bring our genes under our control. That assertion of human freedom is more evidence, of course, that sociobiology is not completely true. What nature has given us will become progressively less important in shaping our lives. We will become freer and, it is tempting to say, more historical beings. We will finally impose on nature our historical or socially constructed goals. Social construction will become more true as the sociobiological account becomes less so.

Human nature triumphed over Communist ideology, but biotechnology may change human nature. Utopian eugenics is finally a realistic proposal for human reform. As E. O. Wilson says, the childhood of human existence, when we were controlled by Mother Nature and Father God, is over; we now have the power and responsibility to decide what we are going to become. In coming to understand that biotechnology has liberated human beings from the constraints of natural evolution, Wilson—the father of sociobiology—became a Nietzschean. Evolution, he says, is becoming conscious and volitional.[17] Because of our defects or sinfulness, we had heretofore thought we needed God's grace really to change. But now we may well be able to fix what is wrong with us without any divine assistance.

EUGENICS AND INDEFINITE LONGEVITY

But how is human nature to be improved? Just because we have new technology, new means, and new equipment, does not mean that we have any idea what to do with it. What do we want to become? The failure of social construction and sociobiology to make us at home in nature causes us to think that what Rousseau regarded as the human being's historical misfortune—his anxious, restless misery—is his natural condition. It turns out that Pascal may have been right; our contingency and our finitude make life almost unendurable without God. The bourgeois person wants to be freed from the misery of knowing about and working against his contingency and mortality. He knows too well that he will die—and at any moment. So biotechnology should extend individual human lives and reduce the dependence of our lives on forces beyond our control. Biotechnology should accelerate the trend long established by modern science and technology. The more we control, the premise is, the less we will fear.

But we also know that if biotechnology is used only to push back death and eliminate genetically based diseases, human misery may actually increase. Objectively, the Bobos may be freer from death and disease than human beings ever have been, but they may be more obsessed with health than human beings ever have been. The more we fend off death in response to fear, the more fearful we seem to become. For one thing, we have more to lose. For another, death comes to seem less necessary or more accidental. It seems more terrible as it becomes more avoidable. And so the practice of the death-defying virtues such as courage, or even ordinary risk-taking, seems more reckless. The coming of indefinite longevity—through the biotechnological, eugenic overcoming of the genetic basis of our natural deterioration—would make death more a matter of chance—because less a matter of necessity—than ever.

If the necessity of death were pushed back indefinitely in each individual case, we surely should still be governed by the fact that we have to go sometime. But with little or no idea of when that time might be, necessity would be quite blurred in one's own particular case. Anxiety about the contingent or increasingly indefinite character of one's own being would grow. Indefinite longevity—as opposed to actual freedom from death—might well make not only human dignity but ordinary human sanity very difficult.

To the extent that death and disease leave the realm of necessity and become accidents to be avoided, human beings are compelled to calculate incessantly about health and safety. Chance can only be resisted by control or planning; the conquest of natural necessity actually intensifies this distinctively human necessity. When we consider the Bobos, we can already see what planning does to human enjoyment, love, and happiness. They claim only to engage in safe sex; Brooks reports that they have even reduced S&M to consensual rules. What is love without dangerous liaisons and other risky business? And what is love without consciousness of the hard responsibilities of birth and death? Strangely, planning about sex with health and safety in mind seems bound to bring reproductive freedom to an end.

The End of Reproductive Freedom

Having children is a way of choosing death. We bring our replacements into the world, as nature intends. Birth without death, obviously, would soon produce a planet that is truly overpopulated. Gloomy scientists not so long ago predicted that the modern science that kept children from dying and allowed most people to get old would create a crisis of overpopulation. That has not happened so far, especially in the most advanced countries, where the birth rate has fallen below the rate of replacement. In those countries the population is getting older and children are getting rarer. Arguably, that is because people are more reluctant than ever to embrace the naturalness or givenness of their timely demise.

Medical science has already won significant victories against evolution. People are on average living far beyond the period of their reproductive utility. So the diseases of old age—the means nature employs to get us out of the way if our environments become too good—are now the most common causes of death. But even they are yielding slowly but steadily to medical advances. Some might argue that our decline in fertility is the way evolution has dealt with our increase in longevity. That is certainly what happens with the other animals. But our decline in fertility has happened too quickly for it to be natural in the evolutionary or unconscious sense. Rather, we are consciously choosing against our natural fertility; we are choosing for our own long lives and against the lives of others—those of our potential children. Our distinctively human choices are being made against natural evolution and for personal preservation. We may be even choosing against life itself: "The inescapable conclusion" reached by our leading experts on aging "is that the biological clocks that are present within organisms exist for one reason only—to support life, not destroy it."[18]

For now, increases in longevity remain compatible with reproductive freedom. But we can imagine that government will eventually have to step in. Not everyone who wants to have a baby will be able to have one. Will those allowed that privilege be chosen by lot or by genetic criteria? The latter would make more sense if we are employing eugenics to enhance health and safety. There would also be a progressively more complete divorce between recreational and procreative sex; procreative sex may disappear altogether. If eugenics eventually advances beyond therapeutic abortion to the actual design of babies, then it will make no sense to allow conception to occur the old-fashioned way. For babies to benefit from all the genetic therapy available, "[p]arents would probably need to go through the processes now used in fertility clinics, where oocytes are harvested from the woman's ovaries and fertilized in a dish with her partner's sperm."[19] Who would not want their baby to have such benefits just to enjoy the pleasure or pride of natural procreation?

And would government be able to allow such irresponsible behavior, given its risks? Any genetically defective baby so conceived might well have every right to sue the parents or government that allowed him to be born.

Sex under today's regime of reproductive freedom may eventually become sex freed from the possibility of reproduction. The absolutely free choice to reproduce or not (reproductive autonomy) seems to be an unstable middle point between being guided or determined by nature and reproductive eugenics. What would life be like if most people were allowed or required to live more than a century without becoming parents? Would monogamy any longer make sense or even be possible? Is a sign of our eugenic future the unfortunate fate of healthy and wealthy old people living in retirement communities, compelled to live lives largely detached from their families and filled with nothing but recreation? Their lives are certainly not easy; nor are they free from anxiety and depression. I think they require a new kind of near-heroic virtue to live in light of the truth and with dignity. We now know how to increase the years of the old, but we do not know how to help them love their many extra days.[20]

DEMOCRACY AS RULE BY THE OLD

To say that democracy culminates in rule by the old contradicts the great thinkers and all human experience thus far. The Socratic view (*Republic*, book 8) is that democracy is rule by the young. Tradition and respect for authority tend to fade in democratic regimes, and so the old no longer serve as role models. The soul seems a weightless and unnecessary idea in a democracy, so that all that remains to distinguish human beings are their bodies. Being old becomes nothing more than a defective form of being young, which is why the old slavishly if futilely imitate the young. The young certainly seem to rule in America today; we are obsessed with our bodies, and the standards of fashion set by youth meet with little resistance. The old scare us because they remind us of death and little else. The more bourgeois a society, the more that signs of the inevitability of death and dying become too hard to bear.

Few really believe that we will be able to reject biotechnological innovations that give us all many more years, even at the expense of children or the young. We are certainly not about to embrace some antitechnological, pro-death policy. I doubt—despite some disturbing trends concerning euthanasia—that suicide among the old will become required, strongly encouraged, or even common. After all, they will become a large voting bloc, and I doubt that their lives will become so miserable that they will rush to their deaths. Furthermore, what medical science can do it will do; it rightly sees its job as keeping us alive and healthy.

Perhaps rule by the old will at least cause us to come to terms with our mortality more effectively than the rule by the young has. But perhaps not: The ugliest thing about the democracy described by Socrates is that rule by the young is rooted in a childish denial of the necessity, and so the morality, that must or should govern every human life. Now we expect the young to be childish, to believe that they will live forever. Uglier by far would be the rule of old people who childishly embrace every technological innovation that allows them to fend off death just a little bit longer. Their childishness may be the source of a world without children, with what at one natural level gives death its meaning. The feckless democracy described by Socrates is at least charming on its surface. The one produced by the eugenic democracy of the future, on the other hand, may be driven by the ugliness of hyperbourgeois calculation.

Regenerative biotechnology designed to keep the old from having anything like a fixed lifespan can only very ambiguously be called eugenic. Can our species really continue to exist in what is close to a postsexual era? Can we really negate the core of our evolutionary inheritance? Can we really act, by ending natural reproduction, to bring natural evolution to an end? As the homey Wendell Berry observes, no breeder of sheep would ever consent to cloning. That interference with nature "is a way to stall the sheep's lineage and make it unimprovable."[21] The least we can do is imagine the resentment of young people compelled to be much more concerned with caring for the old, while being deprived or almost deprived of the joy of caring for children. Surely it is natural that our love for the old be inseparable from our love for the young.

EUGENICS AND SELECTIVE ABORTION

So far, even sophisticated Americans still have children. They usually plan to have them, and they certainly love them. They typically have just one or two. Despite their unprecedented wealth, the burden of raising more would be just too much. Thus, the pressure is on—both stemming from, and contrary to, the impulse of love—to make the few children they have more perfect than children have ever been. The bourgeois obsession with calculation and control—mixed with love of one's own—points in the direction of eugenics.

Genetic testing of the fetus in the uterus now allows us to choose against lives that would be marred by severe genetic effects, to choose against babies being born with Down syndrome, Tay-Sachs disease, cystic fibrosis, and so forth. So far, we cannot choose to instill those human traits we find desirable, but we can keep babies who have undesirable ones from being born. Because we now can choose against what we regard as a low quality of life, successful eugenics has in fact already commenced. We can, in fact, not only choose against those traits which anyone would regard as undesirable, but against any trait at all so long as it can be discovered in utero. We are clearly against the Indian and Chinese practice of aborting girls just because they are girls. But there is evidence that we are increasingly open to using abortion to achieve gender balance in a family. If we are only going to have two children, why not be certain that one is a boy and the other a girl?[22] If the ideal of gender balance causes Bobo parents to have two children instead of one, perhaps the resulting abortion(s) is a small price to pay.

The right thing, according to the reigning principles of reproductive freedom, remains a personal preference, one for which no one can offer the pregnant woman authoritative guidance. Still, experts are nevertheless available to offer advice, and they in turn are guided by the new scholarly field of bioethics. Bioethicists say that it is cruel to choose just for life; nobody should choose misery and pain for another.[23] We have to choose, they say, for quality of life. But their conception of "quality of life" turns out to be maddeningly subjective and surrounded by unhelpful platitudes about dignity, meaning, and pointless suffering.[24] Almost none of those with severe genetic defects are consigned to nothing but pain and misery, after all, while on the other hand every human being experiences some pain and misery no matter what. Suffering sometimes gives us, and sometimes deprives us of, dignity; a life with no suffering at all would be just as undignified as one so full of suffering that thought was impossible.

We also have every right, the bioethicists say, to think about the quality of our own lives, which would purportedly be enhanced by a perfect child and decreased by, say, one with Down syndrome. But when we think about it, whether the lives of family members would really be impoverished by caring for such a loving and needy person—not to mention one who probably does not suffer more than most of us—is certainly open to question. Even if a genetic defect condemns a child to a short life, can we really say that the extreme measures we now take to shield children and even adults from suffering and death really improve the quality of their lives? Surely anything that keeps us from living like real adults—like people aware of the dependence and mortality we all share—impoverishes us. Sharing death and grief—the inevitable result of love—is arguably what makes a family a family.[25]

How are we to know what makes a life not worth living or not worth caring for? Women today must answer this question in deciding whether to allow a child to be born with a genetically based disease with which they often have little or no experience. Thank God (or nature), their judgment is bound to be shaped somewhat by love. But it will also often be distorted by the common but mistaken view that people with severe disabilities are always miserable. And the experts will encourage women to think that terminating life, from that view, is often an act of love. The genetic testing of fetuses, as Lori B. Andrews reports, may be turning the typical woman's view of her pregnancy from "a normal healthy experience into a pathological condition."[26]

Very few women, of course, end up learning that they are carrying a fetus with a significant genetic defect. But studies show that tested women still tend to think of pregnancy as a risk and overestimate their chances for some sort of abnormal birth. Pregnancy has become a more tentative experience. Women recoil from bonding with their babies until the results are in—and even good results do not reassure them all that much. It used to be, as Andrews explains, that the chance a child might be born with a disability was "viewed as a normal risk of reproduction, or even as God's will."[27] The risk was bearable because it came with the territory, and the baby burdened with the disability was regarded as a lovable gift from nature or God.

Genetic testing makes pregnancy objectively less risky, but it also creates the perception that it is more so. As we bring birth more under our control, we are increasingly aware of how incomplete our control really is. Parenting, as one sociologist has noted, has become more paranoid.[28] Even a perfect baby might die or become disabled at any time, despite our best efforts. Our obsession with calculating the quality of our children's lives arises largely out of love, but it also comes at the expense of love. All human beings are imperfect, contingent, and very limited in their possibilities; nonetheless, our first thought used to be that it is good that we all exist. If our "personhood" depends on our autonomy, then none of us is really fully a person, and surely our capacity to be loved is inseparable from our ineradicable dependence on nature, each other, and God. But our eugenic project is based on the thought that our limitations are neither necessary nor lovable.

I should emphasize that I am not arguing for any particular personal choice or public policy at this point. Women, obviously, may be even more anxious if they refuse genetic testing. And it might seem cruel to have the law compel a woman to have a child with Tay-Sachs disease. My only point is that the new dimension biotechnology gives to the modern quest for personal autonomy or freedom from contingency and dependence increasingly isolates and disorients individuals. It might seem comforting that the experts say that it is essential that eugenic decisions remain in personal hands. The danger comes, experience shows, when governments, such as Hitler's, get involved. But from another perspective, it is very disturbing to have the quality of the human future in the unregulated hands of individuals. It is genuinely utopian to believe that government will not get involved in the eugenic project, and only a dogmatic libertarian could really believe that individuals will and ought to be allowed to construct a designer future for themselves and their children.

OUR HUMAN FUTURE

Biotechnological eugenics, as I have described it, is certainly eugenic in the sense that it will allow people to live longer and healthier lives. It is good for the self-preservation and comfort of the particular human individual, and that is apparently the standard that will animate conscious, volitional evolution. Whether it is good according to natural or unconscious evolution is doubtful. By choosing for the individual and against new life—and so choosing against sexual reproduction—we make the natural evolution of our species nearly impossible. But surely what we can do for ourselves will be better than what nature ever did for us, or at least the doctrine of evolutionary biology allows us to believe.

It is not clearly the promise of biotechnology to make human life more enjoyable or happy. Biotechnology also works against the generally acknowledged primary compensations that we have for our mortality—love, family, and children. Through biotechnology we will find ourselves progressively more freed from the responsibilities that have a strong natural foundation and give life natural direction. Even religious freedom and duty may have to give way to the best ways we have to bring birth and health under our control.

Leon Kass recognizes that "the implicit goal of biotechnology . . . could well be said to be the reversal of the Fall, and a return of man to the hedonic and immortal existence of the Garden of Eden." But the creature shaped by biotechnology could not really have the simple innocence of the sinless, unflawed original human beings. Somehow "[h]e will have to be simultaneously an innocent like Adam and the technological wizard who keeps the Garden running."[29] His innocence will not be given to him by God or nature but will be his own technological construction. He, not God, will be responsible for its perpetuation. As a biotechnologically shaped human being, he will necessarily know too much and have too much to do to experience himself as either innocently happy or immortal.

Walker Percy describes in *The Thanatos Syndrome* an experiment in which a few scientists deprive a large population of human beings of their experiences of self-consciousness through chemical treatment. The scientists exempt themselves from the treatment, imagining that their own human disorders or alienation can be cured by controlling subhuman beings, beings who have been deprived of the spirit of resistance to tyranny. What the scientists discover is that they are not satisfied. They have not really raised themselves up to gods, and they are not really satisfied by being able to exploit beings who cannot recognize or love them for who they are. In other words, no biotechnological solution to the problem of human misery is possible unless everyone submits to its consciousness-negating treatment.[30] But most of us, I think, would, in our pride, exempt ourselves. We may hate our distinctively human misery, but we still do not want to be reduced to mere bodies. We surely do not view our quests for perfect children or indefinite longevity as the quests of thoughtless animals. And they are not! That is why I tend to think there will be something irreducibly perverse, thank God, about the consequences of the utopian eugenics of our time.

Chapter 9

Libertarian Fantasy and Statist Reality

To this point, it has been the libertarians more than the old-fashioned liberals or conservatives who have embraced our biotechnological, designer, eugenic future. Libertarians have changed; they've become more cheerful and optimistic. They used to point nostalgically to a past when government was small and people were self-reliant. They used to view the growth of government as more or less irresistible, a cancer caused by democratic envy and the average man's servile preference for security over liberty. But now libertarians believe, and with considerable evidence, that the future is on their side. The free market and political freedom have defeated socialism. A Democratic president signed the bill ending welfare as we knew it, and he was the best friend big, multinational corporations ever had in the White House. We have all witnessed the liberating power of technology in the Information Age. Nobody knows how to regulate the Internet effectively; it seemingly cannot be constrained by national boundaries or political will. It may also be the case that there is no way to regulate biotechnology effectively. One nation may pass some laws—and then watch the breakthroughs occur somewhere else.

September 11th reminded us that the state is not about to wither away. The security-conscious bourgeois bohemians David Brooks describes gratefully accept the protection our government gives them. But that protection, in fact, costs them very little; it is not a real limit on their liberty. The war against terror, so far, has mainly reinforced our opinion that high-tech experts—various kinds of special forces who somehow serve us without dominating us—control the world. They will not be able to protect us perfectly against the dark side of technological progress. But September 11th showed us that we can live well enough with the occasional terrorist attack. Americans have not been tested or even traumatized enough to stall the libertarian drift in their nation and in their souls. Recent neoconservative proclamations that the combination of terrorism and biotechnology has fatally discredited American libertarianism have been bold but quite incredible.

By libertarian we no longer mean members of a tiny third party or even a faction in the Republican Party. There is a developing libertarian consensus in America. Bill Clinton, that brainy "new" Democrat, was a double-barreled libertarian—all for both the free-market and personal permissiveness. And he gushed eloquently about the divine potential for individual control promised by the success of the human genome project. The middle class is now all for moral freedom or autonomy; few believe in government-sponsored redistribution any more. Certainly sophisticated Americans today—though technically children of the sixties—have little interest in government-sponsored or personal charity. They believe they deserve what they have, and their religious involvement promotes inward serenity more than it does service to others.

It is tempting to say that we are all libertarians now. That is an exaggeration, of course. There are religious moralists in both parties, and there is a growing Christian counterculture in America. But the premise of much of that counterculture—by which I mean the homeschoolers and so forth—is that America has become too permissive to be reformed politically, at least for now. It may be possible to rouse the majority of Americans to reject the cloning of human beings. But that seems to be the only biotechnological issue that now grabs their imagination. Certainly neither party is set to wage war seriously against genetic testing or killing embryos for research. It is hard to see from what quarter serious opposition to utopian or libertarian eugenics is going to come.[1]

The libertarians now speak of a designer future, a time when we will be able to arrange our bodies and our souls as we please. Their claim is that the dangers connected with eugenics will disappear when government is kept out of the whole business. One prominent bioethicist, Philip Kitcher, is optimistic about the implementation of what he calls utopian eugenics. People will keep their freedom to choose whether or not to reproduce or have abortions. But most people will choose well because there will be government-sponsored education concerning the consequences of their choices. In school they will learn not to have abortions for racist or sexist reasons. They will also learn that the abortion choice must be based on the quality of life of both the baby that might be born and the persons affected by the new person's existence. They will be informed of the resources that must be diverted to, for example, Down syndrome kids from the unfortunate poor who might really be helped to live a full or high-quality life.

In the utopian future, women will be gently persuaded to have abortions for eugenic reasons, but never coerced. In almost every case, all they will need to choose well, Kitcher says, is to know that "it is permissible, even praiseworthy, to do what we can to prevent human lives whose quality will inevitably be sadly diminished."[2] It is not praiseworthy to choose according to one's inclinations—according to love—alone. What would the consequences be if everyone were that self-indulgent? Still, Kitcher's future society will be humane enough to care for those born with genetically based disabilities, even if the experts recommended against their birth.[3]

Surely this description of the future is too utopian to be plausible. The experts will blur the line between persuasion and coercion. They already have. HMOs, Wesley Smith has reported, are already requiring genetic testing before they will cover the cost of pregnancies. They are already telling women they will pay for aborting but not birthing genetically defective fetuses.[4] The pressure to abort for the good of the fetus and society is already intense, especially but not only for women who are poor or naïve. And will people really be good-humored about their tax or insurance dollars caring for Down syndrome kids whom the experts say need not and should not have been born? Those with such genetic defects will surely seem much more monstrous or less properly human than they have until now. These problems characteristically elude the libertarian imagination. Libertarians tend to assume as a matter of course that the free and reasonable, or "designer," mind will choose abortion for eugenic reasons. For what improves the quality of life is really in the self-interest of everyone.

Once genetic therapy is available actually to improve embryos and fetuses and in some measure design babies, the line between persuasion and coercion will likely disappear. At that point, genetic testing will surely be required, perhaps also the implantation of genetically enhanced embryos into the uterus. Eventually, it may be possible to enhance the quality of babies not only through choosing the best of parents' genetic materials but also through the introduction of enhancements not present in either parent. Parents will be able to choose whatever features they please for their babies, and at that point we might object that parents will be able to wield tyrannical power over their children's very being.[5] But if parents ever have that power, it will only be for a moment. Will parents not be compelled to choose the best available features for their children in terms of health, longevity, intelligence, strength, and so forth? Parental tyranny may well be limited to matters of mere preference, such as hair and eye color. When we read today about two deaf lesbian parents who want to choose deafness for their child, we immediately exclaim that "there ought to be a law!" And there will be a law. We cannot let human perversity and ideology deprive our children of the best possible quality of lives.

Even those who have no moral objection to biotechnological eugenics, such as the libertarian darling Lee M. Silver (author of *Remaking Eden*), worry that it might create two classes, one with the money to design babies and one without that advantage.[6] The result might be the widening of the gap between the haves and have-nots until we really become, in effect, two different species. But I think it is far more likely that whatever reproductive biotechnology is available will be made—at least by the U.S. government—available to all. The poor will demand it, and the rich will feel too guilty not to provide it. The limit to justice here will probably be our national boundaries, at least for a long while. For that reason, even the libertarian Silver believes that in the name of preserving the egalitarian integrity of our species we will eventually have to embrace world government.

Our most respectable—that is, egalitarian—ethicists, such as John Rawls and Ronald Dworkin, say that the power of government may be used to reduce the power of chance in human affairs, to reduce the plight of the unfortunate, in order to create an egalitarian society. So far, one limit to equality that no free government has been able to address very effectively is the diversity and inequality that marks human nature. Some people are naturally or genetically better equipped to acquire and enjoy the good things of life than others. They do not really deserve in the sense of earning for themselves these natural advantages. It is not fair that I am smart enough to make money typing this stuff. It is equally unfair that I have never had the height or strength or hang time required to make money playing basketball. From one view, I have been given by nature the opportunity for a fairly high quality of life; from another I have been condemned to a relatively low quality.

Libertarians believe that it is their right to defend natural inequality and diversity against government. They do not deny that I have not earned what I have been given by nature. But, they say, what I am is largely determined by what I do with what I have been given. What nature has given me is mine. So libertarians believe that women may do what they please with their bodies. They may either kill or enhance their fetuses in whatever way they can. The libertarian view of individual liberty depends on a more or less constant human nature; natural differences must be unchangeable facts. We are stuck with the fact that our chances in life are determined in some large measure by a genetic lottery, and we cannot be held responsible for the outcome of that lottery, for what we have been given. There is little that can or should be done if the clever get more than the stupid because the stupid cannot be made clever.

But what if that lottery could be brought to an end? What if enhancement eugenics could offer everyone the best brains and bodies available? Nature would no longer be a barrier to either egalitarian justice or universal excellence. Would we not have to choose this possibility, even at the expense of human diversity? Libertarians and egalitarians would both agree that it would be foolish to choose against it. And libertarians would have at least a very difficult time arguing against government making this very basic benefit available to everyone. Otherwise, selfish human decisions—instead of blind, pitiless, intractable nature—would too obviously be responsible for making some less competitive in the race of life.

The result is that in the eugenic future government—working with expert scientists—would determine the necessary characteristics of babies. The egalitarian utopia that seems almost coequal with human speculation would become real. We would have equality in excellence and equality in mediocrity at the same time. If everyone had the strength of an NFL lineman and the height of an NBA center, then we would all be the same—mediocre—athletically. The same, of course, could be said about brains and mathematics. Libertarians and egalitarians would have to agree that it is good to be free from the cruelty of the natural lottery. But how could there be human freedom, understood as greatness or individuality, with little remaining natural diversity? It might still be possible; nature— in the sense of genetic endowment—will never determine everything about an individual's existence. But to be genuinely free would be much more difficult than ever.

The boredom and restlessness associated with a combination of the libertarian view of morality with government-imposed natural homogeneity and mediocrity could conceivably be unendurable. Aldous Huxley observed that "In the course of evolution nature has gone to endless trouble to see that every individual is unlike every other individual," and so "Any culture which. . . seeks to standardize the human individual . . . commits an outrage against man's biological nature." Huxley's remark concerned the great project of the twentieth century: "the theoretical reduction of unmanageable multiplicity to comprehensible unity becomes the practical reduction of human diversity to subhuman uniformity."[7] What if our biological nature could be changed so that we could all be, so to speak, very human and still very uniform? Because the addition of various designer features would not change our natures in every respect, can we say that the outrage against our human natures would be even greater?

From one view, the new eugenics will liberate the poor and the unenlightened from their oppression by nature. From another, some of them at least will be subjected to unprecedented tyranny. They will no longer be free to act on their deviant moral and religious opinions.

Even the author of *Brave New World* worried far more about dysgenics than eugenics in our time. "And what about," he asked, "the congenitally insufficient organisms, whom our medical and our social services now preserve so that they may propagate their kind? To help the unfortunate is obviously good. But the wholesale transmission to our descendants of the results of unfavorable mutations, and the progressive contamination of the genetic pool from which the members of our species will have to draw, are no less obviously bad."[8] Huxley's genetic concern expressed here is pre-biotechnological and obviously suspect. He thought that the reproducing and flourishing of the unfortunate—those who are mostly losers in the genetic lottery—was having a bad effect on the quality of life of our species. So Huxley suggests that we think about various ways of keeping them from propagating so much. Few would now endorse his obvious elitism and perhaps racism, not to mention his willingness to constrain human liberty.

But as the biotechnological or eugenic era progresses, government will still probably end up dictating to the unfortunate and unenlightened how and how often (if at all!) they may procreate. Reproductive freedom will eventually, and undeniably, have unacceptably dysgenic consequences. Even the moral or religious arguments such as Catholics or Mormons might make would have to be disregarded. Ironically, those believers—having already lost the pro-life battle to technological imperatives—will be forced to become pro-choicers. That is, they will at least want the freedom to choose when and how to have babies, even if everyone else is killing and enhancing them. And they probably will end up losing again to the biotechnological version of the quality of life argument used by our contemporary pro-choicers.

Government will make designer genetic engineering readily available to raise the poor up to the level of the rich. But it will also require that everyone stop breeding indiscriminately and submit to genetic testing and manipulation. Otherwise, society will be stuck with hordes of kids who will seem to be grossly genetically defective. Not only will they have preventable diseases, they will be much stupider and weaker than normal or enhanced children. So even parents with brains but moral and religious objections to government policy probably will not be left alone. We are just beginning to see why a designer utopia fueled by libertarian premises ends up with unprecedented government determination of the most basic choices that shape our lives.

Ronald Dworkin (in *Sovereign Virtue*) admits, seemingly with no regret, that the advantages of biotechnology must supplant the right of choice: "Suppose it were possible to correct serious defects of different kinds of embryos, for example, either through genetic engineering or more conventional forms of therapy. Then the principle of special responsibility would no longer justify allowing a pregnant woman to refuse tests to discover such a defect in the embryo she carries."[9] The interests of others limit our liberty. But, according to Dworkin, embryos have no interests (and so abortion is permissible). A woman, though, must consider the interests of the baby to be born. The only two legitimate choices available to the pregnant woman are therefore abortion or submission to testing and therapy. We must do everything we can not to leave lives to chance, and so we can't let women choose to be reckless about having babies. Dworkin's position leads inexorably to government regulation of personal reproductive decisions.

Dworkin admits that "modern democracies" tend to embrace the "flat principle of bodily integrity." Women should not be compelled to submit to any procedure, especially when their objection might be founded on "religious conviction." But "the principle of bodily integrity," he concludes, "may . . . be one of those artifacts of conventional morality that seemed well justified before the possibilities suggested by modern genetic medicine were plausibly imagined, but not after."[10] The right to choose, in other words, is not natural but merely a convention that happened to be appropriate for a particular and now-disappearing level of technology. So too, apparently, is government's deference to religious conviction a mere matter of convention. Even if we are repulsed by Dworkin's conclusion, we must admit that he sees further than our libertarians.

One expert, Robert L. Sinsheimer, claims that there is a key distinction between the old eugenics of, say, the Nazis and the new eugenics of designer biotechnology: "The old eugenics would have required a continual selection of breeding of the fit, and a culling of the unfit. The new eugenics would permit in principle the conversion of the unfit to the highest genetic level." Fitness for all is, of course, less murderous and more egalitarian. But "the conversion of the unfit" would have to be coercive. Everyone will have to rise to what is generally regarded as "the highest genetic level."[11] Those who choose against it—at least for their children—would have to be regarded as unfit to choose. Nobel Prize winner James Watson explains why freedom must give way: "Working intelligently and wisely to see that good genes dominate as many lives as possible is the truly moral way to proceed."[12] And the first step to resisting Watson's tyrannical view of freedom is to appreciate how comfortably it rests on libertarian premises.

CHAPTER 10

RELIGION, CONSERVATISM, AND LIBERATIONISM

Is conservatism necessarily grounded in religious faith? The answer depends, of course, on what is meant by both conservatism and religion. I want to answer that question personally, but I hope not too personally. I would not want to say that conservatives must be Catholics, much less think and believe as I do in every respect. So I am going to define conservatism here in an expansive way. And I am going to limit myself to saying that much of Christian psychology and portions of Christian faith must be true for one to be a conservative today, while not forgetting that I know for a fact that there are agnostic conservatives.

What conservatives want to conserve is human life and human liberty, the human being with speech or language who lives open to the truth and must be virtuous to live well. The opponents of conservatives are not so much the liberals, who at their best (say, a Raymond Aron or even an Alexis de Tocqueville) are somewhat confused or ambivalent conservatives, but the liberationists. They say that it is good and possible to liberate human beings from the constraints and miseries of being human. They aim to have the human will transform human nature into something else. They aim to create a new man who is not really a man at all.

We conservatives are quick to remember what most liberal thinkers are too confused to know or too decent to say: Liberal thought is, at its core, liberationist. Liberal theory, as articulated by John Locke and many others, is based on the premise that nature or God give human beings just about nothing worthwhile. So we have no choice but to create value out of nothing; all that exists which is of human benefit is the product of human will and labor. Property, the family, government, and in fact all human relationships are human inventions for the benefit of the individual. Liberal theorists think that government and also the family are ordained by neither God nor nature, and so they can be transformed at will by human beings to suit their convenience.

Human life, say the Lockeans or liberal theorists, is defined by calculation, consent, and contract. And there are no definite limits to how far human beings might move themselves away from an indifferent and penurious nature. Human beings, in fact, constitute themselves (almost) out of nothing, and the idea of willful self-constitution provides hope for a future free from the limits of the past and the present. Human beings are capable of indefinite perfectibility through the progressive negation and transformation of what they have been given by nature.

Liberationists characteristically do not devote themselves to reflection upon the mystery of human freedom. They hold that the point is not to understand nature and human nature, but to transform them. Their task is, in fact, to eradicate mystery from the world, to create a world in which human beings experience themselves as fully at home. As we saw in Chapter 1, their goal is something like the communism described by Marx, a world in which human beings live unalienated in freedom and abundance. And as we saw in the previous chapter, that goal is also shared by our pragmatists, such as Richard Rorty, and perhaps by our new upper class, David Brooks's bourgeois bohemians. If Brooks is right, the Bobos believe that every moment of life should be devoted to a hobby.

Today, the most important and largest group of liberationists consists of extreme libertarians. They say that moral freedom, or the freedom to constitute onself as one wishes, is a necessary companion of political and economic freedom. That freedom requires the embrace of every technological invention that can increase personal freedom and reduce human suffering. So it means the embrace of the biotechnological effort to produce indefinite longevity and designer (designed either through intrauterine interventions or through cloning) children. The libertarian hope is that human beings can live free from the miseries of birth and death and, finally, from the cruel misery of love. Some libertarians hope that biotechnology will do what communism failed to do, create a society in which politics and God wither away. Some share the delusion of Marx that such a world could really be populated by free human beings open to the truth and capable of love.

Let me now explain why, for me, the conservative opposition to liberationism is necessarily religious. Christians maintain that human beings are alienated by the very nature of their being here. As St. Augustine states, we are aliens or pilgrims in the earthly city. Atheistic existentialists, beginning with Rousseau, say that our alienation is merely accidental or absurd, and so the liberationists are right to try to overcome it. If it cannot be overcome, then human life as such is absurdly full of mysterious misery; it is a life not worth living. So twentieth-century atheistic existentialists tended to vacillate between Stalinism (or Hitlerism) and suicide.

But Christian thinkers such as Pascal and Walker Percy believe that our ineradicable alienation is *the* clue to the truth about our being. The mysterious experience of displacement that is the source of our greatness and misery points to the conclusion that our true home is somewhere else. We cannot help asking why we are the only beings "lost in the cosmos," and reason by itself provides no solid answer. But what we really do know about our distinctive natures points in the direction of our being creatures of a personal Creator. Christian faith provides the most plausible answer to questions we must ask about ourselves but cannot answer through reason. That fact, of course, cannot by itself be the source of faith, but it does show our need for it. It also shows that we are constituted by nature so that there is irreducible "space" for faith. We seem to need to believe to live well as whole human persons, to avoid self-denial of one sort or another.

Leo Strauss seems to say that, through reason, some human beings can live in unalienated serenity without God in search of the truth, endlessly unraveling the riddle of Being. The undeniable existence of these rare but real philosophers refutes Pascal's claim that man is necessarily miserably lost without God. But I cannot see how philosophizing overcomes human alienation. The being who wonders is a singular and mysterious exception to the rest of Being. That being, the human thinker, cannot incorporate himself in the cosmos he can otherwise pretty well explain according to impersonal natural laws, and he cannot really show, without faith, that all of existence somehow points to him. Our physicists sometimes now claim that what the human mind can know corresponds to the truth about the cosmos, and so the human mind is fully at home in the world. The problem is that a physicist is not pure mind, but a human being with a body who is subject to all sorts of troubles and perversities that do not fit into the world his mind describes. The real human being who calls himself a physicist is, like the rest of us, an alien. The same goes for those who call themselves philosophers. That is why Walker Percy says that the human being, the wonderer, is necessarily a wanderer. A genuinely self-conscious philosopher, as a Thomist would say, must also be a pilgrim.

What faith does, among other things, is to give us an explanation for why we experience ourselves as aliens or wanderers. It allows us to be ambiguously at home in the world. Knowing why we are not fully at home, we are free to experience the good things of the world for what they are. Christian otherworldliness has produced the thought, made famous by Pascal, that the greatness of man in this world is inextricably bound up with his misery. But if we were created for this life, how could it be nothing but bad? Could original sin, or sin generally, really have been that devastating for our natural existence? The modern, liberal view that man is a solitary and suffering individual by nature is based on that unrealistic abstraction known as "the state of nature," not on a genuinely Christian anthropology or even a plausible rational foundation. Real human beings are social beings, born not only to suffer and die but also to know and love. And we are born not primarily to know and love "the truth," but, above all, other persons, each other, and God. What we know about nature, God, and each other is limited; our knowledge culminates in mystery. But why should we, in liberationist fashion, necessarily equate invincible mystery with a nature or a cosmos that is simply hostile to our existence? Surely human life would be unendurable if purged of all mystery.

For the Thomist, one road to faith is that we can glimpse by nature something of the goodness and gratuitousness of created being. What we really know is the foundation for what I believe to be the conservative virtue of *gratitude*. What we have been given as human beings is good; we are, on balance, privileged beings in the cosmos. What we have been given are personal gifts—qualities of soul—that must have been given by some person, not some impersonal force. By what we know simply through our natural capabilities, the personal source of our gifts is mysterious, although we do know that those gifts are rooted in our distinctive natures. In gratitude under God, we conservatives dismiss the liberationist thought that we would be better off as beings who did not know love, virtue, truth, or even death. The mystery of creation, especially *our* creation, gives us reason to believe that we are more than merely natural beings.

CHAPTER 11

PUTTING LOCKE IN
THE LOCKE BOX

The great social theorist Robert Nisbet concluded *The Quest for Community* (1953) by saying, "I cannot help thinking that what we need is a new philosophy of *laissez faire*," that is, an understanding of the importance of "letting people alone" that is appropriate for our time. The old *laissez faire*, which reached its perfection in the philosophy of John Locke, had the goal, Nisbet observed, of "creat[ing] the conditions in which autonomous *individuals* could prosper" by "emancipat[ing] them from the binding ties of kinship, class, and community." The old *laissez faire* achieved wonderful successes on behalf of liberty and justice, but it also had serious limitations.

The defects of the old *laissez faire* may all be traced to its error of understanding human beings as autonomous individuals and *nothing more*. We are free individuals, it is true, but also friends, parents, children, citizens, and creatures, and our understanding of ourselves as social beings imposes duties on us that both limits our autonomy and makes life worth living. As Nisbet put it, the human being is not "merely" a "socially undifferentiated individual" but a "concrete person" naturally fit to practice virtue in response to various social loyalties and responsibilities. That is why we need to put Lockean individualism in a Locke box made up of a more comprehensive and realistic understanding of human nature.

The old *laissez faire* was, in its principles, unlimited. Its intention was not at all to let us alone. The real goal of Locke and the other old liberals was aggressive and comprehensively transformational, to change all of human life with the abstract or autonomous individual in mind.

The new *laissez faire*, by contrast, resides in the effort to make the extreme individualists—the autonomy freaks—back off, in order to save ordinary human life from being distorted by abstract individualism's most corrosive tendencies, to keep our relentless and self-obsessive pursuit of happiness from destroying our natural and social capability to be happy in the practice of social or communal virtue.

The most clear and confident defenders of the new *laissez faire* in our time are the so-called moral values voters. They should actually be called virtue voters. These voters are often called Fascists by their individualistic enemies, but the truth is they are the very opposite of Fascists. European Fascists, as Nisbet explained, are the most isolated, alienated, and lonely voters, those who experience themselves so much as individuals that they cannot even think of themselves as autonomous. They are so afraid and disoriented that they willingly subordinate themselves to any form of decisive leadership.

But our virtue voters are our least individualistic or least lonely and alienated voters. The typical virtue voter is an evangelical Christian living in a family friendly, community-centered exurb with his wife (or her husband) and kids, experiencing him or herself to some extent as an individual, but more as a friend, parent, creature (or church member), and citizen. Consider just two sets of facts about virtue voters. First, single women voted heavily for Kerry, or for their liberation as individuals; married women with children voted for Bush, or as wives and mothers. Second, our nation's comparatively healthy birth rate apparently depends on the fecundity of observant religious believers. Take them out of the picture, and our birth rate is the same as that of France. France, everyone knows, is fading away. Individualism—unchecked by religious and familial virtue or duty—seems actually to threaten the future of our nation and even our species. The virtue voters are not only on the side of God but also on the side of nature. From both a biblical and a sociobiological view, the virtue voters are the healthiest Americans.

The issue that animates virtue voters more than anything is judicial activism. They want the courts to leave them alone. In the most recent election, they were angered not so much by the thought that same-sex marriage might become legal but by the fear that it would be imposed upon the people by the judiciary. They were angered by the aggressive assertion that laws limiting marriage to a union between a man and a woman had somehow *become* unconstitutional, although nobody had thought them unconstitutional before. Many of the virtue voters, of course, were also angered by the earlier assertion of the Supreme Court that laws restricting even partial birth abortion had *become* unconstitutional. The defenders of the new *laissez faire* believe that the people should be left alone to resolve these controversial moral issues not only according to the principle of individual autonomy but also according to the virtues required for social life.

The new *laissez faire* aims to protect the ordinary social life of Americans from the Court's current way of interpreting the Constitution in light of the Declaration of Independence. There are, of course, conceivably many ways in which that deep and somewhat ambiguous founding document might illuminate our Constitution.

But today's Court, whether the justices know it clearly or not, is focused on the Declaration's Lockean theoretical core—the principled part of the Declaration in which Jefferson paraphrased the great words of the English philosopher. That is the part that speaks of self-evident truths and inalienable rights, the part that says that governments are instituted among men through their consent to protect their rights. Locke understands us as free individuals and nothing more, as beings who are free by nature and are bound to obedience only through consensual contracts and nothing more.

The contemporary Supreme Court interprets the Constitution as progressively and thoroughly Lockean and thus in a progressively more thorough Declaration-of-Independence sort of way. As it sees it, the job of the Court is to use constitutional interpretation to maximize the autonomy of the individual. According to Justice Kennedy in his opinion for the Court in *Lawrence v. Texas* (2003; the case that overturned that state's anti-sodomy law), the authors of the Due Process Clauses of the Fifth and Fourteenth Amendments were humbled by their awareness that they did not know "the components of liberty in its manifold possibilities." Lacking this "insight," they decided not to make the constitutional meaning of liberty "specific." They were aware that "times can blind us to certain truths and later generations can see laws once thought necessary and proper in fact only serve to oppress us." So the Constitution "endures," but "persons in every generation can invoke its principles in their own search for greater freedom." The Constitution does not so much limit us as it functions as a rhetorical weapon to be wielded on behalf of principled novelty. It leads us, or helps us lead ourselves, in the direction of becoming more consistently individuals, which entails the redefinition of every human relationship.

We move toward a more perfect realization of "certain truths" that were far from self-evident to past generations; we gradually liberate our eyes from the blindness that produces oppression. The job of the justices is to position themselves on the cutting edge of this progress of liberty and enlightenment. Our Constitution is a historical project to be pursued, most of all, by the most principled part of our government, the judiciary.

In the Court's view, the fact that none of our founders thought of abortion or sodomy or same-sex marriage as constitutional rights is no impediment to their becoming constitutional rights now. It is important to emphasize that in *Goodrich v. Dept. of Public Health* (2004) the high court of Massachusetts merely followed Kennedy's lead in *Lawrence* by discovering a constitutional right to same-sex marriage, just as Justice Scalia, in his scathing dissent in *Lawrence*, predicted a court soon would. The single word "liberty" in the Fourteenth Amendment, the Court now believes, gives it unlimited or at least indefinite authority to transform state law with the autonomous individual in mind. Nor do the justices believe that their interpretation of the Constitution is arbitrary, or contrary to the will of its framers. The Court understands itself as perfecting the work of our framers.

COMPLETING THE FRAMERS' WORK

I want to present now the evidence that exists in support of the Court's view that it works to complete the framers' work on the basis of the framers' Lockean principles. This view has much truth, but it is not completely true, just as Locke's understanding of the human being as a free individual is only partially true. Our Constitution has plenty of Lockean moments, but it really and truly can be understood to keep them in a Locke box.

From today's Court's principled view, there is no need to read Locke or the Declaration into the Constitution. They are already there. Notice that our Constitution is the first fundamental political document in the history of the world to treat human beings as free individuals. People are never treated as members of classes or categories. That is why our Constitution is silent on race, class, gender, and religion. Our Constitution, it is true, protected slavery as it already existed, that is, as part of the law of some states. But the Constitution itself does not make racial distinctions, and avoiding the use of racial terminology led the framers to engage in some very awkward and euphemistic phrasings. There is also no reason, under the unamended Constitution, why a woman couldn't become president. The exclusion of women from political life was a matter of state law. Women, like blacks, were treated as indistinguishable from free white men, or as free and equal individuals.

And we cannot forget our Constitution's unprecedented silence on God and its prohibition of religious tests for office. From the beginning, Jews and atheists could also be free and equal citizens of the United States because they do not consent to be governed by our Constitution as Jews or atheists but as free individuals. Our unamended Constitution not only does not discriminate on the basis of religious belief, it does not even recognize the existence of our Creator. From the view of today's Court, our Constitution is in principle perfect. But it does not really create a perfect society. The application of the perfect principles of Lockean individualism to all the details of American life is, from this view, the project of American history.

Our framers, from the Court's view, were incomplete and inconsistent in the application of their perfect principles. The main defect of the original Constitution, from this view, was federalism.

State law was, in effect, allowed to remain imperfect or unjust, to continue to countenance distinctions between white and black, male and female, Christian and Jew. Under the original Constitution the states were perfectly free to make laws establishing religions and repressing blacks and women.

But this defect of the original Constitution, from the Court's view, was corrected by the Fourteenth Amendment. Or rather by its constantly expanding view of the scope of this amendment, of the mandate it gives to judicial power. The responsibility it is given by the Fourteenth Amendment makes the Court less and less *laissez faire* when it comes to state law and the contents of ordinary life.

Under the original Constitution, the definition of marriage and virtually all regulations concerning it were reserved to the states. But the Court, in *Eisenstadt v. Baird* (1972), said that the states now must view marriage as nothing but an "association between two individuals" and therefore not privilege individual marital over extramarital decisions concerning reproduction. As the Court elaborated in *Lawrence,* almost anything two intimate individuals consent to do possesses the dignity of autonomy. Both what goes on in what Justice Douglas called "the sacred precincts of marital bedrooms" and hooking up are equally free and dignified contracts between individuals. And we learn in *Planned Parenthood v. Casey* (1992) that state law cannot burden women differently from men; all individuals must be regarded as equally free from natural limitations or differences. The law cannot compel any free individual— man or woman—to have a baby. The unique freedom Justice O'Connor attributes to women is actually their freedom not to be treated as unique. The next step is clear: If marriage is between any two individuals, then it need not be between a man and a woman.

So the Court's project, whether it knows it or not, is at least part of Locke's project to transform all of the conditions of ordinary life with the free individual in mind. Let me emphasize that Locke's intention was not simply to establish a system of limited but effective government but to reconstruct all human relationships on the basis of calculation, contract, and consent. He wanted to free wives, as far as possible, from their husbands; children, as far as possible, from their parents; and even parenthood, as far as possible, from any biological determination. He wanted all of human life to be changed with the goal of maximum conceivable individual liberation. He was, in fact, remarkably optimistic about the success his reform efforts would have: Locke thought there was little chance he could be kept in a Locke box. For us, Lockean principles are the very opposite of *laissez faire;* they are creeping into every facet of our lives.

The Court, in its anti-*laissez faire* efforts, is, in fact, *leading* the people and *following* our mainstream intellectuals. Isaac Kramnick and R. Laurence Moore in *The Godless Constitution* (1997), for example, agree with me that "Locke was the . . . philosopher whose writings most shaped the intellectual and political world of Americans in the eighteenth century." That means, for them, that "liberal social theory" is at the foundation of our "Godless constitution." That theory "posits the autonomous individual as the center of our social universe, for whom social and political institutions are self-willed constructs whose purpose and function are to secure the rights and interests of self-seeking individuals." However we might disagree on what Locke "really" meant, Kramnick and Moore show us what Lockeanism as an ideology for sophisticates means today. The theory of our Constitution demands the reconstruction of all institutions—not only political but social—only with the interests of the autonomous individual in mind. Our intellectuals lead our Court, and our founding philosopher, in turn, leads them.

QUESTIONABLE INTERPRETATION

Now I want to question the justices' method of interpreting the Constitution *only* through a philosophic elaboration of its underlying individualistic principles—that is, their method of interpreting the document with a thoroughly Lockean reading of the Declaration of Independence. First of all, justices are not philosophers, and they have a poor record of thinking through abstract principles or engaging in philosophical speculation. Consider the famous way in which the Court tried to define what liberty means in the Fourteenth Amendment, and by implication in the Declaration, when it reaffirmed the central holding of *Roe v. Wade*: "At the heart of liberty is the right to define one's own concept of existence, of meaning, of the universe, and of the mystery of human life."

The Court's words have been criticized by conservatives as nihilistic and relativistic. And maybe they are. It is just about impossible to tell. They are certainly extremely vague; they read like a flourish from some sophomore's B-plus exam in "Introduction to Existentialism." The Court's opinion hardly provides a definite enough account of what liberty is to be a foundation for constitutional interpretation, and so the most trenchant criticism of them is that they might produce any result at all. And perhaps that is not simply the Court's fault, but also Locke's. Locke was clear that our liberty is liberty from nature, but he was rather vague on what the autonomous individual's liberty is *for*. Still, even Locke would not hesitate to say that defining one's own concept of existence has certain definite limits. The least we can say is that when our justices get existential in defining our liberty, they are pretty clueless.

Justice Scalia—the justice who is most *laissez faire* about the people's view of virtue—is sometimes criticized by well-intentioned conservatives for being a legal positivist, for refusing to root American liberty in our founders' principles, especially as those principles concern nature. But Scalia believes in natural rights and natural law. He just does not employ them, or employ them much, as tools in interpreting the Constitution. He interprets the Constitution as written law that limits in clear ways an otherwise democratic people, not as the foundation for our libertarian or individualistic aspirations. He observed in his dissent in *Lawrence* that "[o]ne of the benefits of leaving [moral] regulation . . . to the people rather than the court is that people, unlike judges, need not carry things to their logical conclusion." The people, when it comes to virtue, think more realistically or less abstractly, and the Constitution gives them plenty of room—but not indefinite room—for moral deliberation.

Scalia sees that the Constitution usually gives the benefit of the doubt to the wisdom and virtue of the American people. That does not mean, for example, that the American people get to deliberate about the wisdom or virtue of slavery or segregation; even without the post–Civil War Amendments, Stephen Douglas was wrong to say that the Constitution "don't care" about slavery. The original Constitution was antislavery and antiracist in structure and purpose and only tolerated racially based slavery where it already existed out of necessity. But it is an error to generalize from race and slavery (or the rights of women and religious minorities) to all controversial moral issues.

If, for example, Aristotle, the Bible, Jefferson, and Darwin, despite their great differences (even on slavery!), think that marriage must be between a man and a woman, a law affirming that view ought to be seen as a reasonable (although not necessary) exception to any attempt to understand human beings as free individuals and nothing more. One reason our framers left laws concerning marriage to the states is that that social institution would be distorted beyond recognition if completely redefined in individualistic terms, and the result would be, if nothing else, devastating for our children. It would actually be devastating, they thought, for men and women too. Women, especially mothers, need the reliable help and protection of men, and studies show that most men cannot live well without the socializing and even moralizing influence of women. Being married with children—that is, being much more than a "free individual"—is still affirmed by most Americans as what makes life most worth living.

Our framers assumed that the Lockean principles of their Declaration and Constitution would not be applied with rigorous consistency to institutions indispensable for the encouragement of social virtue. So, any reasonable interpretation of the Fourteenth Amendment has to be in accord with that reasonable assumption. Part of the true greatness of our framers is that the Constitution and even the Declaration—which speaks of a providential and judgmental Creator—are informed in some ways by a better, more comprehensive view of human nature than that found in Locke's theory.

Considered as a whole—or with additions proposed by other members of Congress that Jefferson graciously accepted—the God of the Declaration is much more active and personal than the Creator or "Nature's God" described in that document's most Lockean part. That Creator not only has given but gives us much for which we should be grateful and to which we are bound. God does not disappear in the Declaration, as he does in Locke's chapter "Of Property" in his famous *Second Treatise*, to be replaced by money—our invention of the means for unlimited acquisition—and by the "wise and godlike prince" who effectually protects our property—what we have made our own by mixing our labor with nature's almost worthless materials. Our Declaration contains more than Lockean principles, in part, because it was a product of legislative compromise. Even our great Declaration does not push Lockean principles to their logical, liberationist conclusions.

Our leading framers, as John Courtney Murray wrote in *We Hold These Truths*, were "building better than they knew" because they were more indebted than they knew to the rational, social, and revelation-friendly premises of premodern natural law. To know that, of course, is not to promote judicial activism based on the wisdom of St. Thomas Aquinas. But it is a good reason for opposing that judicial activism which is based on deducing all the logical consequences of the idea of individual autonomy.

Virtue Voting

Let us look more closely at how the new *laissez faire*—at its best, commonsense natural law thinking—informed the virtue voting of 2004 and at what the *laissez faire* outcome of that election actually was. The virtue voters thought they had two ways to protect themselves from the judicial activism that would not let them alone to define marriage for themselves. The first was to amend state constitutions; the second was to keep a Democratic president from appointing new members of the Supreme Court. Many voters thought the first method alone was sufficient, and so they voted both for marriage-restrictive state constitutional amendments and for Kerry.

The votes in favor of such amendments were overwhelming despite the fact that the average American seems to acknowledge that reasonable people can disagree over same-sex marriage. Surely the progress of our individualism—having produced easygoing divorce and having largely disconnected marriage from sexual exclusivity, fidelity, and parenthood—has made the exclusion of homosexuals from the recognitions and other benefits of the institution seem increasingly arbitrary. That progress, of course, has also shown people that many of our laws oppressed homosexuals in the past. Many moderate Americans have concluded that same-sex marriage, for better or worse, may be an idea whose time has come. But those ambivalent thoughts—products of our confusion about what a human being is—do not produce the conclusion that laws against same-sex marriage are unconstitutional, just as they do not produce the conclusion that laws allowing same-sex marriage are unconstitutional.

The best advocates for same-sex marriage, such as Jonathan Rauch, admitted that they were wounded by the animosity toward homosexuals which lay behind some of the 2004 voting. But Rauch did not despair; he admitted also that the result confirmed his perception that Americans will not accept same-sex marriage until they can see how it promotes virtue. And Rauch expressed his gratitude to President Bush for not closing American discussion on the issue by pushing for an amendment to the national Constitution. Rauch, in other words, thanked the president for affirming the new *laissez faire* ("Saying No to 'I Do,'" *Wall Street Journal*, December 27, 2004).

All along, the best proponents of gay marriage have wanted to make arguments to their fellow citizens about virtue, and so they too have opposed the judicial or constitutional termination of our moral debate. In his book *Gay Marriage* (2004), Rauch argues that same-sex marriage should not become law until most Americans come to see it as not only good for gays, but good for marriage as an institution, and so good for America. Rauch argues that marriage will make gay men less narcissistic and more responsible. Their ability to marry will also strengthen that indispensable institution by keeping the example of homosexual promiscuity from eroding it further. Our country, Rauch stirringly concludes, is best understood as one full of virtuous caregiving couples who are not merely autonomous individuals.

As we saw in Chapter 3, David Brooks also appealed to virtue in his famous column in which he argued that not only should we allow gay marriage, we should *insist* that gay men and women get married. He makes the quite biblical judgment that a life constituted by multiple sex partners and no enduring connections is an "abomination." He embraces the concern of the virtue voters that such morally bankrupt and irresponsible lives are becoming more common—and not just among homosexuals, of course—in our "culture of contingency." Brooks claimed that we need to oppose that trend by encouraging everyone to enter marriage's "culture of fidelity." Nobody should be excluded from the privileges and responsibilities required for the practice of mature social virtue.

The provocative arguments of Rauch and Brooks are meant to start a moral argument among citizens over the possible contribution same-sex marriage might make to marital virtue. The need for such American arguments about controversial moral questions is the reason Brooks believes that our democracy cannot function properly until *Roe v. Wade* is reversed ("Roe's Birth, and Death," *New York Times*, April 21, 2005). Nisbet, for one, would not be dogmatic about how such an argument ought to play out. He said, after all, that to be for community today is not to be thoughtlessly attached to the communal forms of the past. But to be for community of some kind or another certainly is to believe that a reasonable dispute over social virtue and the quality of American life should not be terminated by a one-sided judicial decision about rights—one that promises to do nothing more than to make another contribution to the culture of contingency.

The fact that ordinary Americans experience themselves as

more than free individuals but are fervently attached to the inalienable rights of their Declaration of Independence points to the political compromises they are willing to make in order to keep Locke in the proverbial Locke box. For the proponents of the new *laissez faire*, for those who hope to maintain enough political space to reach livable legislative compromises on issues such as school choice, the content of public education, the accommodation of religion, same-sex marriage, biotechnology, and abortion, there is now no alternative but to vote for the party that most opposes judicial activism. That is not to say there is no role for the Court in setting limits to popular choice when it comes to the individual, only that the contemporary Court has too indefinite a view of what those limits are.

My endorsement of a political life that promotes compromise between our rights- and virtue-oriented voters is not based on any skepticism about the truth all human beings share in common. Both sets of voters perceive part of that truth, and most Americans are caught between them for that very reason. Our evangelical Christians need to be forced to give arguments about the foundation of virtue in human nature that their fellow citizens can appreciate. The natural human good that is the family, for example, can be encouraged without recourse to the absolute truth of biblical revelation. On the other hand, the evangelicals' opponents need to defend themselves against the charge that they do not see that rights can only be good if they are compatible with the social, familial, political, and religious virtues that make life worth living. Compromise, I hope, will approximate the more comprehensive view of human nature that was genuinely characteristic of our founders, as well as the great tradition of natural law. It might even make both sides in our so-called culture war more moderate, which is to say, open to reason.

Now, lest you still think I am employing the deep insight of a great social theorist for shamelessly partisan Republican purposes here, consider this: If the courts were to disavow judicial activism, then the compromises between individual autonomy and social virtue required to defend the goodness of human liberty might be based on concerns expressed by each of our major parties. It was the Supreme Court of Massachusetts, far more than Karl Rove, that was the cause of Kerry's defeat last November. The senator was stuck with both proclaiming that his personal belief that marriage is between a man and a woman and not condemning his state's court for saying that his personal belief is unconstitutional, just as he was stuck with proclaiming his personal belief, as a former altar boy, that life begins at conception while defending a Court that says that laws limiting even partial birth abortion are unconstitutional.

Freed up by the success of the new *laissez faire* to reach realistic legislative compromises on various virtue issues, the Democrats would come to look more moderate and so would be more competitive. Judicial compromise, as Scalia observes, has too often proven to be an oxymoron. Bush's court appointees might actually allow Democratic candidates the luxury of becoming more honest and making more sense about the relationship between indispensable virtue and individual rights.

Furthermore, although I have concentrated here on the danger posed by the abstract individualism or unfettered libertarianism of the Left—cultural or moral libertarianism—there is also a danger from the Right—from economic libertarians, or libertarianism narrowly understood. This danger is much less pronounced for now, but it may grow. There is a fairly influential view of Constitutional interpretation—one that has had quite minimal impact on the Court so far—which says that, in effect, every law that restricts the maximum possible economic liberty for the individual is unconstitutional. And so judicial review should restore the Constitution to its pre-1937 understanding. The efforts to restore what Randy Barnett calls the "lost Constitution" and Douglas Ginsburg calls the "Constitution in exile," especially in their more extreme forms, also represent a form of Lockeanism way, way outside the Locke box.

Some proponents of this view, for instance, have called for a new kind of judicial activism that would declare the Environmental Protection Agency, the Endangered Species Act, and much that other regulatory agencies have done unconstitutional. A very few would go further and declare minimum wage laws, most zoning laws, and even Social Security unconstitutional. The goal seems to be to get much of our relatively minimalist welfare state voided by the Court, including settled, popular programs that pose no obvious threat to political liberty. I can agree that much of the welfare state is inefficient, meddlesome, and demographically unsustainable, and may, for those reasons and others, readily be destroyed and deserve to fade away, but that is quite different from saying that it is unconstitutional. (I do concede that the Court allowed for too much discretion in the use of eminent domain at the expense of property rights in *Kelo v. New London* [2005].)

This sort of libertarian judicial activism—just like the activism of the Left as it relates to abortion, same-sex marriage, and so forth—could also easily err by not giving the benefit of the doubt to the wisdom and virtue of the American people. It might abruptly terminate debate on how best to encourage prosperity, protect the environment, and provide a minimal level of security for all Americans. Once again, the old or individualistic *laissez faire* would not really be *laissez faire* at all. The American people would not be left relatively alone—they should not be left completely alone—to reach livable compromises about conflicting human goods. And we must remember that we can hardly expect justices to be better *economists* than they are *philosophers*.

Consider this possibility, which seems unlikely but is actually in accord with our country's libertarian or individualistic drift: The Court, even with a couple of new G. W. Bush appointees, does not roll back precedents concerning religion, abortion, marriage, and so forth, and even goes a bit further in deducing the social or cultural consequences of the principle of individual autonomy. Meanwhile the Court, with the addition of the Republicans, becomes considerably more principled and aggressive on the economic liberty front. This consistent judicial libertarianism would both direct and mirror our society's creeping libertarianism. It would reflect the current combination in the lives of sophisticated Americans of the "Do your own thing" liberty of the Sixties with the economic freedom let loose in Reagan's Eighties. Even with the compassionate efforts of President Bush, the nonlibertarian side of the Sixties—activist government compassion for the poor, the unfortunate, and the oppressed (not to mention "the environment")—and the nonlibertarian side of the Eighties—concern for the unborn, children of narcissists, the effects of unlimited biotechnological development, and the impoverished cultural climate—have already fallen on hard times. The emergence of what might be called "the consistent constitutional ethic of individual autonomy" would provide more evidence of our progress as individuals.

Whatever happens, one thing is for sure: we will remain stuck with virtue.

NOTES

CHAPTER 3

THE PROBLEM OF TECHNOLOGY

1. Tyler Cowen, *Creative Destruction: How Globalization Is Changing the World's Cultures* (Princeton, NJ: Princeton University Press, 2002), 152 *et passim*.

2. William Leach, *The Destruction of Place in American Life* (New York: Vintage Books, 1999), 181.

3. Alan Ehrenhalt, *Lost City: The Forgotten Virtues of Community in America* (New York: Basic Books, 1995).

4. Alexis de Tocqueville, *Democracy in America*, volume 2, part 3, chapter 12.

5. Wilson Carey McWilliams, "Science and Freedom: America as the Technological Republic," *Technology in the Western Political Tradition*, ed. A. Melzer, J. Weinberger, and R. Zinman (Ithaca, NY: Cornell University Press, 1993), 101. I am indebted to several other essays in this collection, especially those by Melzer, Weinberger, and Galston.

6. Alexis de Tocqueville, *Democracy in America*, volume 2, part 1, chapter 10 with volume 2, part 2, chapter 8.

7. Martin Heidegger, "The Question Concerning Technology," *The Question Concerning Technology and Other Essays* (New York: Harper, 1977), 6-7.

8. Leo Strauss, *The Rebirth of Classical Political Rationalism* (Chicago: University of Chicago Press, 1989), 42.

9. Jacques Ellul, *The Technological Society* (New York: Random House, 1967), 401.

10. Wendell Berry, *The Art of the Commonplace: The Agrarian Essays of Wendell Berry*, ed. Norman Wirzba (Washington, DC: Counterpoint, 2002), 172.

11. Ibid., 178–79.

12. Ibid., 181.
13. McWilliams, "Science and Freedom," 85.
14. Berry, *Art of the Commonplace*, 36.
15. Alexis de Tocqueville, *Democracy in America*, volume 1, part 2, chapter 10.
16. Berry, *Art of the Commonplace*, 11.
17. Ibid., 11.
18. Ibid., 14.
19. Ibid., 24.
20. Ibid., 23.
21. Ibid., 26.
22. Ibid., 27.
23. Ibid., 25.
24. Ibid., 30.
25. Pascal, *Pensees*, fragments 102, 168 according to the numbering system found in the Honor Levi translation (Oxford: Oxford University Press, 1995).
26. Bruce C. Thornton, *Plagues of the Mind: The New Epidemic of False Knowledge* (Wilmington, DE: ISI Books, 1999), 93.
27. Ibid., chapter 6.
28. See chapter 8 of this book, "The Utopian Eugenics of Our Time."
29. Leon R. Kass, *Life, Liberty, and the Defense of Dignity* (San Francisco: Encounter Books, 2002), 10.
30. Ibid., 253.
31. Ibid., 21.
32. Ibid.
33. Ibid., 268.

CHAPTER 4
THE LIMITS OF THE AMERICAN UTOPIAN IMAGINATION

1. Richard Rorty, *Achieving Our Country: Leftist Thought in Twentieth Century America* (Cambridge, MA: Harvard University Press, 1998), 86.
2. Ibid., 130.
3. Michael Barone, *Hard America, Soft America: Coddling and the Battle for America's Future* (New York: Crown Forum, 2004).
4. David Brooks, "How to Reinvent the GOP," *New York Times Magazine*, August 30, 2004, 35.
5. David Brooks, *Bobos in Paradise: The New Upper Class and How They Got There* (New York: Simon and Schuster, 2002).
6. Walt Whitman, *Leaves of Grass*, as quoted by Rorty, 22.

7. Brooks, "How to Reinvent the GOP," 35.

8. Page numbers in parenthesis in the text are to David Brooks, *On Paradise Drive: How We Live Now (And Always Have) in the Future Tense* (New York: Simon and Schuster, 2004).

9. Rorty, *Achieving Our Country*, 22.

10. Kay S. Hymowitz, *Liberation's Children: Parents and Kids in a Postmodern Age* (Chicago: Ivan Dee, 2003), 153.

11. Brooks, "How to Reinvent the GOP," 56.

12. Virginia Postrel, *The Substance of Style: How the Rise of Aesthetic Value is Remaking Commerce, Culture, and Consciousness* (New York: HarperCollins, 2003).

13. David Brooks, "The New Red-Diaper Babies," *New York Times*, December 7, 2004.

14. David Brooks, "The National Creed," *New York Times*, December, 30, 2003.

15. David Brooks, "The Power of Marriage," *New York Times*, November 22, 2003.

16. Sara Issenberg, "Boo-Boos in Paradise," *Philadelphia Magazine*, April, 2004.

17. Alan Wolfe, *The Transformation of American Religion: How We Actually Live Our Faith* (New York: Free Press, 2003), 24.

18. Ibid., 38.

19. "Understanding American Evangelicals: A Conversation with Mark Noll and Jay Tolson," *Center Conversations* (Washington DC: Ethics and Public Policy Center, June 2004), 5.

20. Clifford Orwin, "The Unraveling of Christianity in America," *Public Interest*, 155 (Spring 2004), 29–30.

21. David Brooks, "Who Is John Stott," *New York Times*, November 30, 2004. See also Brooks, "Stuck in Lincoln's Land," *New York Times*, May 5, 2005.

22. Philip Longman, "From Here to Maternity," *Washington Post*, September 2, 2004. For more on this topic, see Longman's book, *The Empty Cradle: How Falling Birthrates Threaten World Prosperity and What to Do About It* (New York: Basic Books, 2004).

23. Stanley Hauerwas, *Resident Aliens: Life in the Christian Colony* (Nashville, TN: Abingdon Press, 1989).

24. Wolfe, *Transformation of American Religion*, 256.

25. Brooks, "The Power of Marriage."

26. Jonathan Rauch, *Gay Marriage: Why It Is Good for Gays, Good for Straights, and Good for America* (New York: Times Books, 2004); Andrew Sullivan,

Virtually Normal: An Argument About Homosexuality (New York: Vintage Books, 1996).

27. Waller Newell, *The Code of Man: Love, Courage, Pride, Family, Country* (New York: Regan Books, 2003), xi.

28. Ibid., 356.

CHAPTER 5

COMPASSIONATE CONSERVATISM AND BIOTECHNOLOGY

1. Franklin Roosevelt, "Address to the Young Democratic Clubs of America" (1935) and "Fireside Chat on Party Primaries" (1938), both in *American Political Rhetoric*, ed. P. Lawler and R. Schaefer (Lanham, MD: Rowman and Littlefield, 2000).

2. I have usually used the translation of Mansfield and Winthrop (Chicago: University of Chicago Press, 2000).

3. On this view of the connection between Rorty and Bloom, see my *Postmodernism Rightly Understood: The Return to Realism in American Thought* (Lanham: Rowman and Littlefield, 1999).

4. Alasdair MacIntyre, *After Virtue: A Study in Moral Theory* (South Bend, IN: University of Notre Dame Press, 1997); James Davison Hunter, *The Death of Character: Moral Education in an Age Without Good or Evil* (New York: Basic Books, 2001).

5. See Randy Barnett, "Do Unto Others: The Vices of Bill Bennett," *National Review Online* (May 9, 2003), where Bennett's hypocrisy is revealed not to be in his moralism, but in his prohibitionism. True libertarians don't mind people preaching against smoking, drinking, drugs, or gambling, but they shouldn't try to outlaw them. But the libertarians who are rigorously and consistently anti-prohibitionist are a small group.

6. Peter D'Adamo, *Eat Right for Your Type* (New York: Putnam, 1996); D'Adamo, *Live Right 4 Your Type* (New York: Putnam, 2000).

7. See Leon Kass, *Life, Liberty, and the Defense of Dignity* (San Francisco: Encounter Books, 2002).

8. Eduardo Nolla, critical edition of Alexis de Tocqueville's *Democracy in America*, (Indianapolis: Liberty Fund, 2005), vol. 2, part 1, ch. 8, notes.

9. See my "Tocqueville on the Doctrine of Interest," *Government and Opposition* 30 (Spring 1995), 221–39.

10. Pascal, *Pensees*, trans. A. J. Krailsheimer (New York: Penguin, 1966). References to Pascal are according to the fragment numbers that appear in this edition.

11. Antoine-Nicholas de Condorcet, *Sketch for a Historical Picture of the Progress of the Human Mind,* trans. J. Barraclough (New York: Noonday Press, 1955), 200.

12. Ibid., 199.

13. See Virginia Postrel, *The Future and Its Enemies: The Growing Conflict over Creativity* (New York: Touchstone Books, 1999). For a stronger account of the connection between the libertarian vision of indefinite perfectibility and the biotechnological near-conquest of death, see Ronald Bailey, "Forever Young: The New Scientific Search for Immortality," *Reason Online* (August 2002).

14. See chapter 8, "The Utopian Eugenics of Our Time," in this volume. The change from natural or blind to conscious and volitional evolution is developed nicely as a sort of subordinate Promethean theme in the work of E. O. Wilson, especially in *On Human Nature* (Cambridge, MA: Harvard University Press, 1978) and *Consilience: The Unity of Knowledge* (New York: Knopf, 1998).

15. Kass, *Life, Liberty, and the Defense of Dignity.*

16. See chapter 9, "Libertarian Fantasy and Statist Reality," in this volume.

17. This is from *Griswold v. Connecticut* (1965), in which the Court declared unconstitutional a law prohibiting a married couple from using contraceptives. The law a very consistent libertarian would strike down in the future would probably require the separation of sex from procreation. But in truth our Constitution is not that consistently libertarian.

18. Harvey C. Mansfield and Delba Winthrop, "Liberalism and Big Government: Tocqueville's Analysis," *Tyranny and Liberty: Big Government and the Individual in Tocqueville's Science of Politics* (London: The Institute of United States Studies, University of London, 1999), 5.

19. Kass, *Life, Liberty, and the Defense of Dignity,* 271–74.

20. Quoted by Bailey in "Forever Young." Bailey himself is a true libertarian follower of Allen, believing that the government is evil because it may want to discourage biotechnological development that will indefinitely postpone the death of Bailey.

21. See Jerry Weinberger, "What's at the Bottom of the Slippery Slope: A Post-Human Future?" *Perspectives on Political Science* 32 (Spring 2003), 93.

22. Fukuyama, *Our Posthuman Future: Consequences of the Biotechnology Revolution* (New York: Farrar, Straus, and Giroux, 2002), 71.

23. Jacob Sullum, *Saying Yes: In Defense of Drug Use* (New York: Tarcher/Putnam, 2003), 262.
24. See Peter D. Kramer's thoughtful *Listening to Prozac* (New York: Putnam, 1997) and his silly "Why I'm in Favor of Sadness," *Self* 23 (July 2001), 88. His new book, *Against Depression* (New York: Viking, 2005), is an impressive return to the themes of *Listening*.
25. Randolph Nesse, "What Good Is Feeling Bad? The Evolutionary Benefits of Psychic Pain," *The Sciences* (November/December 1991), 30–37.
26. Randolph Nesse, "Evolutionary Explanation of Emotions," *Human Nature*, no. 3 (1990), 261–89.
27. Stephen Braun, *The Science of Happiness: Unlocking the Mysteries of Mood* (New York: John Wiley, 2000), 165–66.
28. Ibid., 180.
29. Ibid., 181.
30. Fukuyama, *Our Posthuman Future*, 56.
31. Carl Elliott, *Better Than Well: American Medicine Meets the American Dream* (New York: W. W. Norton, 2003), 55, 58–59, 229, 233.
32. Walker Percy, *Lost in the Cosmos: The Last Self-Help Book* (New York: Farrar, Straus, and Giroux, 1983).
33. Ronald Bailey, *Liberation Biology: The Scientific and Moral Case for the Biotech Revolution* (Amherst, NY: Prometheus Books, 2005), 231.
34. Alexis de Tocqueville, Letter to Madame Swetchine (February 26, 1857) in *The Tocqueville Reader: A Life in Letters and Politics*, ed. O. Zunz and A. Kahan (Oxford: Blackwell, 2002), 334–37. I altered the translation in one place.
35. Pierre Manent, *Modern Liberty and Its Discontents*, ed. and trans. D. Mahoney and P. Seaton (Lanham, MD: Rowman and Littlefield, 1998), 33–43.
36. See Percy, *Lost in the Cosmos*, especially the two-part Space Odyssey that concludes the book. See also my *Aliens in America*, chapter 3.
37. Harvey Mitchell, "Reclaiming the Self: The Pascal-Rousseau Connection," *Journal of the History of Ideas* 54 (October 1993), 639.
38. Kass, *Life, Liberty, and the Defense of Dignity*, 270.

CHAPTER 6

THE CAREGIVING SOCIETY

1. Chantal Delsol, *Icarus Fallen: The Search for Meaning in an Uncertain World*, trans. Robin Dick (Wilmington, DE: ISI Books, 2003), 150, 154.

2. *Long-Term Care Report: Findings from Committee Hearings of the 107th Congress* (June, 2002), 13.

3. Ibid., 14.

4. Richard J. Martin and Stephen J. Post, "Human Dignity, Dementia, and the Moral Basis of Caregiving," *Dementia and Caregiving: Ethics, Values, and Policy Choices*, ed. R. Binstock, S. Post, and P. Whitehouse (Baltimore: Johns Hopkins University Press, 1992), 62.

5. Delsol, *Icarus Fallen*, 153–54.

6. Alexis de Tocqueville, *Democracy in America*, volume 2, part 3, chapters 10–12.

7. David Brooks, *On Paradise Drive: How We Live Now (And Always Have) in the Future Tense* (New York: Simon and Schuster, 2004) and *Bobos in Paradise: The New Upper Class and How They Got There* (New York: Simon and Schuster, 2002).

8. Thomas R. Cole, *The Journey of Life: A Cultural History of Aging in America* (New York: Cambridge University Press, 1992), 259.

9. Robert B. Hudson, "The History and Place of Age-Based Public Policy," *The Future of Age-Based Public Policy*, ed. R. Hudson (Baltimore: Johns Hopkins University Press, 1997), 7.

10. For the history of the Sisters of Mercy in America, John J. Fialka, *Sisters: Catholic Nuns and the Making of America* (New York: St. Martin's, 2003). Pay attention to Fialka's remarkable stories of their early years and the facts about their decline; ignore his analysis.

11. This, I think, is the tough subtext of Virginia Postrel's perky and libertarian *The Substance of Style: How the Rise of Aesthetic Value Is Remaking Commerce, Culture, and Consciousness* (New York: HarperCollins, 2003).

12. Diane E. Meier and R. Sean Morrison, "Autonomy Reconsidered," *New England Journal of Medicine* 346 (April 4, 2002), 1087.

13. Audrey R. Chapman, "The Social and Justice Implications of Extending the Human Life Span," *The Fountain of Youth: Cultural, Scientific, and Ethical Perspectives on a Biomedical Goal*, ed. S. Post and R. Binstock (New York: Oxford University Press, 2004), 359. To support this conclusion, the author cites Francis Fukuyama, *Our Posthuman Future: Consequences of the Biotechnology Revolution* (New York: Farrar, Straus, and Giroux, 2002). Fukuyama says that one result of our medical success is that more and more people are reaching a point "when their capacities decline and they return increasingly to a childlike state of dependency. This is the period that society doesn't like to think about . . . , since it flies in the face of ideals of personal autonomy that most people hold dear" (68).

14. Chapman, "Social and Justice Implications of Extending the Human Life Span," 354.
15. Robert Morris and Francis G. Caro, "The Young Old, Productive Aging, and Public Policy," *The Future of Age-Based Public Policy*, 94.
16. Carl Elliott, *Better Than Well: American Medicine Meets the American Dream* (New York: W. W. Norton, 2003), 283.
17. Daniel Callahan, *Setting Limits: Medical Goals in an Aging Society* (New York: Simon and Schuster, 1987), 158.
18. Fukuyama, *Our Posthuman Future*, 68.
19. Chapman, "Social and Justice Implications of Extending the Human Life Span," 357.
20. Martin and Post, "Human Dignity, Dementia, and the Moral Basis of Caregiving," 58.
21. Ibid., 60–61.

CHAPTER 8

THE UTOPIAN EUGENICS OF OUR TIME

1. See Francis Fukuyama, *Our Posthuman Future: Consequences of the Biotechnological Revolution* (New York: Farrar, Straus, and Giroux, 2002).
2. My analysis of Marxism and feminism here is indebted to Alexandre Kojéve's brilliantly idiosyncratic, perfectly modern view of Hegel. See my *Postmodernism Rightly Understood: The Return to Realism in American Thought* (Lanham, MD: Rowman and Littlefield, 1999), chap. 1.
3. Francis Fukuyama, *The End of History and the Last Man* (New York: Free Press, 1992).
4. On the connections between Bloom and Rorty, see my *Postmodernism Rightly Understood*, chap. 2.
5. Edward O. Wilson in *Sociobiology* (Cambridge, MA: Harvard University Press, 1975) and especially in *On Human Nature* (Cambridge, MA: Harvard University Press, 1978) very consciously and polemically attempted to change the way sophisticated Americans looked at the world. He attempted (and in some measure succeeded) to create an era of sociobiology. Leon Kass tries to explain that "certain substantive teachings of science—most notoriously Darwinism, but also corporealism and mechanism—are, *in their cultural effect*, ethically subversive" (*The Hungry Soul: Eating and the Perfection of Our Nature* [New York: Free Press, 1994], 5). The distinction between the modesty of real scientific teaching and cultural misunderstanding that Kass puts forward is accepted by Wilson, but his sociobiological task is actually to exploit that

misunderstanding to change the culture. That is why Philip Kitcher, with considerable justice, says that what we ordinarily call sociobiology ought to be called "pop sociobiology" (*Vaulting Ambition: Sociobiology and the Quest for Human Nature* [Cambridge, MA: MIT Press, 1985], 14–15).

6. Cf. Fukuyama's *The Great Disruption* with my "Francis Fukuyama as Teacher of Evil," chap. 2 in *Aliens in America*.

7. See Larry Arnhart's conclusion in *Darwinian Natural Right: The Biological Ethics of Human Nature* (Albany, NY: State University of New York Press, 1998), 273–75.

8. Edward O. Wilson, *Consilience: The Unity of Knowledge* (New York: Knopf, 1998).

9. Ibid., 7.

10. Carl Sagan, *Pale Blue Dot: A Vision of the Human Future in Space* (New York: Random House, 1994).

11. See S. J. Olshansky and Bruce A. Carnes, *The Quest for Immortality: Science at the Frontiers of Aging* (New York: W. W. Norton, 2001).

12. Philip Kitcher, *The Lives to Come: The Genetic Revolution and Human Possibilities* (New York: Simon and Schuster, 1996), 212.

13. Ibid., 213.

14. Nicholas Wade, *Life Script: How the Human Genome Discoveries Will Transform Medicine and Enhance Your Health* (New York: Simon and Schuster, 2001), 170.

15. Alan Wolfe, *One Nation, After All* (New York: W. W. Norton, 1998) and *Moral Freedom* (New York: W. W. Norton, 2001).

16. David Brooks, *Bobos in Paradise: The New Upper Class and How They Got There* (New York: Simon and Schuster, 2000).

17. Wilson, *On Human Nature*, with *Consilience*.

18. Olshansky and Carnes, *The Quest for Immortality*, 69.

19. Wade, *Life Script*, 167.

20. See Kass, *Toward a More Natural Science: Biology and Human Affairs* (New York: Simon and Schuster, 1990), 32.

21. Wendell Berry, *Life Is a Miracle: An Essay against Modern Superstition* (Washington, DC: Counterpoint, 2000), 26.

22. See Margaret Talbot, "Jack or Jill? The Era of Consumer-Driven Eugenics Has Begun," *Atlantic Monthly* (March 2002).

23. Kitcher, *The Lives to Come*, is the best and in some ways most moderate yet still unhelpful example of bioethical expertise.

24. On bioethicists as a new class of bureaucratic schoolmaster-despots

who undermine democratic and theological views of the value and purpose of human life, see John H. Evans, *Playing God: Human Genetic Engineering and the Rationalization of the Public Bioethical Debate* (Chicago: University of Chicago Press, 2002). See also the critical and illuminating analysis of Daniel Callahan, "Bioethics," in *Encyclopedia of Bioethics*, ed. W. Rush (New York: Macmillian, 1995).

25. See Kass, *Toward a More Natural Science*, 95.
26. Lori B. Andrews, *Future Perfect* (New York: Columbia University Press, 2001), 60. My discussion of this pathological condition is indebted to Andrews throughout.
27. Ibid., 65.
28. Frank Furedi, *Paranoid Parenting: Why Ignoring the Experts May Be Best for Your Child* (Chicago: Chicago Review Press, 2002).
29. Kass, *Toward a More Natural Science*, 34n.
30. Cf. Walker Percy, *The Thanatos Syndrome* (New York: Farrar, Straus, and Giroux, 1987) with my *Postmodernism Rightly Understood*, chap. 4.

CHAPTER 9

LIBERTARIAN FANTASY AND STATIST REALITY

1. Even Fukuyama, in *Our Posthuman Future*, says at one point that "Any case to be made against human genetic engineering should . . . not get hung up on the red herring of . . . the prospect of government coercion" (88). He also regards the "scenario" in which "the indefinite postponement of death will force societies to put severe constraints on the number of births allowed" as "extreme" (96–97). Fukuyama's public adversary, Gregory Stock, actually gives a troublingly strong case for the inevitability of our, in some way or another, genetically created, pro-choice future. See Stock's *Redesigning Humans: Our Inevitable Genetic Future* (New York: Houghton Mifflin, 2002). My analysis throughout this chapter is indebted to both Fukuyama and Stock.
2. Philip Kitcher, *The Lives to Come* (The Free Press, 1997), 237.
3. On the argument supporting "utopian eugenics," see ibid., 187–238.
4. Wesley J. Smith, *Culture of Death: The Assault on Medical Ethics in America* (San Francisco: Encounter Books, 2001).
5. Dinesh D'Souza, *The Virtue of Prosperity: Finding Values in an Age of Techno-Affluence* (New York: Free Press, 2000), chaps. 9 and 10.
6. Lee M. Silver, *Remaking Eden* (New York: Morrow, 1997).
7. Aldous Huxley, "Brave New World Revisited," *Brave New World and Brave New World Revisited* (New York: Harper and Row, 1965), 16–17.

8. Ibid., 13.
9. Ronald Dworkin, *Sovereign Virtue: The Theory and Practice of Equality* (Cambridge, MA: Harvard University Press, 2000), 450.
10. Ibid., 450.
11. Robert L. Sinsheimer, "The Prospect of Designed Genetic Change," in Ruth F. Chadwick, ed., *Ethics, Reproduction, and Genetic Control* (New York: Routledge, 1992), 145.
12. James Watson, "Fixing the Human Embryo Is the Next Step for Science," *Independent* (UK) (April 16, 2001).

INDEX